The Complete
Illustrated Guide to
Astrology

★ ★ ★ ★ ★

The Complete
Illustrated Guide to
Astrology

★ ★ ★ ★ ★

Janis Huntley

element

Element
An Imprint of HarperCollins*Publishers*
77-85 Fulham Palace Road
Hammersmith
London W6 8JB

The Element website address is www.elementbooks.co.uk

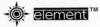

and Element are trademarks of
HarperCollins*Publishers* Limited

First published in Great Britain in 1999 by
ELEMENT BOOKS LIMITED
Shaftesbury, Dorset SP7 9BP

This paperback edition published by Element in 2003

Designed and created for Element Books with
THE BRIDGEWATER BOOK COMPANY LIMITED

Printed and bound in Hong Kong by Printing Express

Library of Congress Cataloging in Publication
data available

British Library Cataloguing in Publication data available

ISBN 0-00-715274-4

The publishers are grateful to the following for
permission to reproduce copyright material:
Bridgeman Art Library: pp. 67 (Rafael Valls Gallery,
London), 133B (Chester Beatty Library)
e.t. archive: p. 127T (Uffizi Gallery, Florence)
GSF Picture Library: p. 13L
Hulton Deutsch: pp. 175T, 181T, 182B, 184B,
Image Bank: pp. 42B, 105B, 146T
Images: p. 37B
JS Library International: pp. 168B,172T, 183B
Keystone: p. 176/177B
Kobal Collection: p. 178B
Popperfoto: pp. 152, 157T, 160T, 161, 168T,174L,175B,
180B, 183T, 185T
Redferns: pp. 176B, 177T, 179T
Science Photo Library: pp. 8B, 28R, 41R, 69BR, 78B, 11B,
139B, 141B, 142, 145, 146/47, 158, 172T
Stock Market: pp 13B, 18B, 26T, 27T, 34, 46L, 49B, 71,
77R, 79T, 103R, 119B, 120L, 120B, 141T
Superstock: pp. 52B, 70L,
Tony Stone Images: pp. 16B30B, 39T, 43L, 50T, 51T, 55T,
58B, 64, 75B, 76T, 77T, 91R, 93T, 94T, 94B, 96B, 96T,
99T, 99B, 103T, 113T, 115B, 117B, 121B, 122T, 122B,
124T, 126, 138, 139, 140, 157B, 165T

Special thanks to Mary Armstrong, Michael Attree, Clare
Bayes, Deirdre Bridger, Stephanie Brotherstone, Andrew
Brown, David Burton, Adam Carne, Charlotte Carter, Yana
Casquero, Rob Chappell, Rukshana Chenoy, Jasmine Clowes,
Lisa Clowes, Roger Cooper, Guy Corber, Lisa Dando, Rowan
Dando-Wilson, Sorrel Dando-Wilson, Tansy Dando-Wilson,
M.G.C. Davis, Maggie De Freitas, Peter Dudley, Jana Elliot,
Angela Enahoro, Cassandra Fellingham, Steve Freedman,
Helen Furbear, Annette Gerlin, Zoe Hall, Harriet Hart, Sam
Hollingdale, Chloe Hymas, Pat Infanti, Fleur Jones, Anu
Juvonen, I.Kaskero, Maria Lloyd, Wendy Oxberry, Donna
Poplett, Pat Poplett, Max Rashand, Morgan Rashand, Sharon
Rashand, Caron Riley, Michelle Sawyer, P.B. Sawyer, David
Scott, Emma Scott, Wendy Scott, Francesca Selkirk,
D.Simpson, S.Simpson, Chrissie Sloane, Nadia Smith,
Nicholas Smith, Joseph Smurthwaite, Andrew Stemp,
Caroline Stemp, Lauren Sword, Sheila Sword, Andrew Tong,
Louise Williams, Alain Yahiaoui, Fabien Zecchino for help
with photography

Special thanks to Buxtons, Furnishers, Carpets and Flooring
Contractors, 27-35 Ditchling Road, Brighton, BN1 4SB, for
help with properties

CONTENTS

* * * * * * * * * * * * * * * * *

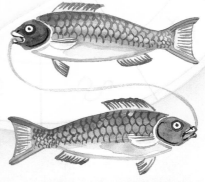

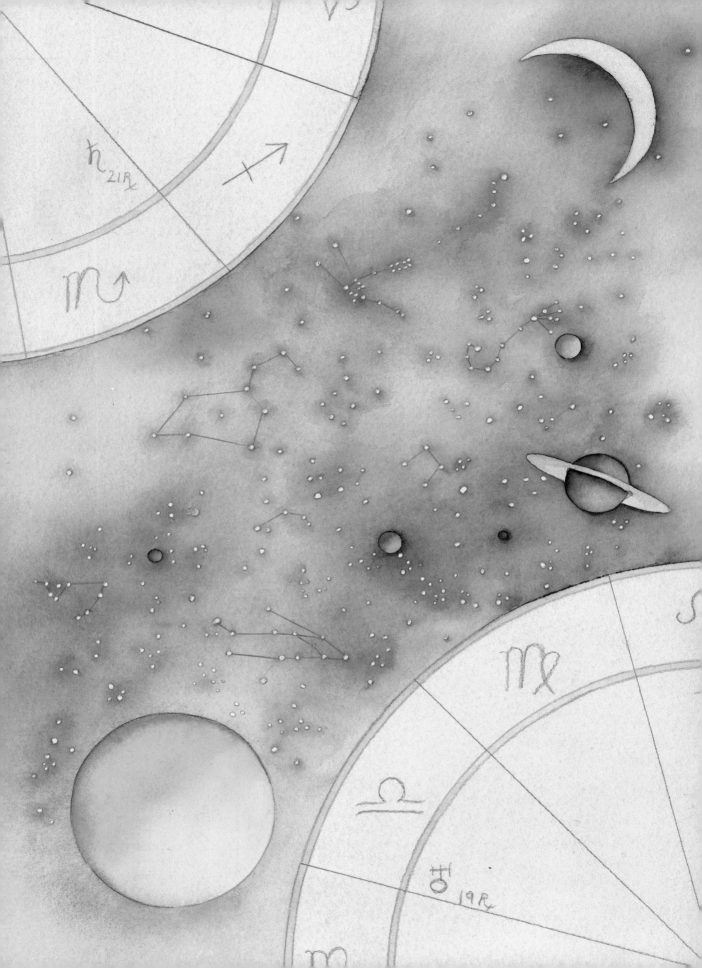

DISCOVERING ASTROLOGY

★ ★ ★ ★ ★

We have all read our horoscope in one of the thousands of Sun-sign columns which appear daily in newspapers and magazines all over the world. However, these entertaining columns reveal only the tip of the iceberg – astrology encompasses so much more than just Sun signs. It is an art, a science, a method of psychoanalysis, and a doorway to the future. With the advent of computers, the ancient art of divination using astrology has become highly accessible and comprehensive. Our fascination with it has expanded over thousands of years and as we move into the Age of Aquarius – a sign which combines scientific advance with ancient wisdom – the 21st century should herald an even greater upsurge of popularity.

ABOVE The birthchart is split into 12 segments (houses) in which the siting of the planets is mapped.

Astrology is a science but it can be great fun, too. The biggest reward of all is to see astrology at work – to know that the planetary energies do affect our lives as predicted in our personal birthcharts. Astrology is a tool for all of us to use – a gift of understanding the complexities of human character and a key to unlock this knowledge in a helpful way.

THE PRINCIPLES OF ASTROLOGY

* * * * * * * * * * * * * * * * *

Aries the ram

Taurus the bull

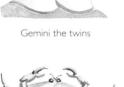

Gemini the twins

Cancer the crab

Leo the lion

Virgo the virgin

MODERN ASTROLOGY IS a no-nonsense application that will help us open doors of perception into every area of our lives and the lives of those around us. The twelve Sun signs are the foundation of astrology which reveal a small but highly potent brew of our innate characteristics. They lead to the complexity of the individualized birthchart which leaves no stone unturned in its capacity to delve deep into our true inner nature, the invisible spaces of our psychic realm. Astrology helps us to understand ourselves and others through all the stages of emotional, physical, mental, and spiritual development.

Astrology has developed over thousands of years as a system of divination to help us survive in times of darkness and uncertainty – but during the last few centuries it has evolved into a means of personal analysis. Throughout the 20th century, psychiatrists and counselors in the Western world have discovered they can understand and help

RIGHT An astrologer will prepare a birthchart for you and explain the effects that the positions of the various planets have on your life.

HOW ASTROLOGY HAS EVOLVED

The Egyptians claim to be the founders of astrology, but it is known that the Babylonians in ancient Mesopotamia (now Iraq), used divination for agricultural purposes based on astronomical data perhaps 3,000 years ago. This included the so-called fixed stars, or planets. The ancient Greek, Roman, and Egyptian astronomers refined this predictive art into systems which are similar to those used by astrologers today. Records show that the Egyptians used the "equal house" method of Zodiacal division which is popular today.

RIGHT Divination using the stars and planets is an art that dates back back 3,000 years.

The discovery of the three outer planets, Uranus, Neptune, and Pluto, which have all coincided with major progressive changes during the last few centuries, has opened up the study of astrology and it is likely that other undiscovered planets exist in our universe.

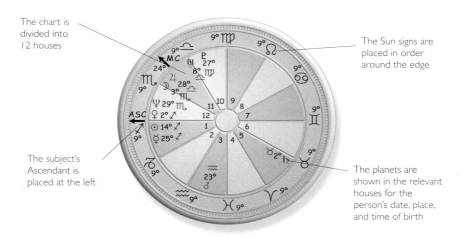

The chart is divided into 12 houses

The Sun signs are placed in order around the edge

The subject's Ascendant is placed at the left

The planets are shown in the relevant houses for the person's date, place, and time of birth

Libra the scales

Scorpio the scorpion

ABOVE A person's birthchart contains all the information an astrologer needs to be able to assess their personality and offer guidance or advice.

their clients more successfully when accurate birthcharts are available. Awareness that astrology is more than just a guide to the future has generated a tremendous surge in its popularity during the last 50 years and many people today consult an astrologer or create and analyze their own birthcharts.

Although many astrologers today like to emphasize that astrology is a science which bears no resemblance to fortune-telling, the art of predictive astrology, or divination, remains popular and appears in the Sun-sign forecasts in newspapers and on TV.

It matters not whether astrology is an art or a science, or a combination of both, as its main principle is to help and guide us. Astrology can help with career development, relationship problems, health concerns, financial status, social outlets, sexual matters, travel plans, educational worries, political and environmental changes – the list is endless. It provides an overview of how we should react to life and is a mirror for the hidden energies and potentials in our lives.

The unique energy of the planets used in astrological interpretation endeavors to guide us in the direction that is right for us as individuals. The position of the planets within the

RIGHT Astrology gives you vital knowledge that can help you find true love and fulfill your ambitions.

birthchart tells us what areas of life we should concentrate on, and their daily movement indicates the important changes we should be making within our attitudes and lifestyles at any given time.

Astrology gives us vital knowledge about ourselves which tells us how to be positive, how to change ourselves for the better, and, most important of all, how to lead successful, fulfilling lives.

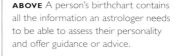

Sagittarius the archer

Capricorn the goat

Aquarius the water carrier

Pisces the fishes

PART ONE

Sun Signs

★ ★ ★ ★ ★

The 12 signs of the Zodiac are the foundations on which the ancient science of astrology is built. They are called the Sun signs and are based broadly on the night-sky constellations known to astronomers for thousands of years. Sun signs became popular during the second half of the 20th century because they are easy to work out. The orbit of the earth around the Sun is constant — it spends about 30 days in each constellation every year — which ensures that in any given month the Zodiacal Sun sign is always the same. The planets, on the other hand, are more variable in their orbit. Character interpretations based on Sun signs alone can, however, be misleading. A person with the Sun and several more planets occupying the Sun sign will always be more typical of the Sun sign than someone who has only the Sun in that sign. (It is possible, but extremely rare, for all ten planets to occupy different signs of the Zodiac.) Predictive astrology based upon solar (Sun sign) charts can be surprisingly accurate when forecast by a good astrologer.

ABOVE Ancient astronomers organized the stars into constellations that are the basis for the Sun signs.

ARIES

* * * * * * * * * * * * * * * *

March 21 to April 19

Aries is ruled by
the planet Mars

Aries is ruled by
the element Fire

Aries rules
the head

BELOW Typical
characteristics of
Arian appearance.

KEYWORD CHARACTERISTICS

energetic, enthusiastic, impatient,
impulsive, self-centered, outspoken,
thoughtless, strong-minded, hot-tempered,
adventurous, excitable,
domineering, extroverted

THE NATURE OF ARIES

Aries is the first sign of the Zodiac and Arian subjects often possess a sense of self-importance and a strong desire to be at the head of the line. The loud voice in the crowd that shouts "Me first!" or rushes blindly forward is nearly always a Sun Aries or a person with a lot of Aries in their birthchart. This sign, more than any other, needs to lead. A natural-born warrior, fearless and courageous when positive, but foolhardy and reckless when

ABOVE The Aries Sun sign is depicted as a ram. True to their position at the head of the Zodiac, Arians are strong-willed, competitive, extrovert people – born to lead.

negative, an Aries person is difficult to ignore, highly competitive, hard to beat, insufferably annoying, but strangely likeable.

Aries people are strong-willed, adventurous, naturally extrovert, and impulsive. They can be dynamic and utterly implacable when sparked into active mode. Loaded with energy and vitality, they charge at full power into their endeavors and expect people to keep up with them; then suddenly they become bored, and inexplicably lose interest in what they were doing. At this point they beat a hasty retreat, leaving others to pick up the pieces. Aries people are essentially starters in life, but unless there are a lot of fixed signs in their chart (Taurus, Leo, Scorpio, or Aquarius), they are rarely known to complete a lengthy project.

Arian subjects are warm and ardent in their relationships with others – sometimes too much so. Their keenness can become pushy and their zest for life seems like aggression. True, there are some Arians who are bossy, impatient, and hot-tempered, but even the most frenzied of Aries subjects will quieten down if they have to stop and think what they are doing. Because they are so rash, Aries people are totally unaware of any negative impact they may be producing – automatically assuming that everyone is on their wavelength. Aries is essentially the baby of the Zodiac – at the beginning of creation – and very much involved with self and its basic needs. But it

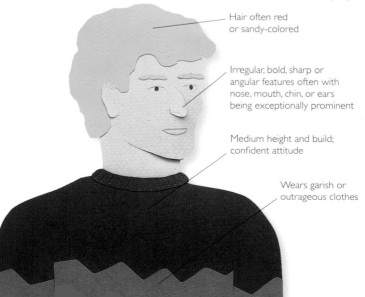

Hair often red
or sandy-colored

Irregular, bold, sharp or
angular features often with
nose, mouth, chin, or ears
being exceptionally prominent

Medium height and build;
confident attitude

Wears garish or
outrageous clothes

This sign has links with bright reds

Tuesday is Aries lucky day

The birthstone of Aries is bloodstone

is possible for Arians to be made aware of other people's needs. When pulled up and forced to face their own actions a typical Arian will invariably be full of remorse and make a concerted effort to please others – for a while at least.

Most Arian people are direct, outspoken and uncomplicated. They don't hide their lights under a bush, nor do they exude kindness or tolerance, but they are enormously exciting, highly demonstrative, generous to a fault, and at times oddly affectionate. They enjoy combat, will always stick up for themselves – and others – and will automatically take the lead in most areas of their lives. In a bad temper or if unable to get their own way, Arians can strike out and hurt, both mentally and physically, but they are just as quick to forgive and forget.

ARIES IN LOVE

Although ardent, warm, and passionate, Aries can be too hasty when involved in loving or sexual relationships. They pursue their quarry relentlessly, are quickly aroused and can be very forceful in their approach. Many Arians find the chase more exciting than the surrender. They are possessive and protective toward loved ones, but will not tolerate dependency. Partnerships are often shortlived because they invariably have no idea how to handle their relationships, and when things do go smoothly, they get bored and are quick to move on.

ABOVE Arians put their heart and soul into the chase and find it very exciting. Once successful, however, they can quickly lose interest and look elsewhere.

LEFT Arians have a zest for life and are highly adventurous. Fearless in their pursuit, they favor activities that will get them noticed.

ARIES AT WORK

Enthusiastic and keen to get moving, Aries at work can be dynamic or disastrous. Lack of planning and too much urgency over a situation can leave the Aries subjects flat on their backs and out of a job. Arians cannot bear being told what to do but love having command over others. They are therefore suited to positions of authority. Their active nature also draws them toward dangerous occupations and military regimes.

ARIAN OCCUPATIONS

executive, police officer, fire fighter, film stunt person, film director, ambulance driver, sales representative, soldier, iron or steel worker, racing driver, circus performer, athlete

ARIES AND LEISURE

Speed is the essence where Aries is concerned. Aries people crave excitement and adventure, love taking risks, and hate to conform. Their leisure time should be spent in a wide variety of physically strenuous or demanding activities but because of their short attention span, they should not involve themselves in sports or leisure activities that require a great deal of concentration. They like to finish first, are very competitive, and usually extremely capable provided they are allowed to do things at their own superfast pace and in their own unique style. They are attracted to dangerous, daredevil activities, wild stunts, fairgrounds, wargames, assault courses, fast sports, hunting, horses, large dogs, motorcycles, motor-racing, vibrant or rousing music, and any creative outlet that

RIGHT The typical Arian will enjoy activities that feed their desire for adventure. They are lovers of speed and will happily fly in the face of danger.

combines strength with freedom of movement and little need for concentration. Aries subjects who do not, or cannot satisfy their strong physical urges in stren-uous activity are likely to become short-tempered or physically abusive. Aries people hate to lose, and less evolved souls of this sign are prone to tantrums and cries of "unfair" when thwarted or relegated to second position. Although they love their homes – it's often the only place where they feel they can relax – it is vital that all Arians spend time each day pursuing open-air activities. When Arians are confined in small spaces for more than a few hours, they tend to suffer from sleepless nights and bouts of frustration. Jogging, sprinting, or aerobics are excellent forms of exercise in which they can work off some of their abundant energy.

ARIES AND HEALTH

Aries people tend to suffer from all kinds of headaches, particularly migraines, as well as many other problems relating to the head and face. Bumps, lumps, and skin defects often occur around the head, and due to their extreme impulsiveness and careless approach, Arians tend to be accident prone.

The Arian, however, is also tough and strong and their bodies can endure pain and strife more easily than most other signs. All Arians benefit tremendously from rest and relaxation but they are afraid to sit still even for a moment, considering this a sign of weakness or laziness on their part.

HEALING FOODS

ginger, horseradish, red peppers, chilies, leeks, onions, garlic, cilantro, mustard, watercress, paprika

ARIES AND DIET

Food is vital to the Aries sense of well-being. Their seemingly inexhaustible supply of energy must be well stoked, preferably by small quantities of high energy foods such as carbohydrate and protein (meat, beans, nuts, bread, pasta, rice) throughout the day. Many Arians bolt down large meals when they can grab a spare moment and often resort to junk or convenience foods. Fortunately, they tend to burn off fat fairly quickly and rarely suffer from indigestion. It is also unusual to find a really fat Arian. A deep love of exercise through sport or in other ways also helps to keep their weight down.

Despite the fact that most Arians enjoy hot, spicy, sustaining food such as curries, fried and Mexican food, they also respond well to a strict vegetarian regime.

ABOVE Arians are highly competitive and love games where they can show their strength. and superiority

ARIES SPORTS AND EXERCISE

motor-racing, boxing, squash, aerobics, fitness training, working out, judo, tennis, sprinting, skiing, Rugby football

POSITIVE ARIES
I came, I saw, I conquered!

NEGATIVE ARIES
Fools rush in where angels fear to tread.

TAURUS

★ ★ ★ ★ ★ ★ ★ ★ ★ ★ ★ ★ ★ ★ ★

April 20 to May 20

Taurus is ruled by the planet Venus

Taurus is ruled by the element Earth

Taurus rules the neck and throat

This sign has links with green and brown

THE NATURE OF TAURUS

Taurus is the second sign of the Zodiac after Aries. People born under this laid-back sign are seldom in a hurry to go places or do anything. They are content to take second place in a venture and follow their Arian leaders. Taurean people relate well to the saying "more haste, less speed" as they hate being rushed into anything. After much deliberation, however, they will usually take decisive action and eventually complete the task in hand.

Taureans are quiet, gentle people, but they know their own mind and nothing will dissuade them once they are convinced they are on the right track. This sign is so set in its ways that it is not uncommon for a typical Taurean to become completely stuck and unable to move or adapt to the times. Taureans want everything to be as it always was. They do not enjoy being disturbed or forced into change. The thought of too much action can sometimes make a Taurean feel physically sick. They desperately want life to be a bed of roses but often find that to achieve peace and harmony is an uphill struggle. Luckily, this sign possesses a lot of tenacity and is usually strong enough, physically and mentally, to overcome all but the toughest obstacle.

Despite innate slowness and aptitude for inertia, most Taureans possess an uncanny knack for personal gain. Taurus people love

ABOVE Represented by the sign of the bull, Taureans are steady individuals who enjoy their creature comforts.

money, wealth, and status more than anything else, and it is rare to find a truly poor Taurean. They know how to handle their finances, despite being spendthrifts, and like to be seen as the people who have everything. Taurean women are skilled at making a little money go a long way – personal possessions, accumulated in abundance, are lovingly and meticulously cared for, simple food is made up into gourmet feasts, and bargain clothing is transformed into designer outfits. Such is the natural cleverness of Taurean subjects that others rarely think to question or suspect the origins of their apparent affluence.

Taurus is an Earth sign, like its companion signs Virgo and Capricorn, but it is the most earthy of them all and also the

ABOVE The home of a Taurean is his castle and must be secure and comfortable with the luxuries Taureans enjoy.

The birthstone of
Taurus is emerald

Friday is the
Taurean lucky day

LEFT Taureans are
loving, loyal partners
who, once smitten,
are unlikely to stray.

most basic. Taureans feel
trapped or imprisoned if
denied physical access to the
land. They are always green-
fingered in some way. Many work
outdoors in agriculture, farming,
gardening, and similar occupations
while those unable to do so can be
found pottering in gardens or tending
to indoor plants.

TAURUS IN LOVE

Taureans are very slow and deliberate in forming attachments but once their heart is opened they make wonderfully loyal and endearing partners. They are not interested in flirtation or a wide variety of partners. Unfortunately, Taureans are not the most romantic of people and in a happy family rela-tionship, they tend to become even more habitual, rigid, and unadventurous than usual. They love to come home from work, eat a finely prepared supper, put their feet up, and watch TV all night. The most stoic and tolerant of partners eventually find this behavior unacceptable and try to nudge the Taurean out of their chair. Variety is defi-nitely not the spice of life for Taureans.

They are extremely sensual and both male and female Taurean subjects need a great deal of good, earthy sexual bonding to get them through life. Taurus without sex is like a bear with a sore head, and once aroused only the real thing will quench their desire. Taureans in love are loyal, sexy, domesticated, and easily pleased. Is it any wonder that this sign proudly holds the record for the lowest divorce rate of all the twelve signs?

Thick,
lustrous hair

Rounded
or pug nose

Full lips
and generally
heavy features

Square-set face,
particularly
around the jaw

Dresses in classic,
conservative style,
but appreciates
good quality

Well-built, solid,
short to medium
height and prone
to overweight in
later years

LEFT A typical
Taurean will display
some of these
characteristics of
appearance.

TAURUS AT WORK

Taureans learn and adapt slowly, so they need a career in which they can move at their own pace. They work on a simplistic structured level and are often attracted to outdoor or manual occupations. At the other end of the scale, their financial acumen can lead them into working with money, or their love of music may direct them to the world of entertainment.

TAURUS AND LEISURE

Mention the word "leisure" to a Taurean and they will visualize a deserted sun-

TAUREAN OCCUPATIONS

farmer, landscape gardener, construction worker, carpenter, forest ranger, home help, domestic worker, cook, stockbroker, accountant, financial adviser, architect, hotelier, bank manager, musician, singer

drenched beach on which they are relaxing beneath a large palm tree. Such fantasies are common to the Taurean psyche because, unlike Aries, this is a sign which likes to take everything slowly and carefully. In fact, most Taureans actually enjoy doing nothing at all in their spare time. To them, leisure is an opportunity to relax and unwind although they are strong and physically able to compete with any sign of the Zodiac, including Aries. They dislike taking part in speedy or dangerous activities. Slow-moving, quiet sports and

POSITIVE TAURUS
Fortune comes to those who stand and wait.

NEGATIVE TAURUS
Like a bull in a china shop.

endeavors such as snooker, golf, tai-chi, and yoga appeal to them along with anything that involves sitting in a comfortable armchair. Watching TV is a favorite pastime but they also enjoy occupations with a high level of concentration, such as needlework, embroidery, jigsaw puzzles, and reading. Despite their addiction to luxury and comfort and their reputation for being lazy, Taureans are not afraid of hard work especially in the form of leisure. Their innate love of the land and attunement with nature ensures that outdoor pursuits like hiking, orienteering, birding, fishing, and gardening rate highly on their list of pleasant activities. Taureans are naturally green-fingered and most enjoy messing about in a garden. A passion for food and eating encourages them to dine out regularly but the experience has to be savored slowly – fast food does not match discerning Taurean standards.

Look in on any local choir, operatic group, or music society and there are bound to be a number of Taureans in attendance. Some Taureans enjoy heavy, classical music, while others prefer ballads and light classics, but the younger generation of Taureans are often attracted to earthy music with a powerful beat, such as reggae.

Friends born under more active Sun signs will find Taureans slothful and unimaginative, but look more closely and you will see complete absorption and utter contentment on their faces as they indulge in their favorite leisure pursuits.

HEALING FOODS

mint, gooseberries, thyme, rosemary, olives, apples, pears, grapes, rhubarb, green beans, cherries, spring cabbage

TAURUS AND HEALTH

Taurus people are usually strong and hearty with few major health problems in their early years but due to the rulership of the neck and throat, they are liable to suffer from niggling sore throats and neck pains throughout their lives. Taurean singers, especially, need to look after their throats with appropriate sprays and careful diet.

TAURUS AND DIET

Inertia, lack of exercise and overeating are common among Taureans – factors which inevitably encourage them to put on weight and some of the most overweight people in the world are born under this sign. Taureans have much to gain by cutting down on food intake and adopting a vegetarian or near vegetarian diet. Most are unhappy to do so, however, and prefer to suffer the consequences.

LEFT Taureans enjoy slow-moving activities involving concentration such as tai-chi or yoga.

TAURUS SPORTS AND EXERCISE

judo, tai-chi, boxing, yoga, snooker, golf, walking, hiking, discus, hammer-throwing, cricket

GEMINI

* * * * * * * * * * * * * * * * *

May 21 to June 21

KEYWORD CHARACTERISTICS

lively, communicative, adaptable, highly strung, multifaceted, moody, unemotional, highly expressive, independent, sharp-witted, mentally active

Gemini is ruled by the planet Mercury

Gemini is ruled by the element Air

Gemini rules arms, chest, and lungs

This sign is linked to yellow and silver

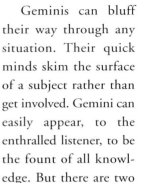

Geminis can bluff their way through any situation. Their quick minds skim the surface of a subject rather than get involved. Gemini can easily appear, to the enthralled listener, to be the fount of all knowledge. But there are two sides to every story just as there are two sides to every Gemini. The twin-sign of the Zodiac, Gemini people rarely act the same way twice with the same person. They tend to forget what they have said because their minds are constantly racing ahead and moving onto something new. However, they do learn extremely quickly and are good at passing examinations.

The birthstone of Gemini is crystal

Wednesday is Gemini's lucky day

ABOVE The first thing you'll notice about a Gemini, whose Sun sign is depicted by the faces of twins, is their mental agility.

THE NATURE OF GEMINI

The quicksilver element of Mercury endows its Geminian subjects with restlessness, versatility, and a constant desire for mental activity. This sign does not possess the physical strength of Aries or Taurus, but compensates by being top of the Zodiac in mental agility. Words spill easily from the Geminian mouth but they are not always words that others wish to hear.

Sometimes Gemini people cannot stop talking but it's mainly gossip or their own personal experiences. "Bigmouth" is an apt description for many a Geminian subject. Geminis are clever. Their talent with words also makes them good writers and orators – in the right mood they can sell you absolutely anything. But their love of communication at any cost can sometimes lead them into trouble. Truth becomes distended, their imagination runs riot, and what the Geminian regards as storytelling can often be outright lying.

ABOVE
Their way with words and vivid imaginations, make Geminis good writers.

RIGHT As well as these typical traits of appearance, Geminis also tend to gesticulate expressively.

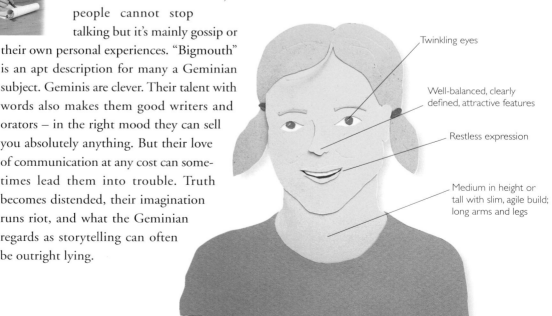

Twinkling eyes

Well-balanced, clearly defined, attractive features

Restless expression

Medium in height or tall with slim, agile build; long arms and legs

Relatives, friends, and companions are very important to Gemini people and they will chat to anyone, anywhere. Their restless nature leads them to travel by road, rail, and air (boats are too slow) but they prefer short-distance to long-haul journeys.

The Geminian life may appear to be chaotic, but this is how they like it. Unlike Taureans, Geminis do not wish to be bogged down by routine. Gemini people are seldom boring even when they talk too much. They make interesting companions, and are usually much sought after. While admiring their talents and attempting to keep up with their lightning speed, the wise listener will, however, take everything a Gemini says with a pinch of salt.

LEFT Geminis love to chat and have much to say. They are great gossips and will talk at length.

GEMINI IN LOVE

Mercury, the ruler of Gemini, is an androgynous planet, preferring speech and mental activity to physical expressions of love. A strongly Geminian person (someone with more than just the sun in Gemini) is not particularly concerned with love matters. Ironically, most Geminians are very attractive and can be pursued constantly by admirers, and the more Gemini turns its back on a lover, the more besotted that person becomes. When a Gemini does fall in love, it is usually the communicative values of the partner which were the main attraction. They are turned on by loving or sexy language, especially in the form of poetry or erotic tales. They are stimulated by change and variety within a relationship and are sometimes accused of being flirtatious and unfaithful; these are misconceptions because all Gemini truly requires is someone to talk with and if this can be achieved by flirting and tossing aside boring, unresponsive people then they will go ahead and do so.

BELOW Geminians need their partners to communicate, and if this is by means of poetry – all the better.

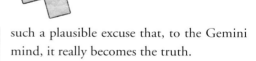

RIGHT Geminians prefer games for the quick-witted rather than the physically strong. When outdoors they are attracted to sky-bound activities such as hot air ballooning or parascending.

GEMINI AT WORK

Geminians are mind people and are rarely attracted to heavy physical work. Because they like to get everything done quickly, they are not always as thorough as some of the other signs of the Zodiac, but they will come up with some ingenious ideas and work well in areas which interest them. The Gemini person is often called a Jack-of-all-Trades, Master-of-None. They scatter their talents in all directions but communication is always involved in whatever they do. People of this sign work badly on their own or from home, or in a job with a set daily routine. Positions that involve lots of movement suit them. Timekeeping is rarely important to them but they are as likely to be early as late – or not turn up at all because something else grabbed their attention. When this happens, they do genuinely forget prior engagements, but later they'll be on the phone having thought of

GEMINI OCCUPATIONS

journalist, writer, telesales executive, sales representative, lawyer, dancer, entertainer, model, acrobat, teacher, orator, airport worker, railroad conductor, sales person, travel consultant

such a plausible excuse that, to the Gemini mind, it really becomes the truth.

GEMINI AND LEISURE

Any activity which stimulates the brain in short, sharp bursts is enjoyable for people of this sign. Like Aries, sustained concentration is difficult for most Geminians, but they compensate by absorbing information like a sponge. Rapid mental and physical pursuits are favored. Cerebral activities such as card games, boardgames, gambling, reading (in short bursts), and word games are more likely to appeal to them than highly physical sports. Geminis are often slim and agile with nimble hands and feet: they tend to enjoy table-tennis, badminton, dancing, gymnastics, acrobatics, and running.

LEFT Often slim with long limbs and radiant beauty, Geminian women are well-suited to modeling.

GEMINI AND HEALTH

Constitutionally, Gemini is one of the weaker signs of the Zodiac. People with this sign featured strongly in their birthchart need to look after themselves but most Geminis do not consider their health to be very important. They are not interested in regular exercise – many of them do not have the physical strength – nor do they possess much of an appetite. Geminis eat to live and when their mind is distracted, they will forget to eat and then, like Aries, pile in loads of junk food.

Coughs, colds, lung and chest infections, arthritis, and general aches and pains are common as the Gemini subject grows into middle age. Even young Geminis do not escape as childhood asthma is frequent. The rulership of Mercury can make Geminians highly strung and prone to mental problems and diseases involving constant or jerky movements such as epilepsy and Parkinson's disease.

GEMINI SPORTS AND EXERCISE

sprinting, ice-skating, table tennis, tennis, football, dancing, skiing, long jump, high jump, pole-vaulting, badminton, gymnastics

Geminian women can be very attractive and enjoy beauty contests, but the most favored leisure occupation of all is talking, rarely pausing for breath or allowing the listener to respond. Unlike the Taureans who prefer to keep their feet planted firmly on the ground, Geminians thoroughly enjoy raising themselves above the earth and reaching for the sky: air travel, hot-air ballooning, parascending, parachuting, and almost any short-term activity which takes place in the sky. Geminis love a wide variety of music but tend to prefer light, breezy tunes with rhythm but not too much noise. Lyrics are important but, conversely, many Geminians are great jazz fans.

HEALING FOODS

carrots, dill, marjoram, valerian, hazelnuts, walnuts, oats, fish, licorice, apricots, squash, turmeric

GEMINI AND DIET

Geminians need light, nutritious food including lots of cooked vegetables and soups. They burn up fat quickly and so need more than most in their diet but can tolerate it in only small amounts They also require plenty of protein (meat, eggs, fish, beans, nuts) but dairy foods are bad for their lungs and asthmatic tendencies.

CANCER

★ ★ ★ ★ ★ ★ ★ ★ ★ ★ ★ ★ ★ ★ ★ ★ ★

June 22 to July 22

Cancer is ruled
by the Moon

Cancer is ruled by
the element Water

Cancer rules
the stomach
and breasts

THE NATURE OF CANCER

The sign of Cancer is the first in the Water element triad and is related to the seas and oceans. Cancerian people have deep emotions and fathomless longings that are like the depths of these waters. They are serious, caring, sensitive people with complex psyches who do not believe in half-measures – it's all or nothing with them but it's the nothing which usually wins out. Rather than take a risk and put all their energy into something that might fail, they prefer to wait, moving slowly with crab-like steps. When the time is right, they pounce and dart forward with amazing speed and efficiency.

KEYWORD CHARACTERISTICS

quiet, sullen, home-loving, sensitive, nurturing, kindly, sentimental, emotional, taciturn, protective (perhaps overprotective), security-conscious

This is a sign that dislikes taking unnecessary risks. When the going gets tough, they are perfectly content to dig in and surround themselves with domestic comfort and security. Not that they are weak, or cowardly – far from it. Subjects of this sign can be extraordinarily strong-minded, resilient and brave when faced with an emergency but they prefer to live their lives without drawing too much attention to themselves. Moon people invariably emphasize that they value peace, seclusion, home and family life above all else, but bear in mind that there are two faces to the Moon, and when an unobtrusive Cancerian is forced into the limelight, they may appear to change beyond recognition. Given the opportunity at the right time, people of this sign cope remarkably well with fame, fortune, and responsibility.

ABOVE The Cancer Sun sign is depicted by a crab and is related to the oceans.

Sensitive, caring, domesticated, and nurturing, the wonderful mother-father figure of a positive Cancerian is sometimes too good to be true. But sensitivity can become vulnerability, caring may transmute into dominance, and nurturing can become smothering. Many Cancerians do not know where to draw the line. They want to help and love to be needed. The mother who encourages her children to overeat and then wonders why they are overweight does so

Sharp-featured, with fine, dark, sparse hair and slim build (New-Moon type), or pale face, rounded features, fair-haired and plump (Full-Moon type)

Short to medium height though some New-Moon types are very tall; self-protective attitude

LEFT A typical Cancerian will display some of these traits.

RIGHT Cancerian mothers can inadvertently smother their children with their constant nurturing love.

out of love, but this is a classic case of killing by kindness. People sooner or later will run away from a Cancerian who is stifling them and when this happens, the Cancer subject feels deeply hurt and prepares for battle. This is emotional warfare of guilt, reproach, sulking and pinching and out come their small crablike claws which usually remain tightly controlled beneath their outer shell. A wounded Cancerian is not an easy person to deal with and many surrender to this form of attack rather than face such hostility. Conversely, many Cancerians will simply turn their backs on emotional situations rather than risk getting hurt.

This sign is linked to white and black

The birthstone of Cancer is moonstone

Monday is Cancer's lucky day

Money and a sense of security play an important part in the Cancerian scheme of life. They need to own-and-belong in order to feel safe. Although careful with money, they give as good as they get and are kind, generous, and thoughtful when their feelings are reciprocated.

CANCER IN LOVE

Cancerians love wholeheartedly. They are loyal and dependable, if sometimes moody and difficult to understand. They respond well to big hugs, words of love, and frequent reminders as to how wonderful they are. Their love of nurturing may lead them to act like a parent to their partners though occasionally it is the Cancerian who becomes the dependent partner in a relationship seeking a maternal-paternal figurehead. Cancerian men like to be cosseted and well fed, and Cancerian women usually enjoy the role of cosseting. Sex as a means of expressing love is very important to Cancer subjects. Sometimes, however, a love-starved Cancerian will turn to promiscuity as a mistaken substitute for the love they crave. Within a mutually caring relationship Cancerians can be wonderfully supportive and make excellent lovers, but when things go wrong they can become impenetrable, vindictive, and callous.

LEFT Cancerians have a continuous need to feel loved and respond well to private displays of deep affection.

CANCER AT WORK

Although Cancerians are generally loyal, hardworking, and unafraid of menial tasks, they do not enjoy performing unnecessary or extraneous work. They are efficient and systematic in their approach and are often found in positions of authority or high esteem. Their emotional sensitivity sometimes lets them down but most Cancerians are adept at creating a protective shell of control and austerity. They invariably face all that is thrown at them at work and burst into tears of anger or frustration when they get home. Cancer's love of money and security usually enables them to become a success in whatever career they choose.

CANCER OCCUPATIONS

domestic help, hotelier, caterer, business executive, accountant, financial adviser, welfare officer, plumber, subaqua diver, sailor, antique collector, furniture restorer, real estate agent

Because they cannot bear to part with anything (this would weaken their sense of security), Cancerians surround themselves with clutter both at home and in the workplace. They love collecting things and are often found in careers which involve accumulation of some kind.

CANCER AND LEISURE

Cancerians make the most of their leisure time either by working extremely hard at home improvements or by curling up in a comfortable armchair listening to their favorite music – often with a lapful of children or pet animals. When Cancerians commit themselves to a leisure pursuit they are keen, enthusiastic, and utterly dedicated. If they can be persuaded to leave the security of their homes, this watery sign will often be found indulging itself beside rivers, lakes, oceans, or just plain rainwater – all are fascinating to this emotional Water sign and virtually all Cancerians enjoy watching or taking part in at least one

LEFT Cancerians love the sea, music, the company of animals, and collecting.

RIGHT The Cancerian is often to be found messing about in boats, a sure reflection of their natures as a Water sign.

watersport. On vacation they enjoy getting their feet wet in or around boats. Many Cancerians take their leisure interests so seriously that they get involved competitively in water sports such as rowing, canoeing, boating, swimming, or scuba diving.

Most Cancerians enjoy looking backward and reliving the past and therefore many of them take up leisure interests such as history, photography, and furniture restoration. They are avid collectors of anything old – stamps, coins, books, antiques, even clothes – and are swift to grab a bargain when they see one. Because most Cancerians are highly domesticated, both sexes tend to enjoy cooking and eating – especially when it comes to preparing the dessert course! Many female Cancerians take up needlework or knitting and males of this sign enjoy pottering about the home. They have a weakness for sentimental music, most classical music, and works that build up to a splendid finale. Sounds of the sea and birdsong in relaxation music work well for them.

POSITIVE CANCER
Love lasts long while money endures.

CANCER AND HEALTH

Cancerians ignore their health and do not take sufficient exercise. In addition, acute vulnerability and over sensitivity are at the core of their health problems. Every little hurt or suffering is taken in via the stomach where it festers and causes digestive problems. Indigestion, stomach ulcers, colitis, and Crohn's disease are but a few of the problems which may occur.

CANCER SPORTS AND EXERCISE

swimming, diving, ice-skating, boating, rowing, golf, cricket, rifle shooting, water polo, surfing

CANCER AND DIET

Cancerians love sweet, milky foods such as chocolate and dairy desserts but these types of foods can cause overacidity in the stomach so care must be taken not to overindulge. Women of this sign are prone to breast ailments such as mastitis. Overeating and overweight are also a problem for the Full-Moon type of Cancerian. This sign is not renowned for its physical prowess, and exercise must be taken slowly and regularly in small doses.

NEGATIVE CANCER
If the Moon rises haloed around, others will be treading on deluged ground.

HEALING FOODS

cabbage, pumpkin, cucumber, seaweed-kelp, mangoes, bananas, mushrooms, melon, strawberries, watercress

5 LEO

★ ★ ★ ★ ★ ★ ★ ★ ★ ★ ★ ★ ★ ★ ★ ★

July 23 to August 22

Leo is ruled by
the Sun

Leo rules the heart
and the spine

Leo is ruled by the
element Fire

**KEYWORD
CHARACTERISTICS**

loyal, proud, egocentric, pompous,
determined, generous, theatrical, lazy,
fun-loving, affectionate, attention-seeking,
bossy, humorous

Thick hair, often fair
or red, drawn back
from the face

Strong features
on square set face

Love of facial or
body adornment

Height medium
to tall, corpulent
in later years

THE NATURE OF LEO

Proud and regal, fiery and determined, the subjects of this sign are
always a bit larger than life. Leos
love to be noticed, admired,
and adored and will do
anything to gain your attention. This is usually achieved
by showing generosity, open-heart-
edness, affection, and good humor,
but when the desired result is not
forthcoming, Leos occasionally
reveal another, less amenable, side to their
natures – they roar loudly, bellow, and
exhibit a terrible anger which frightens all
but the hardiest of souls. By this time, Leos
have usually made their point and won the
battle but if victory still eludes, they may
either charge with ferocious energy and killer

ABOVE Leos often
have a regal expression
as well as some of
these typical traits.

instinct or just as readily back
down and stroll away – it really
depends how hungry they are for
victory. Innately lazy and
good-natured, it is often quite
difficult for Leo subjects to make
an effort to assert themselves,
especially if they are happy with
the way their life is going.

This sign is linked
to orange and gold

Leos are loyal, likeable, and
often quite lovely people, but they
can also be self-indulgent, stubborn, and prone to sulkiness if
they don't get their own way. Leos
who find that negative behavior
often gets results will play the
same tune again and again rather
than improve their way of doing
things. Leos are renowned for
being eternal children who hate to
grow up but it is unpleasant to see
adult Leos stamping their feet and

The birthstone of
Leo is diamond

Sunday is Leo's
lucky day

BELOW Leos can
tend to be slow to
mature and will sulk
or throw a tantrum
regardless of time
or place.

having temper tantrums if they can't get their own way. A wise person ignores Leo at this time because there is nothing Leo hates more than being ignored. When left to ponder their behavior, they soon understand that positive actions breed positive results and quickly revert to being the sweet, kind, amusing people we know and love.

When Leos commit themselves to something or someone, they do so for life or as long as possible. However, relationships built on love and affection can sometimes turn sour and Leos are unable to escape from them because of their unswerving loyalty as well as their fear of being disliked or rejected for being seen to let people down.

Most Leo subjects smile and laugh a great deal, even to excess. They are warm, demonstrative, and theatrical and love pageantry, glitz and glamour. Leos who are well-respected and admired possess hearts of gold which dispense an abundance of love but Leos who feel unloved or unappreciated become depressed, self-pitying, or self-destructive.

LEFT Like the lion that represents them, Leos can roar loudly if things don't go their way.

RIGHT A happy Leo is fun to be around. They are demonstrative and magnetic, displaying great warmth.

LEO IN LOVE

ABOVE Leos love wholeheartedly and genuinely want their relationships to work and last.

Leo is the sign which rules the heart the center of love in its purest, most giving form. Leos love wholeheartedly, without reserve and with utter commitment. Leos always feel devastated if their partner lets them down in any way. A partner who stops adoring or respecting their Leo is felt to be unfaithful or disloyal —even if it was Leo's own fault. Leos can become so egocentric that they lose sight of what is happening in a relationship: it is not always possible for their partner to give unconditional love constantly. A positive, caring Leo is, however, a joy to be with. They can be magnetic, funny, extremely sexy, and remarkably thoughtful. When Leo's relationships work well we can only admire, but a broken Leo relationship is a sorry sight indeed.

POSITIVE LEO

The king sits upon his throne bestowing wondrous gifts on his subjects.

LEO AT WORK

To an onlooker it may seem that Leo at work is achieving very little but this is not so. Leos do not like to hurry over anything: they appear relaxed – even lazy – just like a sleeping lion, but in fact they are always alert and ready to sprint into action at a moment's notice. However, even when moving fast, a Leo can sometimes appear to be going slowly. Leos actually work harder than most when inspired and happy and are their usual loyal and dependable selves. Good old Leos are always there when you need them. They are not as easy-going as they seem, however, and will not tolerate being undermined or dictated to under any circumstances. Some rebel openly against situations they dislike while others develop a slow resentment that eventually erupts into anger, leaving their employer or colleagues wondering what on earth has happened. Leos need to occupy positions of respect and authority and earn this with dedication and hard work. It is vital that they choose a career where they can be happy, as tedium, and a lack of respect and friendship can soon turn laughing Leo into lamentable Leo. A position which allows creativity is also very important within the Leo workplace.

LEO OCCUPATIONS

actor, model, fashion designer, company executive, film director, fire fighter, artist, entertainer, animal trainer, police officer, musician, horse rider, agent, jewelry maker

LEO AND LEISURE

Leo is the lazy lion who loves to sleep, lie back, survey the world with regal aplomb, and generally remain inactive during leisure hours, but when it decides to move, it has strength, courage, speed, and tenacity. Most Leo subjects are remarkably similar to their ruling lion. They love lazing in the sun, but when real action is called for, they are off like a bullet from a gun. Leos are physically strong and capable of great achievements in sports such as marathon running, field athletics, football, and wrestling. They have a great affinity with horses and enjoy equestrian activities such as riding, horseracing, polo, and horseback-hunting. They like to lead and are unhappy following the crowd. Leo ladies love adornment and often work in the world of fashion. Designing and creating clothes or jewelry are excellent pastimes for these women. Occupations

which require an invest-ment of both time and patience are also highly suited to the Leo temperament. Yoga and tai-chi, origami, painting, and music, are all popular. In active mode, Leos enjoy loud, bombastic music with a powerful rhythm and lots of brass and percussion: classical music with large orchestras, for instance, or heavy metal. But in their lazy, quieter moments they prefer to be lulled to sleep with soft, sweet sounds. They enjoy acting and the world of theater and often become involved with amateur dramatic groups. They are easygoing but highly competitive. They are bad losers and always aim to perform at their very best. They try hard once committed but just as they appear to be winning the game, the lazy lion aspect of their natures demands a rest and they break off to recuperate in time for the next one.

LEO AND HEALTH

Leos have a strong con-stitution which can take a great deal of wear and tear. Too much abuse, however, weakens the susceptible Leo heart, making this

NEGATIVE LEO
Pride comes before a fall.
All that glitters is not gold.

sign more prone to heart problems than any other. The natural pride of Leo subjects is apparent from an early age when they automatically assume an upright posture when sitting and walking. It's as if they know their spinal column can be weakened by slouching. Leos who do slouch and hold them-selves badly (especially teenagers) will eventually find themselves paying for it later in life.

LEO AND DIET

Leos possess a hearty appetite and find it hard to thrive on a vegetarian diet. The lion is a natural carnivore and meat seems necessary to the Leo diet. They put on weight easily, and too much fat and sugar can be damaging to their hearts.

HEALING FOODS
citrus fruits, olives, almonds, saffron, cornmeal, pineapple, mangoes, natural honey, cinnamon, bananas

LEO SPORTS AND EXERCISE
running, aerobics, equestrian sports, horse-racing, polo, wrestling, weight-lifting, discus-hammer-javelin, yoga, football, bowls and bowling

LEFT Leos show an aptitude for sports which require unfal-tering strength and have a desire to win against any odds.

VIRGO

★ ★ ★ ★ ★ ★ ★ ★ ★ ★ ★ ★ ★ ★ ★ ★ ★

August 23 to September 22

The Virgo Sun sign is depicted by a woman holding a flower

Virgo is ruled by the planet Mercury

Virgo is ruled by the element Earth

KEYWORD CHARACTERISTICS

intelligent, critical, fussy, discerning, modest, diligent, restless, analytical, practical, serious, smallminded, capable, worrying

LEFT A typical Virgo will show some of these characteristics and will generally be quiet but talkative.

Serious expression, prominent eyes

Medium to tall build; men tend to be slimmer than the women, who can be either glamorous or gawky

THE NATURE OF VIRGO

Virgo is situated midway on the Zodiac in sixth position – and as a result many Virgoans seem to sit on the fence looking backward with confidence and at the same time displaying a certain timidity in moving forward. Unlike neighboring Leos, Virgoan subjects are happy to remain in the background, employing their organizational skills to help those with extrovert talents. Virgos are practical, sensible, logical, and clever. They can make mountains out of molehills in both a positive and negative context. They are often underestimated and ignored while lesser souls receive more opportunities in life because they push themselves to the front of the line. Virgos know they have as much ability as anyone else but shyness and lack of confidence prevent them from showing it and so it is easy for others to walk all over them. Virgoans become indignant when this happens and can be quite caustic in their verbal abuse. This sign is ruled by Mercury, planet of communication, so despite their many inhibitions, Virgoans can talk the hind leg off a donkey and be quite presumptuous and witty in the process.

Virgos are renowned for their fussy, worrying, critical natures – traits which can be very irritating to other signs. They are perfectionists who need to have everything just right and who often feel misunderstood when they are accused of being critical or of complaining too much: they view these qualities as positive expressions of their own needs rather than verbal assaults upon other people. No sign is more critical or more

BELOW Lack of confidence can hold a talented Virgo back and stop them from standing up for themselves.

demanding of itself than Virgo, and if they do not like it when the tables are turned on them, this is because they are fully aware of their own shortcomings and are quite capable of reprimanding themselves and adapting to a change in circumstances.

Fussiness, which borders on obsession at times, is apparent with most Virgoans – some are fussy about anything and everything while others exhibit this trait only occasionally. And there are those who appear seemingly unfussy, rather sloppy Virgos who apparently have no pride in anything. But look closely, however, and you are bound to find that even this type will be highly critical or fussy about something.

The things that matter to Virgo are usually regarded as trivial by others but Virgo knows that big oaks grow from tiny acorns and that you should concentrate on minor and more practical details first. In this they are often proved right.

LEFT Virgos like to keep their affairs in order and can be meticulous about filing and refiling paperwork.

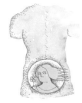

Virgo rules the intestines

Virgo is linked to shades of yellow and green

The birthstone of Virgo is agate

Wednesday is Virgo's lucky day

VIRGO IN LOVE

The sign of the Virgin is often said to be cold, unaffectionate, and lacking in sexual desire. Sometimes this is true, but more often than not these traits are a cover for inherent sensuality. This is an Earth sign and all the Earth signs need strong physical contact with their partners. Unfortunately many Virgoans are secretly ashamed of their desires and brush them to one side. It is only when they are older that they begin to learn that sex as a demonstration of love is nothing to be ashamed of and they begin to lose their inhibitions and become good lovers. Like Mercury-ruled Gemini, they respond well to words, but Virgoans can surprise everyone with their natural ability to write about sexual matters on a very deep level.

Another surprising Virgoan trait is their love of change. Marriage and partnership to them mean variety, communication, and earthy action, but they do need to be careful that their constant carping, nagging, and desire for verbal exchange do not scare partners away.

LEFT Virgoans can express their sexual feelings easier in words than actions.

connections within their birth charts (planets in Fire or Air signs) they can go far within their chosen career, but they have to learn how to push themselves and make others sit up and take note.

VIRGO AND LEISURE

The practical nature and restless psyche of this sign ensure that its subjects seldom relax in their spare time. Virgo loves to be on the move and needs to feel useful in either mental or physical activity. Although they have a weaker constitution than many of the other signs, Virgoans are physically capable of short bursts of energy but, given the choice, they prefer to exercise their brains rather than their bodies. They love doing crosswords, jigsaw puzzles, and all kinds of word games, and are one of the most well read signs of the Zodiac. Not overly competitive, they are, however, highly adept at games involving skill such as chess and bridge. They are equally happy by themselves or joining in with a group activity providing it is not too physically challenging. They prefer less physically demanding, earthy sports such as golf, bowls, and snooker in which their clever, logical minds usually enable them to take the lead and become very successful. Figures, of the mathematical kind, fascinate them and many enjoy lending their skills as treasurer, accountant, or auditor to leisure and charity work. Not known as great lovers of music, Virgoans will

ABOVE Virgos enjoy being out of doors but would rather hone their mental agility than test their muscles.

VIRGO AT WORK

Virgos will often take on the jobs that nobody else wants – tedious humdrum tasks that take time, organizational skills, and concentration. Virgos love to be occupied and need to be of service to others. They work well behind the scenes in almost any kind of situation except highly strenuous

VIRGO OCCUPATIONS

secretary, filing clerk, nurse, welfare officer, cartographer, architect, estimator, banker, accountant, domestic help, writer, draughtsman or draughtswoman, computer operator, alternative therapist, nutritionist

ABOVE Virgos are attracted to careers which allow them to help others – as long as they are not too strenuous.

occupations. Because their own brains work quickly and efficiently, they are sometimes impatient with those less able than themselves. They like to look after others and are often attracted to jobs in the caring professions. They are good with financial matters and their logical approach makes them ideally suited to banking or accountancy work. Virgo is a truly adaptable sign with many capabilities. With the right planetary

NEGATIVE VIRGO
Vice is often clothed in virtue's habit.

POSITIVE VIRGO
Good industrious work produces fine rewards.

ABOVE Virgos can literally worry themselves sick suspecting various ailments when they are in perfect health.

only listen to their favorite pieces for short spells at a time. They have lots of natural rhythm and musical ability but are usually too busy doing other things to take music seriously; however, music and literary critics are common among this sign. They enjoy being out in the open and many take up hiking or rock-climbing. Computers and other hi-tech equipment fascinates them and they enjoy surfing the Internet.

VIRGO AND HEALTH

The sign of Virgo is the central figurehead for all health concerns. People of this sign thrive on health matters – and sometimes become obsessed by them. This is the sign of the true hypochondriac. Most Virgos worry constantly about their health – some in a positive sense by taking care of their diet and lifestyle, others in a negative way by imagining they have every disease under the sun. The worrying in itself can often produce the symptoms Virgo is determined to alleviate.

ABOVE Virgos are more suited to deliberate skillful sports than fast and furious ones.

Always a tense sign, Virgos need to learn to relax and accept that they are just as healthy as everyone else - in fact they are usually one of the healthiest of the 12 signs. Their constitutions are sound and they grow old gracefully, often retaining a remarkably youthful appearance. Virgos seem to thrive on the attention that ill-health can bring – sometimes it's the only way for them to be cossetted and get the affection they crave – but eventually, Virgo cries wolf once too often and loved ones turn away.

VIRGO AND DIET

Virgoans rarely possess a hearty appetite and can sometimes survive on very little. They are always fussy eaters and are often plagued with food allergies, both real and imagined. They need a diet that is high in carbohydrates and a variety of vegetables with just a little protein as this can sometimes be difficult for them to digest. Whatever they choose to eat, they often suffer from indigestion and intestinal problems such as diverticulitis, irritable bowel syndrome, and Crohn's disease.

Virgoans need plenty of physical exercise in short sharp bursts, but many Virgoans shun exercise in favor of mental pursuits.

HEALING FOODS

parsnips, green beans, apples, parsley, carrots, watercress, dill, cilantro, marjoram, mint, caraway seeds, alfalfa, brown rice

VIRGO SPORTS AND EXERCISE

golf, walking, yoga, tai-chi, billiards, bowls, table tennis, badminton, cricket, gymnastics, triple-jump, darts, snooker, orienteering, hiking

LIBRA

* * * * * * * * * * * * * * * *

September 23 to October 22

Libra is ruled by
the planet Venus

Libra is ruled by
the element Air

Libra is linked with
blue and red

KEYWORD CHARACTERISTICS

charming, polite, indecisive, refined,
well-balanced, sociable, impractical,
self-seeking, cool, well-read, quietly
extroverted, romantic

THE NATURE OF LIBRA

Libra is the seventh sign of the Zodiac, ruled by Venus the planet of love, harmony, and beauty and Libran subjects tend to center their lives around love and relationships. People born under this sign need a partner in order to be at their best and feel fulfilled.

Aware of every option in any situation, Librans are reluctant to select a direction until they are absolutely certain it is the right one. For this reason they tend to be thought indecisive. Librans love to impose a sense of order in their lives – everything must look perfect – appearance, clothing, possessions, home, and environment must be scrupulously clean and tidy. They cannot bear dirt, squalor, ugliness, bad language, aggressive attitudes, and hypocrisy – though they are not averse to employing double standards when it suits them.

Although Librans are inherently self-seeking and lack emotional depth, they are generally well-liked for their calm, friendly manner and polite demeanor. Libran children are popular with adults as they are often well-behaved, intelligent, and respectful toward their peers. Underneath all the sweetness and light, however, most Librans possess a hard, cold, steely core. When they are confronted and forced to show their true colors, subjects of this sign can turn out to be remarkably hard, aggressive, and verbally self-protective, more akin to the opposite sign of Aries than Venus-ruled Libra. It may seem that Librans are easy to dupe, take for granted, or ride roughshod over, but those who attempt this will soon realize their mistake. Librans know what they want and they use all the tools of their sign to achieve these ends. If charm and pleasantness do not bring results, they eventually resort to tougher measures.

ABOVE The Libran Sun sign is a set of scales. This reflects the Libran struggle to achieve a balance in their lives.

ABOVE Librans may appear indecisive but are actually looking at every possible angle to be absolutely sure of the best direction.

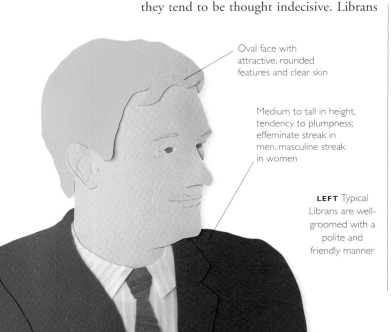

Oval face with attractive, rounded features and clear skin

Medium to tall in height, tendency to plumpness; effeminate streak in men, masculine streak in women

LEFT Typical Librans are well-groomed with a polite and friendly manner

BELOW Libran children are popular for their good behavior.

The birthstone of Libra is opal

Libra rules the kidneys and bladder

Friday is Libra's lucky day

Outwardly likeable, gracious, and caring, it comes as a surprise when, at the slightest hint of trouble, Librans quickly vanish. When they reappear sometime later, once everything has returned to normal, they will be full of apologies and highly plausible excuses. They are invariably forgiven for this apparent lapse in conduct and are rarely considered disloyal or cowardly. But Librans will, in fact, remain loyal to a person or a cause only as long as it suits their own needs and interests. They are highly adept at managing to get their own way without anyone realizing it. They will, however, turn up the charm and fight tooth and nail, or whatever it takes, to see fair play for themselves and others if they consider that an injustice has taken place. They will also readily give support to the underdog. To achieve balance in all aspects of their lives is the ultimate aim of most Librans, but sometimes the means does not justify the end.

LIBRA IN LOVE

Libran subjects tend to live and breathe in a heady atmosphere dominated by themes of love. Forever seeking a soul mate, they are often convinced they have found the right one until the inevitable cracks in the relationship begin to appear, causing the Libran perfectionist to crumble into despair, lament their lost love and then move quickly on in order to find their true soul mate. Librans want their partners to be perfect – loving, romantic, caring, and intellectually supportive – qualities which Librans themselves can supply in abundance within a relationship that is working well. Librans believe that to give is to receive and that equality and balance are vital, though their partners are not always able to match up to these requirements.

Librans are sexually attractive and rarely short of prospective partners. They can be affectionate, glamorous, and romantic, but they can also be petulant, cool, and impersonal when thwarted. They form relationships swiftly and easily but are just as likely to abandon them in the same manner.

BELOW Romance is the key to Libra's love life, but if the romance wears off, the Libran perfectionist will quickly disappear in search of their ideal.

ABOVE Librans exude charm and elegance, and with their love of high fashion, can make good models.

LIBRA AT WORK

Librans are imaginative and creative, intelligent and diplomatic, and are an asset to many working environments. Under no circumstances will they get their hands dirty however, or be harassed into doing something they do not want to do. They are adept at charming someone else into doing the monotonous and messy tasks that make them cringe. In the right environment with a salary to match their abilities, they are capable of great achievements. Many Librans charm their way to the top in whatever they choose to do. However, if they are unable to complete a task to the highest of standards, they prefer not to attempt it in the first place. Sometimes they appear slow, lazy, or unhurried, but this is the manner in which Venus-ruled signs (Taurus and Libra) operate – it rarely means that they are not trying. They are far more suited to artistic, creative or intellectually oriented careers than manual or physical jobs.

LIBRA AND LEISURE

Venus-ruled Librans prefer to take things easy during their leisure hours and there is nothing they enjoy more than curling up in an easy chair with a good book. They also enjoy watching TV but usually dislike programs containing violence, bloodshed, or vulgarity. Librans like everything to be nice and appreciate peaceful, harmonious environments. When they make the effort, they can spend hours of leisure time improving their homes and transforming them into attractive and sophisticated places. They won't do the hard, dirty work, of course – someone else will have to do that. Librans are surprisingly strong when forced into physical exercise and

LIBRAN OCCUPATIONS

florist, librarian, fashion model, fashion designer, publisher, journalist, artist, air steward, musician, receptionist, beauty consultant, hairdresser, judge, lawyer, arbitrator, counselor, media representative, presenter

RIGHT Librans appreciate the beauty of nature and favor activities involving graceful movements.

LIBRA AND HEALTH

Generally speaking, people with this sign possess a sound constitution with good health but too many excesses in food and love – they tend to overeat if they are unhappy within a relationship – can eventually lead to the development of health problems often involving the kidneys, the adrenal glands, and the bladder. Cystitis is a common complaint among female Librans and often occurs when they consider their partner is not giving them enough attention. Librans who are unable to find love will often develop kidney stones.

LEFT Librans like to feel a sense of harmony and tend toward artistic forms of exercise like synchronized swimming.

can enjoy such activities as ice-skating, tennis, trampolining, and badminton. Their love of beauty can draw them toward dancing, particularly ballroom and sequence dancing, while their strong musical ability leads them to join choirs and singing groups. They also like operas, ballet, musicals, ballads, light classics, meditational music, and easy-listening pop music. Libran women (and often the men, too) enjoy attending fashion shows and shopping for clothes and luxuries.

All Librans appreciate fine art and objects of beauty. They like to be seen at all the fashionable places, especially when being wined and dined. They love to be in the company of other people and enjoy communicating and socializing. Flower-arranging, yoga, and aerial activities such as flying, hot-air ballooning, and paragliding also appeal to their breezy temperaments.

HEALING FOODS

cinnamon, basil, pennyroyal, raspberries, sorrel, artichokes, blackberries, almond oil, pears, cashew nuts, dates

LIBRA SPORTS AND EXERCISE

ice-skating, gymnastics, badminton, yoga, tai-chi, high jump, long jump, pole-vault, bowls, bowling, cricket, synchronized swimming, ballroom dancing

LIBRA AND DIET

Librans love to eat good quality, nutritious food but they also have a sweet tooth and may become chocoholics. Too many candle-lit dinners with copious amounts of alcohol can also lead them to put on a great deal of weight in later years. Vanity, and a desire to retain their youthful looks, can sometimes save them from self-destructive habits but they usually resist taking any exercise until it becomes absolutely essential.

SCORPIO

✶ ✶ ✶ ✶ ✶ ✶ ✶ ✶ ✶ ✶ ✶ ✶ ✶ ✶ ✶ ✶ ✶

October 23 to November 21

Scorpio is ruled by
the planet Pluto

Scorpio rules
the bowels and
reproductive
organs

This sign has
links with deep
red and black

The birthstone
of Scorpio is
malachite

Scorpio is ruled by
the element Water

Tuesday is Scorpio's
lucky day

KEYWORD CHARACTERISTICS

possessive, intense, emotional, secretive,
sexy, determined, intuitive, penetrating,
shrewd, powerful, controlled, magnetic,
resilient, loyal

THE NATURE OF SCORPIO

Scorpio is probably the most feared and yet the most revered sign of the Zodiac. The symbolic scorpion with the poisonous sting in its tail has much to answer for. True, Scorpion subjects can sometimes turn and lash out viciously but only after they have been harassed or pushed beyond endurance, a quality they possess in abundance. Most Scorpios would not hurt a fly for they are as gentle, caring, and generous as they can be hard, cruel, and mean. It really depends how they are treated. This is a sign which demands respect and usually gets it. But things occasionally go wrong and Scorpio is unwisely rejected, ignored, or treated harshly for no apparent reason. This is the

ABOVE Push a
Scorpio too far
and you'll soon wish
you hadn't.

moment when Scorpio strikes back, sometimes immediately with an emotional physical or verbal attack but more often with a calculated act of revenge. Scorpio thus confirms its reputation, leaving its victims – and those who know them well – wondering what they have done wrong.

Although they rarely admit it, Scorpions are highly sensitive, emotional creatures who are so easily hurt that they cannot bear to show their feelings for fear of being ridiculed. The other Water signs (Cancer and Pisces) cry easily and let their feelings out, but Scorpios develop from an early age the ability to control such outer expressions of emotion, and remain dry-eyed. However, they weep bucketfuls when they do finally release themselves. Because their emotions are so deep and strongly felt, undesirable traits such as jealousy and possessiveness are difficult to control.

ABOVE The
presence of a sting
in the Scorpion's
tail demands that
it be feared
and respected.

RIGHT As well as the typical
characteristics of appearance
shown here, Scorpios have a
serious, intense look about them.

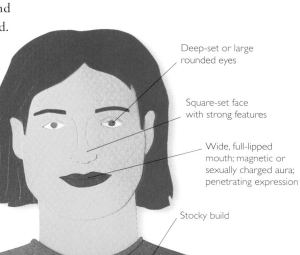

Deep-set or large
rounded eyes

Square-set face
with strong features

Wide, full-lipped
mouth; magnetic or
sexually charged aura;
penetrating expression

Stocky build

RIGHT Scorpios are deeply emotional and easily hurt but will hide their emotions from others for fear of being laughed at.

Intrinsically loyal themselves, they can neither understand nor accept deceitfulness in others. Scorpios do not forgive easily, if even at all, and are capable of holding a grudge for the rest of their lives.

Scorpio subjects are hard-working, generous to a fault, and very determined. Once they begin a task, they will be dedicated to finishing it. They can become obsessively devoted to a person, a cause, or a project and when this happens, the Scorpion seems to be wearing blinkers. Nothing exists apart from their current obsession. Trying to persuade a Scorpio to change their mind once it has been made up is like trying to make the stars fall from the sky: then even major distractions have only a minor effect.

This is the sign which is ruled by Pluto, the planet linked to destructive events such as volcanic eruptions and nuclear warfare. Scorpios think that they have the power to shift mountains and, figuratively speaking, it is amazing how often they come close to achieving this.

ABOVE Scorpio is ruled by the planet Pluto which is linked to volcanic eruptions and warfare.

SCORPIO IN LOVE

Scorpios love deeply, loyally and possessively. They are highly sexed, extremely magnetic and make marvelous lovers. In a loving relationship there is nothing Scorpio will not do to make their partner happy. They are protective toward loved ones and always stand up for them even when their partner is in the wrong. Unfortunately, they expect this support to be reciprocated and are devastated when it is not forthcoming. Scorpios can love too much. Once they commit themselves it is truly for better or for worse — on both sides, for they will cling tenaciously to any relationship, using every weapon known to them to prevent someone else from taking what they perceive as rightfully theirs regardless of how unhappy they are. Hence Scorpio's reputation for jealousy and possessiveness is realized. Marriage to a Scorpio will either be a wonderful, all-consuming experience, or a prison from which there is no escape.

LEFT A Scorpio will do everything they can to keep a partner in a loveless relationship.

employers. Their shrewd
business sense can lead
them into the world of
high finance, stock-
broking, and company
ownership. It is difficult
to pull the wool over the
eyes of Scorpio and woe
betide anyone who tries.
The penetrating, accu-

ABOVE Scorpios
are serious souls
with an abundance
of energy which
must be correctly
channeled.

SCORPIO AT WORK

Give Scorpio a job that requires tenacity and
dedication and they will be supremely
happy, but if adaptability, communication,
and mobility are required, then think twice
about employing a person born under this
sign. Scorpios prefer to stay in one place and
work quietly at their own efficient pace. If
challenged, however, they can be aggressively
verbal in their own defence. Despite their
somewhat rigid approach, they are
marvelous at organizing others and make
excellent, if somewhat demanding,

sing stare of a wronged Scorpio can turn
even the strongest legs to jelly.

Scorpios are secretive creatures regarding
their affairs and their innermost motives, but
they are remarkably adept at prizing
information from others. This talent makes
them ideal for psychiatric or detective work.

SCORPIO AND LEISURE

The natural intensity of the Scorpio subject
demands that leisure activities be taken
seriously, yet many Scorpios find it hard to
involve themselves as much as they would
like – mundane duties and responsibilities
often seem to get in the way. Scorpio is
reckoned to be the most determined sign of
the Zodiac, however, and come what may,
most of them insist they are thoroughly
relaxed and able to enjoy their free time. The
sheer tenacity of this sign makes them
excellent players in almost any sport which
demands intense concentration and physical
endurance. Weight-lifting, boxing, wrestling,
marathon running, field athletics, and yoga
are but a few. The Water element of Scorpio
also attracts them to all kinds of water sports,
but scuba diving, swimming, and boating
activities suit them best. Unlike Librans,

BELOW The alert
nature of Scorpio
combined with
their love of water
makes the job of
lifeguard ideal.

SCORPIO OCCUPATIONS

stockbroker, private detective,
police officer, gynecologist,
surgeon, midwife, company
director, psychiatrist, alternative
therapist, army officer, lifeguard,
undertaker, butcher

POSITIVE SCORPIO
Silence is golden. Still waters run deep.

NEGATIVE SCORPIO
He who despises his own life is soon master of another's.

SCORPIO SPORTS AND EXERCISE

weight-lifting, tennis, yoga, marathon running, snooker, fencing, pistol and rifle shooting, darts, swimming, scuba-diving, fishing, canoeing, sailing, all endurance activities

Scorpios enjoy tense, gritty television programs with plenty of violence and bloodshed. Their musical taste is often extreme and always heavy; anything from Beethoven to the Sex Pistols is appropriate to their brooding temperaments. Music is often one of the few outlets through which Scorpios can release their pent-up emotions and tears. People of this sign like to read – somewhat slowly and carefully – and take up serious studies such as psychiatry and

astrology. They are drawn to magic and the occult, and enjoy analyzing the reactions and behavior of other people. They excel at mind games, board-games, and cards, and love solving riddles and puzzles. The tremendous mental and physical strength of this sign makes them formidable opponents.

ABOVE Scorpios enjoy watersports, while the patience and concentration required by fishing suits them well.

SCORPIO AND HEALTH

Despite a remarkably strong constitution, Scorpio subjects seem to fall prey to both major and minor illnesses throughout their lives. Psychologically, this could be due to the constant suppression of very powerful emotions and deep-rooted feelings of guilt and inferiority. The recuperative ability of this sign, however, is quite remarkable and many a Scorpio has survived to a ripe old age after a multitude of serious operations or illnesses. The planet Pluto indicates that Scorpios have the ability to rise rejuvenated from the ashes and ready to start over from where they left off.

Scorpio is one of the most intuitive signs of the Zodiac and many highly developed souls of this sign experience prophecies, miracles, or true enlightenment concerning emotional or health matters at some time during their lives. Scorpios can achieve great highs or sink to the lowest depths of despair or depravity. Illnesses such as venereal disease, syphilis, and Aids are all related to this Pluto-ruled sign. Retention of emotion also causes constipation and bowel problems. Scorpio women are prone to womb, vaginal, or menstruation difficulties while Scorpio men need to take care of their prostate gland.

SCORPIO AND DIET

Subjects of this sign usually enjoy eating meat and other animal proteins, and although they need to balance their intake with a variety of nutritious fruit and vegetables, like Leo, they do not thrive on a wholly vegetarian diet.

HEALING FOODS

kelp, watercress, brown rice, aloes, garlic, onions, beets, spirulina, potatoes, carrots, brazil nuts

9 SAGITTARIUS

★ ★ ★ ★ ★ ★ ★ ★ ★ ★ ★ ★ ★ ★ ★ ★ ★

November 22 to December 21

Sagittarius is ruled by the planet Jupiter

Sagittarius rules the thighs and liver

Sagittarius is ruled by the element Fire

THE NATURE OF SAGITTARIUS

The influence of the planet Jupiter enables the subjects of Sagittarius to express themselves in an expansive, larger-than-life manner. People of this sign cannot bear their lives to be confined or controlled and their urge to break free from shackles, real or imaginary, is so strong that when the "No Escape" signal goes up they panic and become verbally aggressive, self-pitying, self-destructive and uncontrollable. Given freedom, they are warm, affectionate, funny,

RIGHT True to the depiction of this sign as half horse, half archer, Sagittarians are changeable and must have freedom.

and interesting companions. Ironically, when an escape route opens ahead of them, most Sagittarians are happy to stay where they are – but this is part of the enigma of the duality of this mutable sign. The adaptability of Sagittarius gives ambidexterity to its subjects and enables them to tackle more than one thing at a time. Concentration is not their strong point, however, and they often become unstuck when taking on too much. Their love of change and variety makes them fascinating but unreliable: what was important to them last week has been completely forgotten this week. Projects are started but not finished, appointments and promises are made but not kept, and words are spoken which mean nothing a few days later. Sagittarians listen earnestly to advice but rarely follow it. They have a mind of their own and go through life

This sign has links with dark red, orange, and indigo

The birthstone of Sagittarius is carbuncle

THU

Thursday is the Sagittarian lucky day

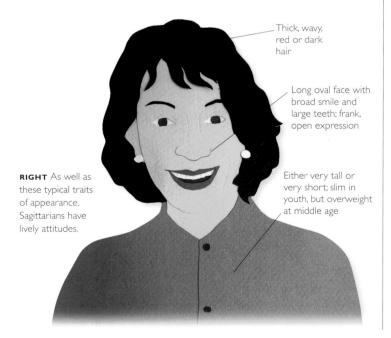

RIGHT As well as these typical traits of appearance, Sagittarians have lively attitudes.

Thick, wavy, red or dark hair

Long oval face with broad smile and large teeth; frank, open expression

Either very tall or very short; slim in youth, but overweight at middle age

learning things the hard way. Fortunately, they are easily able to forgive and forget – tears or temper tantrums turn to fun and laughter within a short space of time, and when Sagittarians smile or laugh, their happiness is infectious. The sunny aspect of their nature turns even the angriest tide in their favor. Regarded as the luckiest sign of the Zodiac, Sagittarians always appear to land on their feet. They can be reckless and foolhardy, and children of this sign are often prone to accidents. Their adventurous, exploring natures are rarely deterred, however, and typical Sagittarians when hurt or thwarted will howl loudly, complain bitterly, then simply pick themselves up, and move on to the next adventure.

Sagittarians are known for their bluntness and what they perceive as plain honesty. Diplomacy is an alien word to them. Ask for their opinion and you will get it in no uncertain terms. This makes them unintentionally hurtful, rude, and ungracious. They are great storytellers. The realm of make-believe means a lot to them, and their tales, though convincing, are usually far from true.

LEFT Although Sagittarian children are often accident prone, it rarely distracts them from seeking adventure.

ABOVE Local gossip can be transformed beyond recognition in the hands of a Sagittarian.

SAGITTARIUS IN LOVE

The fickle, adaptable nature of Sagittarius does not make it easy for its subjects to remain constant in love. They fall in and out of love like a yo-yo, sometimes with the same person. To be trapped in an unhappy relationship or marriage is unendurable for a Sagittarian. At the slightest hint of difficulty they are off – some return quickly, others arrive back on their partner's doorstep months or years later as if nothing had happened, and a few are gone for good. Sagittarians can become remorseful when separated from their partners – here, absence certainly does make the heart grow fonder – but even though they return full of goodwill and good intentions they soon feel trapped again and so the cycle is repeated – if the partner will allow it, and many will. This is because a Sagittarian who is truly in love is a wonderfully warm, generous, affectionate and highly entertaining person.

LEFT Time apart is important for a Sagittarian partner and can help the relationship.

SAGITTARIUS AT WORK

The key to keeping Sagittarians happy at their jobs is variety and lots of freedom to complete tasks at their own convenience. Sagittarians dislike being trapped in a nine-to-five routine. They have gregarious natures

ABOVE A job that involves constant movement such as a cab-driver will suit the Sagittarian's restless nature.

and love to communicate – to them, the office party or long lunch are part of the job. The Fire signs (Aries, Leo, and Sagittarius) take an enthusiastic approach to life, but Sagittarians can be effusively keen in the initial phases of a job or career and then, like Aries, quickly lose interest and need to move on to something else. However, unlike Aries, they will often return to what they were doing in the first place. Occupy their minds with different activities, give them time and plenty of leeway, and chances are they will finish the job – though sometimes it can be too late. Fortunately, the jovial charm of the Sagittarian can usually run rings around an employer – but when the system eventually breaks down, as it invariably does, they have already resigned and moved on.

Jobs that involve travel, communication, selling, and variety are ideally suited to the Sagittarian temperament.

SAGITTARIUS AND LEISURE

Subjects of this sign are restless, imaginative, and adventurous. The prospect of sitting still is absolutely abhorrent to them. For most Sagittarians the word "leisure" means "activity" and they are willing to try anything that involves physical movement. Both sexes of this sign know how to enjoy themselves – often to extremes. They enjoy most activities but have problems with slow, earthy sports such as golf or bowls. They make excellent, enthusiastic, and optimistic team-mates and enjoy team games such as baseball, basketball, football, and hockey. In common with the other two Fire signs, Aries and Leo, they are also keen on equestrian sports like horse-racing, polo, and hunting, but their concentration and physical stamina are not as strong. Good communicators, Sagittarians enjoy reading and storytelling. Their minds are ever alert and prepared for the next exciting activity. Young Sagittarians are often hyperactive, constantly seeking movement and pleasure, but as they grow older, most Sagittarians learn to conserve energy to their advantage. All target sports such as archery, rifle-shooting, and darts appeal to their sharp

SAGITTARIAN OCCUPATIONS

sales representative, truck-driver, cab-driver, fire fighter, travel representative, croupier, jockey, odd-job person, comedian, entertainer, short-story writer

mental ability but although they may be highly talented, many Sagittarians fail to win awards in sport because of sudden lapses in their concentration. Though not overly musical, they have an excellent sense of rhythm and are particularly keen on modern music, powerful percussion, and rock music.

SAGITTARIUS AND HEALTH

Sagittarians have a fairly strong constitution but too many indulgences – food, drink, gambling, sex, and exercise – cause health problems from middle age onward. Too much drink is particularly bad for them as their livers are highly susceptible to alcohol. Likewise, too much fat in the diet can also be dangerous. Most Sagittarians take part in vigorous sporting activities and usually have strong legs but thighs are often weak in some

---

SAGITTARIUS SPORTS AND EXERCISE

archery, horse-riding, polo, hockey, pistol and rifle shooting, aerobics, athletics (good decathlon competitor), triple jump, darts, football, baseball, basketball

---

way. The innate optimism of Sagittarius convinces its subjects that they will never have health problems but this, of course, is not so.

SAGITTARIANS AND DIET

Sagittarians are very seldom health-conscious or aware of their diet and will pay no heed to advice warning them about their excesses. As a result they tend to fall ill far more frequently than they should. They are natural born hunters and survive well on a carnivorous diet but too much animal produce can lead to high blood pressure, florid complexions, and a shortness of breath. They should be encouraged to balance their meat intake with a variety of nutritious fruit and vegetables.

ABOVE Sagittarians can be heavy drinkers which is unsuitable for them as their livers are particularly vulnerable to alcohol.

HEALING FOODS

asparagus, mint, olives, dandelion leaves, mulberries, hawthorn berries, rose hips, chestnuts, pure maple syrup, sage, thyme, nutmeg

10 CAPRICORN

★ ★ ★ ★ ★ ★ ★ ★ ★ ★ ★ ★ ★ ★ ★ ★

December 22 to January 19

Capricorn is
ruled by the
planet Saturn

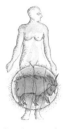

Capricorn rules
the skin, bones,
and knees

Capricorn is ruled
by the element
Earth

BELOW
Capricorns have a
tendency to carry
the world on their
shoulders which
can sometimes be
reflected in their
appearance.

THE NATURE OF CAPRICORN

The heavy Saturnine influence on this sign endows Capricorn subjects with a sense of duty and responsibility toward themselves and others. Capricorns like to be seen to be doing the right thing, and although they can take in their stride everything that life throws at them, they are seldom able to deal lightly with any problems. The art of living in itself can sometimes be difficult for them but their powerful will to succeed gives them the ability to grit their teeth and struggle on regardless. Slowly but surely Capricorns soldier on down the road of

ABOVE Like the goat, Capricorn is sturdy and can survive hardship.

success. Unfortunately, they can sometimes be ruthless or unsympathetic toward others as they strive to achieve those goals. Because they work hard at everything they do, they expect everyone else to be the same. Laziness, apathy, and lack of ambition are alien words to Capricorns who firmly believe that others must also pull their weight – and those who don't deserve to get trampled on. When forced to stop and consider their actions, many Capricorns are mortified by what they are doing and try to make amends but others are too stubborn to correct their behavior, and so it is not without justification that the Capricornian reputation for hardness, coolness, and cruelty has evolved.

From a very early age Capricorns seem to have old heads on their young shoulders. Baby Capricorns have fewer tantrums than other children and seldom misbehave as often. They prefer to watch and wait until the right moment comes along and then show just how clever, witty, and lovable they really are. Even the sternest of Capricorn subjects will usually possess a droll, dry sense of humor hidden deep beneath that hard outer skin.

Capricorns need masses of respect, recognition, and security in their lives and with this level of support they can develop

KEYWORD CHARACTERISTICS

sensible, reserved, cautious, ambitious,
hard-working, reliable, cold, insecure, wise,
moralistic, earthy, serious, determined,
sensual, dutiful

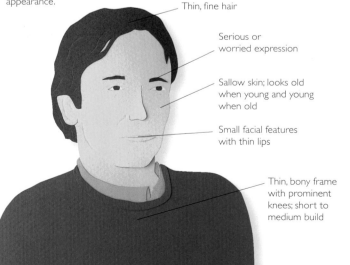

Thin, fine hair

Serious or
worried expression

Sallow skin; looks old
when young and young
when old

Small facial features
with thin lips

Thin, bony frame
with prominent
knees; short to
medium build

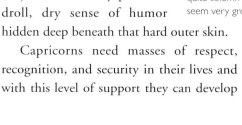

ABOVE Baby Capricorns can be quite solemn and seem very grown-up.

CAPRICORN IN LOVE

The insecurities and fears inherent with most Capricorns are rarely more apparent than when they fall in love. Fear of being rejected or humiliated makes them resist showing their true feelings until absolutely sure of complete acceptance – a tall order even for the most ardent of lovers. If this is forthcoming Capricorns become affectionate and uninhibited creatures, allowing their sensuality to flow freely. As long as love and security remain intact, Capricorns will be content forever. They would never dream for a moment of being disloyal, unfaithful, or even slightly flirtatious with anyone else as monogamy for them is almost a moral duty. But if things do go wrong Capricorn, instead of letting go gracefully, hangs on, ashamed to admit defeat and desperate to be loved again. It is uncommon for Capricorn to desert a partner even when love has died but they can become bitter, resentful, and vindictive toward a straying partner on one hand while at the same time hanging on grimly with the other. Generally, Capricorns make loyal, caring partners who fight hard to make a relationship work.

RIGHT Capricorns do not like to give up on love and will hang on grimly to a relationship, even when spurned.

Capricorn is linked to gray, dark brown, green, and black

The birthstone of Capricorn is jade

Saturday is Capricorn's lucky day

into greatly loved and revered members of society. Without these factors, however, they are likely to be miserable, miserly, withdrawn, and calculating. Once set on a negative course, it is difficult for them to grow into the pillars of society they would dearly love to be. Capricorns of all types are intrinsically loyal, reliable, honest, hard-working, and astute, but when their desire to reach the top outweighs all else, they can become hypocritical, judgmental, and status-seeking. Some adult Capricorns appear formidable or unapproachable, especially toward children or those weaker than themselves, but it is worth making an effort to get to know people of this sign as their bark is always worse than their bite and their inner core is surprisingly soft, sensitive, and loving.

BELOW Capricorns strive to reach the top of their career, which may involve a duty to others.

CAPRICORN AT WORK

The influence of Saturn as the ruler of this sign endows Capricorns with the ability to work long and hard for little reward. Their endurance usually pays dividends, however, and many of them reach the highest positions of authority, respect, and affluence within their chosen careers. But no matter how high they go, or how wealthy they become, Capricorns always want to step onto the next rung of the ladder. Sometimes, they climb so high that it is impossible for them to go any farther but it happens that in their constant striving, they take one step too many and find themselves tumbling back down to the bottom again. But, like their figurehead, the goat, they quickly dust themselves off, lick their wounds, and start over.

RIGHT Capricorns are not afraid of hard work and long hours and like jobs which require skill and efficiency.

CAPRICORN OCCUPATIONS

judge, lawyer, police officer, high-ranking military officer, civil servant, traffic warden, prison guard, bank executive, tax official, insurance sales executive, secretary, engineer, auto mechanic, shopkeeper

The moral attitudes that Capricorns hold in high esteem lead them into careers within the armed forces, civil service, legal profession, and occupations which require discipline, efficiency, and hard work.

CAPRICORN AND LEISURE

The slow, serious side of the Capricorn temperament is invariably carried over into their leisure activities. Capricorns do enjoy themselves but more gregarious signs of the Zodiac find this hard to accept. To more active signs it is a mystery that anyone can

RIGHT The quiet, serious nature of Capricorn is usually reflected in their choice of leisure pursuits.

HEALING FOODS
raisins, beech nuts, pine nuts, barley, spinach, carrots, beets, turnips, sloes, tamarind

enjoy their leisure pursuits in such a dull, dour manner as a Capricorn. However, wise subjects born under this sign will firmly reply that you do not have to fling your arms about, or yell and shout in order to have fun. Capricorn people enjoy their own company and are quite happy to sit and read for hours on end. But they are cool and shrewd when competing in sports and should not be underestimated. They seldom admit defeat in anything and that includes their leisure pursuits, too. Favored sports are the slow earthy ones such as snooker, bowls, bowling, cricket, gentle hiking, and mountaineering. Their small, bony frames are well suited to gymnastics and long-distance running but their weak constitutions sometimes make it hard for them to undertake heavy physical activity, especially when they're young. They are surprisingly musical and, in common with Taurus, enjoy both singing and listening to music, usually with a preference for something classical or serious and heavy. Many Capricorns dislike spending money and will avoid pastimes that are costly. Solitary hikes in the cold or rain are often enough to satisfy their meagre tastes.

CAPRICORN AND HEALTH
Because of their thin, wiry build, Capricorns often look unhealthier than they really are but, when young, they do seem more prone to illness than other children. Born in the height of winter, they need to be well looked after and kept warm. But they are great survivors. Capricorn children who are weak or unhealthy often grow into remarkably healthy adults who not only feel good, but look years younger than their actual age. Many elderly Capricorns who have aged gracefully also tend to rediscover their lost youth and the sight of an active Capricornian senior laughing and playing like a child is a wonderful experience. Of course, even healthy Capricorns eventually succumb to illness: arthritis is the commonest problem, followed by skin and knee ailments. Capricorns who have not been able to release emotions or reach the heights they strove for can suffer from a variety of different problems – rheumatoid arthritis, paralysis, ME, and severe mental depression, for instance.

CAPRICORN SPORTS AND EXERCISE
rock-climbing, mountaineering, golf, rambling, hiking, potholing, snooker, bowls, jogging, skiing, yoga

CAPRICORN AND DIET
As babies and young children, Capricorns need to be encouraged to eat properly but their appetites improve as they grow older. They need to nibble or graze constantly on energizing, healthy snacks such as carrots, dried fruit, and nuts. Heavy meals are not easily digested by this sign and should be avoided.

RIGHT Endurance and the courage to meet a challenge can lead adventurous Capricorns to climbing activities.

AQUARIUS

★ ★ ★ ★ ★ ★ ★ ★ ★ ★ ★ ★ ★ ★ ★

January 20 to February 18

Aquarius is ruled by the planet Uranus

Indigo and deep blue are linked to Aquarius

Aquarius is ruled by the element Air

Aquarius rules the legs and ankles

The birthstone of Aquarius is sapphire

Saturday is the Aquarian lucky day

KEYWORD CHARACTERISTICS

friendly, humane, detached, eccentric, intelligent, cool, aloof, self-opinionated, magnetic, unique, stubborn, unemotional, gifted

THE NATURE OF AQUARIUS

Aquarius is one of the hardest signs of the Zodiac to understand – perhaps because its symbol the Water Carrier represents emotions and a sensitivity that are at odds with the element of Air which governs the sign. The wavy lines of the Aquarian symbol that look like water are, in fact, electrical currents or brainwaves and are particularly appropriate to this sign. Aquarius is not an emotional sign, especially on a personal, one-to-one level. Friends and partners expect Aquarians to show lots of feelings and are puzzled when this doesn't happen. As a result, Aquarians are often felt to be unfathomable when in reality they live almost entirely on the surface. True, they carry their emotions in the water urn, but these rarely spill over and Aquarians will not reveal their innermost feelings no matter how hard others may try to persuade them, simply because they are unable to do so. Emotion? Aquarians do not even know the meaning of the word.

ABOVE This sign carries what emotions it has in the water urn, and rarely spills a drop.

Aquarius is a mentally active sign and if we could peer inside their brains, we would be amazed at the constant level of highly-charged activity going on in there. Aquarians exploit this sharp intellect and knowledge to get what they want from life. People of this sign have a reputation for being enigmatic, difficult to understand, and different from everyone else, and cleverly play on this to gain power and attention. They are extremely friendly yet detached at a personal level, sociable in large gatherings, but unsociable at smaller meetings and parties which require greater intimacy. They are helpful and compassionate when involved with charities or group activities but appear cold or heartless in close relationships – contrary behavior to the rest of us but logical and altruistic to Aquarians.

BELOW Aquarians will enliven a large, anonymous gathering, but they close up in a more intimate group.

Thick, medium-brown to dark hair

Attractive, even features on square-set face; small well-shaped nose

Tall, slim build

Can be unusual or eccentric in dress or speech

LEFT A typical Aquarian will be friendly and alert with some of these traits.

Ruled by Uranus, the planet of sudden, major change and modern technology, Aquarians are usually forward thinking in both speech and action. They are often highly intelligent, bordering upon genius (or madness), and gifted with unusual talent. They love to talk and offer their opinions – and can often appear insufferable know-it-alls who insist they are right – and unhappily for the rest of us they usually are. Aquarians are outwardly patient with those unable to think or react as swiftly as themselves, but inwardly they can sometimes be highly intolerant – another contradiction of the unique Aquarian makeup.

AQUARIUS IN LOVE

No other sign finds it as hard to fall in love or understand what love is as Aquarius. There are exceptions, usually when the Moon or Venus are in prominent positions within their birthcharts, but in general, Aquarians struggle to relate at an intimate level. They are remarkably loyal when they do find someone whom they think they can love and try hard to make their partner happy but their strange habits and cold attitude mean they usually end up making a mess of it all. Aquarians sometimes walk away from emotionally charged situations simply because they cannot handle them. They do not mean to hurt or bewilder, but inevitably it seems that way. When Aquarians are confident that emotions have simmered down and their minds are working logically once more they will re-emerge from their hideaways and try to make amends. Their natural magnetism and ability to talk their way in or out of anything usually helps and many remain with the partner of their choice for a lifetime. Others will, from time to time, seek excitement elsewhere while still regarding themselves as a devoted partner. They make love with their minds – which are aroused by the unusual or perverse.

ABOVE When in love erotic literature can be the first step to thawing out the ice surrounding the Aquarian persona.

AQUARIUS AT WORK

The rulership of the planet Uranus sums up Aquarians as needing constant change in their lives – but the word constant itself is a steadfast word and so long as Aquarians ensure that their chosen career offers both variety and stability, they will be happy to stay put and work hard. However, it can sometimes take a long time for Aquarians to find the right job and they grow easily bored with what they are doing. Like the other two Air signs (Gemini and Libra) they are happiest when communicating with others. Aquarians possess a vast repertoire of knowledge which they feel compelled to pass on, and although they like to be alone occasionally, and can appear totally disinterested in what is going on around them, this is purely a facade because their antennae are picking up everything that is happening. Clever indeed!

Aquarians expect to be appreciated for their intelligence and hard work and they usually are. They consider it their right to be given plenty of opportunities and can be rebellious in their attitudes if they feel they are being badly treated. They love all kinds of scientific and modern technology, and also have a powerful affinity with airplanes, the Universe, and the great beyond…

AQUARIUS AND LEISURE

Although they possess a great deal of stamina and a surprising amount of strength, most Aquarians prefer to indulge in cerebral leisure pursuits rather than tough physical sports. Aquarians love to talk and pass on their broad knowledge. If they do not know the answer to something, they will pretend they do or else ignore the question. Often called the genius of the Zodiac, they are capable, talented people who excel in many different activities. Reading, mind games,

AQUARIAN OCCUPATIONS

pilot, airport worker, computer operative, electricity worker, scientist, astronomer, astrologer, group activist, brain surgeon, psychiatrist, stunt person, entertainer

RIGHT
Fascination with science is a strong Aquarian trait, and many Aquarians will pursue careers that explore the farthest reaches of man's knowledge of the world – and beyond.

LEFT The last
of the Air signs,
Aquarians feel at
home with sky-
borne activities –
the more unusual,
the better.

chess, bridge, and all games that require diplomacy and skill appeal to their cool analytical temperaments. They are whizz kids with computers, electrical gadgets, and modern technology. Aquarius is the last of the Air signs and is therefore thoroughly at home in airplanes or any activity that takes place in the sky. Space travel would suit them perfectly, given the opportunity, as they are happy to sit still in one place for hours on end. As long as their minds are active, Aquarians are content. Unusual activities attract their attention and they are quite capable of carrying on more than one mental pursuit at the same time. Astronomy and new scientific discoveries interest them and some Aquarians spend hours trying to invent crazy new gadgets. They love music of all kinds and possess a good sense of rhythm. Modern jazz, synthesized music, and contemporary classics are particularly

appealing to them. They enjoy dancing, especially when given the chance to express their own unique individuality.

AQUARIUS SPORTS AND EXERCISE

flying, hang-gliding
parachute jumping,
abseiling, high jump, pole-
vault, badminton, aerobics,
dancing, skiing, ice-skating,
speed-skating, cycling

AQUARIUS AND HEALTH

Aquarians possess strong constitutions and are usually fairly healthy throughout their lives. Too much mental activity, however, can cause damage to their nervous systems and lead to mental illness, epilepsy, Parkinson's disease, multiple sclerosis, brain tumors, and other problems originating in the brain. Their attraction to electricity makes them prone to shocks. Aquarius is physically stronger than the other two Air signs and possesses good powers of recuperation. Their ankles can be weak, however, and falls are common in old age.

AQUARIUS AND DIET

Despite slim agile builds, most Aquarians eat well but tend to stick to restricted and rigid diets that create an imbalance of vitamins and minerals in their bodies. They sometimes develop unusual eating habits or strange cravings and are quite content to eat the same meals day after day for months or even years on end. They should vary their diet and eat food which nourishes the brain such as fish and nuts.

HEALING FOODS

oily fish, coconut,
walnuts, hazelnuts,
sunflower seeds,
carrots, licorice,
caraway seeds,
parsley, wheatgerm

LEFT Aquarians
are not adventurous
eaters and are
content to eat the
same monotonous
food day after day.

PISCES

★ ★ ★ ★ ★ ★ ★ ★ ★ ★ ★ ★ ★ ★ ★ ★ ★

February 19 to March 20

Pisces is ruled by
the planet Neptune

The element Water
rules Pisces

Pisces rules the feet

Pisces is linked to
purple, sea blue,
and green

The birthstone of
Pisces is amethyst

Thursday is the
Piscean lucky day

KEYWORD CHARACTERISTICS

emotional, sensitive, dual-natured,
introverted, artistic, vague, adaptable,
confused, escapist, enigmatic, kind,
self-sacrificing, moody, dependent

THE NATURE OF PISCES

The full circle of the 12 signs of the Zodiac reaches completion with Pisces. This is the sign which contains a little of every other sign and is often the hardest of all to understand. It is often an enigma to everyone, including itself. The two symbolic fishes swimming in opposite directions – one looking backward, the other facing forward, are indicative of the true feelings and characteristics of Pisceans. The urge to go backward and escape into an imaginary, fearless world is strong within the Piscean psyche, yet at the same time people of this sign are often highly gifted and feel compelled to drive themselves toward the spotlight in order to show their talents. As a result of this, Pisceans are rarely content. In the outer world of ambition, success and wealth, they yearn to escape into their own world in search of peace and sustenance for their souls, but their creative energy and desire to set the world right cannot be stilled and sooner or later their private sanctuary becomes a prison.

Eyes either large
and attractive,
protuberant and
staring, or small
and inquisitive

Enigmatic, dreamy,
or confused attitude

Variable height
and plump build

LEFT One Piscean
can look very
different from
another – everything
about this sign is
complex.

The complexity of Piscean emotions makes them difficult people to understand, and it's been said that nobody can ever completely know a Piscean person. Just when you think you have them fathomed, they do something different or react in a totally unexpected manner. In this respect many people find Pisceans irritating or unsociable, although others view their multi-faceted personalities as charismatic.

Most of the time, however, typical Pisces subjects are quiet and introspective, preferring to watch and wait rather than dive straight in. They are generally kind, sympathetic, and supportive, and readily offer a listening ear for people with problems and a shoulder for friends to cry on. But when the time comes that they need to be comforted themselves, they find it hard to express their feelings to others and often turn away and console themselves in private.

ABOVE The sign of two fish swimming in opposite directions gives a clue to this sign's complex psyche.

RIGHT Although Pisceans tend to deal with their own emotions in private, they make good listeners.

The Piscean capacity to reach great heights and sink to the lowest depths leaves them vulnerable to addictions – not only drugs and alcohol but sex, food, and other, stranger, compulsions. Pisceans are gullible and easily tempted, especially when young. In addition to being self-sacrificing, Pisceans in negative mode can be self-demeaning and self-destructive, but on a higher level, this is the sign of saints and priests and ordinary loving, caring people. Pisceans hate to see anything or anyone (apart from themselves) hurt or destroyed and will always offer support to the underdog. However, their acute sensitivity can sometimes get them into all sorts of trouble.

The main enigma of this sign is the diversity of its subjects. No two fish are alike. Each Piscean will react differently to recurring situations according to the mood of the moment. Nothing is too much for them to handle when they are in a positive mood but when negativity seeps in, Pisceans can sometimes drown in their own sorrows.

PISCES IN LOVE

The flowing stream that represents the waters of Pisces is usually shallow and fast and, as a result, Pisceans tend to fall in and out of love quickly. Their need to give and receive love is strong and despite their inner desire to remain unencumbered by relationships many Pisceans become dependent on their partners. The complexity of Pisces is never-ending. Many become promiscuous or obsessed by emotions and sex from a young age but most are strangely naïve switching from partner to partner in the search for perfection. Strong men are often attracted to the sweet innocence and dependency of the Piscean woman, but are shocked to find her strength and determination leave him in the shade. Pisceans are adept at carrying on more than one relationship simultaneously and although Pisceans themselves can slither easily away from a relationship, those who fall in love with them are usually entangled forever.

BELOW Pisceans can be extremely flirtatious and are easily distracted from what seemed a good relationship.

POSITIVE PISCES
A good saver is a good server.
A good heart never lies.

NEGATIVE PISCES
The fish that nibbles at every
bait will soon be caught.

PISCES AT WORK

The acute sensitivity and intrinsic shyness of this sign make it difficult for Pisceans to be fully accepted and appreciated within a strict or controlled working regime. Mundane work, harsh words, and performance targets do not suit the temperament of the Piscean individual at all. They are far happier when allowed to work at their own pace among few people in a more relaxed atmosphere. Piscean talents are many and diverse but they will not flow in a tough environment.

Highly creative and artistic by nature, Pisceans are best suited to careers which develop these talents such as artist, musician, or writer. Many Pisceans are not concerned with material rewards but those who are usually manage their finances very well. Along with everything else in its life, Pisces is capable of working at all levels – from the lowest to the highest and it is often difficult to gauge how they will handle a particular work situation. They often find themselves in subordinate positions when their hearts are crying out for recognition. However, when they do assert themselves, they are a force to be reckoned with and cannot be overlooked. Pisceans will work tirelessly to achieve good results when they are appreciated and respected for who they are.

PISCES AND LEISURE

The Piscean love of variety and change is not so readily apparent in their leisure activities. This sensitive sign thinks twice before getting involved in anything they do not understand or enjoy because constant defeat in sport or games is demoralizing for them. Though lively, talented, and creative, when it comes to physical activity many Pisceans appear to have two left feet, no balance at all, and little endurance. Tough physical regimes are often too demanding for the weak Piscean constitution. The best sports for this changeable sign are those involving water such as swimming, diving, surfing, canoeing, rowing, or sailing. The restlessness of Pisceans makes them light on their feet and many good dancers and footballers are born under this sign. Slow, earthy sports requiring concentration are not suitable, although they do enjoy fishing.

The most rewarding activities for Pisceans are those which require little physical strength such as writing, poetry, art, or music. They love sad, soulful music and will cry their hearts out listening to it. But they also enjoy lively dance music, pop

PISCEAN OCCUPATIONS

musician, artist, poet, writer, pharmacist, service engineer, gas fitter, coastguard, plumber, meteorologist, fisherman, oil-rig worker, sailor, nurse, psychic or medium, social worker, counselor

BELOW When employed in non-creative positions, Pisceans often seek jobs close to or on the water.

PISCES SPORTS AND EXERCISE

surfing, fishing, football, dancing, ice-skating, roller-skating, running, aerobics, yoga, whitewater rafting, gymnastics, swimming

music, and classics – in fact there is not much that they do not appreciate at some time or another. Meditation and yoga appeal to them – provided they can sit still long enough to reap the rewards. Pisceans also love the theater and despite their introverted, kindly natures can become remarkably good actors – transforming themselves completely on stage. Above all, Pisceans enjoy their own company where they can act out imaginary scenes and compete with themselves in games such as solitaire and patience.

PISCES AND HEALTH

Renowned for their weak constitutions and a tendency to consume harmful addictive substances, Pisceans can become highly toxic and shorten their lives accordingly. On the other hand some of the longest-lived people in the world are born under this sign. The broad spectrum of experiences which occur during a Piscean lifetime are also apparent within the physical make-up of this sign. Pisceans need to keep warm, especially around the hands and feet, as they are prone to rheumatism and blood circulation problems. They also suffer from foot ailments, diabetes, and all illnesses that stem from their personal addictions. Anorexia is common, as is obesity.

PISCES AND DIET

Emotionally disturbed Pisceans will either stop eating altogether or eat for comfort. They need a varied diet, rich in liquid, minerals, and seafood.

ABOVE When they are not messing about in the water, Pisceans are usually seeking new outlets for their creativity.

HEALING FOODS

watercress, brown rice, cucumber, dandelion leaves, poppyseeds, sesame seeds, oily fish, pears, seaweed, melon

SUN SIGN GROUPINGS

★ ★ ★ ★ ★ ★ ★ ★ ★ ★ ★ ★ ★ ★ ★ ★

THE 12 SIGNS of the Zodiac are divided into three distinct groupings which form the basic foundation for birthchart interpretation. These are called *The Polarities, The Elements,* and *The Quadruplicities.* They provide deeper insight toward understanding the essential motivations and characteristics of the 12 signs.

ACTIVE/PASSIVE SIGNS

ACTIVE SIGNS	PASSIVE SIGNS
Masculine, Positive	*Feminine, Negative*
Aries	Taurus
Gemini	Cancer
Leo	Virgo
Libra	Scorpio
Sagittarius	Capricorn
Aquarius	Pisces

THE POLARITIES

The Zodiac is divided into two groups, each containing six signs known as *The Polarities*, which are traditionally designated *Masculine* and *Feminine* but it has become fashionable in recent years to label them *Positive* and *Negative*. These terms have proved equally unsatisfactory, however, because the word "negative" implies weakness and lack of character. Nowadays, many astrologers prefer the terms *Active* and *Passive* which are more appropriate to the qualities of the signs and sound less judgmental. The polarities are easy to work out – commencing with Aries (an *Active* sign), every alternate sign from there is also *Active*. Likewise, starting with Taurus (which is *Passive*) every alternate sign is also *Passive*. Generally, the *Active* signs tend to be extrovert and confident while *Passive* signs are introverted and quiet.

THE ELEMENTS

This is a major division of the signs into four 90-degree sectors (triangles) which are called *Fire, Earth, Air,* and *Water.* Each element (triangular grouping) is composed of three compatible signs. All the elements are vital to life as they

BELOW Active signs like Aries and Gemini tend to be extrovert and are often the life and soul of the party.

RIGHT Sun sign groupings showing element, polarity, and quadruplicity help the astrologer to interpret how one sign interacts with another.

Capricorn, passive, Cardinal Earth

Aquarius, active, Fixed Air

Pisces, passive, Mutable Water

Aries, active, Cardinal Fire

Taurus, passive, Fixed Earth

Gemini, active, Mutable Air

interact with one another. *Fire* needs earth as a base on which to ignite, and is fanned into action by the breezes of air. If and when it rages too fast, it can be tempered or put out by water. *Earth* needs the warmth and power of fire in order to regenerate itself, the substance of air to give it life and allow new growth, and the addition of water to nurture that growth. *Air* needs fire to warm it up, earth to impound and regulate its actions, and water to enable the formation of rain and the continuance of life. *Water* needs fire to dry it out and prevent it from swamping the earth. It requires the earth to stabilize its flow, and the

THE ELEMENTS

FIRE	EARTH	AIR	WATER
Aries	Taurus	Gemini	Cancer
Leo	Virgo	Libra	Scorpio
Sagittarius	Capricorn	Aquarius	Pisces

air to fan it into action and help form tidal surges. In general, *Fire* sign people are warm and enthusiastic, *Earth* sign people are practical and earthy, *Air* sign people are communicative and congenial, and *Water* sign people are sensitive and emotional.

THE QUADRUPLICITIES

The third division of the signs of the Zodiac is called *The Quadruplicities* and comprises three groups of four incompatible signs – one from each element – which are at a 90-degree square angle to one another. These sectors are entitled *Cardinal, Fixed,* and *Mutable.* To the beginner it can be hard to fathom why these signs are grouped together and what they can possibly have in common but they can reveal remarkably accurate insights toward the motivations of individuals. In general, *Cardinal* signs are self-seeking and pushy, *Fixed* signs are rigid and uncompromising, while *Mutable* signs are restless and adaptable.

ABOVE In general, passive signs like Cancer and Virgo are quiet souls, keeping themselves to themselves.

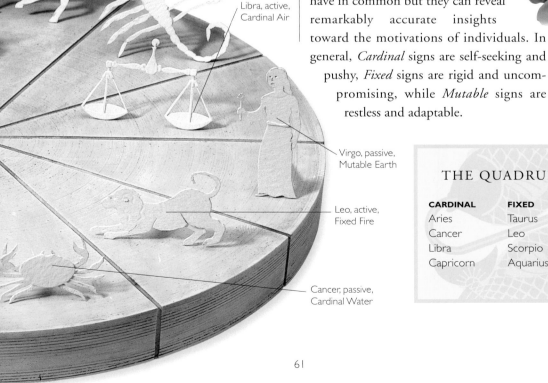

Sagittarius, active, Mutable Fire

Scorpio, passive, Fixed Water

Libra, active, Cardinal Air

Virgo, passive, Mutable Earth

Leo, active, Fixed Fire

Cancer, passive, Cardinal Water

THE QUADRUPLICITIES

CARDINAL	FIXED	MUTABLE
Aries	Taurus	Gemini
Cancer	Leo	Virgo
Libra	Scorpio	Sagittarius
Capricorn	Aquarius	Pisces

POLARITIES AND ELEMENTS

★ ★ ★ ★ ★ ★ ★ ★ ★ ★ ★ ★ ★ ★ ★ ★ ★

THE POLARITIES
ACTIVE: *Aries, Gemini, Leo, Libra, Sagittarius, Aquarius*

The three Fire signs (Aries, Leo, and Sagittarius) and the three Air signs (Gemini, Libra, and Aquarius) combine to form this compatible grouping. All six signs are inherently extroverted and confident in nature. They tend to react in a direct confrontational manner, often without a great deal of introspection. They are objective, dynamic, and uninhibited during adult life and tend to be noticed more quickly than the Passive signs.

PASSIVE: *Taurus, Cancer, Virgo, Scorpio, Capricorn, Pisces*

The three Earth signs (Taurus, Virgo, and Capricorn) and the three Water signs (Cancer, Scorpio, and Pisces) group together to form this compatible polarity. Predominantly passive people, they are naturally introverted and quiet by nature. They usually think before they act and prefer to work quietly behind the scenes. They are subjective and constrained, especially in childhood, and until they are able to develop a more self-assured approach, they tend to be overlooked in favor of the Active signs.

THE ELEMENTS
FIRE: *Aries, Leo, Sagittarius*

Like the fire they represent, subjects born under these signs are warm, magnetic, and highly flammable. Once ignited, their flames burn quickly, sparking in all directions with powerful, physical central force. A constant, well-controlled fire is a glorious sight which can enthral the crowds. Fire sign subjects are energetic, outgoing, and enthusiastic in nature, but sometimes their flames can burn too strongly and surge out of control, rendering them dangerous, hot-headed, and thoughtless in their actions. Those who stand too close at this stage can get severely burned – the wise will keep their distance and treat those born under the Fire signs with the respect and caution they deserve.

EARTH: *Taurus, Virgo, Capricorn*

Those born under the three Earth signs are practical, materialistic, logical, and above all down to earth. They are solid and sensible and possess an innate love of the earth and all that nature represents. They need to spend time each day outside in all weathers in order to feel confident and secure within their daily lives, absorbing the feel of the ground beneath their feet. The natural diversity of the composition of the earth caused by differing weather patterns indicates that there is more to the Earth signs than meets the eye. They are not as single-minded or lacking in enthusiasm as they appear, and when the equilibrium of the earth is disrupted by major disasters such as earthquakes, floods, hurricanes, and forest fires, the character of the earth can be irrevocably

ABOVE Fire signs are powerful with an abundance of energy which must be positively channeled.

ABOVE Earth signs are sensible, down-to-earth people but if pushed too far, they can explode in a tumult of anger.

altered. Similarly, when people born under the Earth signs are persuaded or forced into destructive action the results can be catastrophic. The normal passive temperaments of these subjects can turn into volcanoes of unrepressed anger. One wilful act is capable of negating a lifetime of everything that the Earth signs hold most dear, and although many succeed in rebuilding their lives, the foundations are rarely as secure.

AIR: *Gemini, Libra, Aquarius*

Air sign people are the natural communicators of the Zodiac. They are lively, chatty, intelligent, and full of ideas but are often thought to have their heads in the clouds. They like to hover above the ground, sometimes static and observant but more often than not flitting from one thing to another as the wind moves them in ever-changing directions. Subjects of this sign need to have the freedom that allows them to exercise their highly inventive minds.

What Air signs should always bear in mind, however, is that a little wind, especially when warm, is highly refreshing but too much hot or cold air can cause damage. Air signs who talk too much or try too hard to impress others with their mental prowess can be asking for trouble. Air sign people are usually easy-going and lack emotional depth, but they can be verbally abusive when angered.

WATER: *Cancer, Scorpio, Pisces*

All Water signs are emotional. Whether it be the oceans of Cancer, the deep, still lakes of Scorpio, or the shallow rivers of Pisces, water envelops these three signs as they struggle to survive in what they often view as a harsh, material world. Sensitive, vulnerable, protective, and passionate in everything they do, Water signs are innately passive and caring – sometimes to their own detriment. They are secretive, intuitive, and artistic but often deeply insecure and unable to show their true feelings. The emotions of Water signs do, however, need careful handling – water can be dangerous if treated recklessly.

People born under these signs can take as much as they give and expect others to respond positively to their sentiments. A gentle lapping tide can suddenly change into a dangerous, destructive tidal wave when Water signs feel unloved or unappreciated in life. Those who feel happy and at home in the water must always beware of the dangers that lurk unseen beneath the surface.

LEFT Air signs are born talkers which can make them highly entertaining, overpowering, or know-it-all bores.

THE QUADRUPLICITIES

* * * * * * * * * * * * * * *

CARDINAL

Cardinal signs are self-seeking. They know what they want and how to go about getting it. They like to be at the front of the line making their voices heard and initiating action. They are thought to be selfish, or unfeeling, when their urge to push forward overrides all else. Each sign does, however, assert itself in a different manner.

ARIES *Cardinal Fire* Aries people assert themselves with physical force, elbowing their way to the front of the line, totally oblivious to the needs of others as they seek to fulfil their own urgent demands, but although they can be aggressive or brutal in the process, they rarely intend others any harm.

CANCER *Cardinal Water* Cancer subjects assert themselves with sidewise, crablike movements around the back of the line until they reach their destination, rarely pouncing until they are sure of acceptance. If this fails, they will attempt to appeal to the emotions of others to get what they want.

LIBRA *Cardinal Air* Librans assert themselves politely and with great charm, pushing their way to the front of the line without anyone realizing that they have done so. Success falls

easily into their laps, and they are usually admired for their harmonious dispositions.

CAPRICORN *Cardinal Earth* Capricorns assert themselves quietly and cautiously with a steel-like determination as they creep unnoticed to the front of the line, then surprise everyone with their powerful, demanding voices. They never give up and will eventually reach the top in all their endeavors.

FIXED

Fixed signs are aptly named as they appreciate routine and can be rigid or stubborn in their attitudes. They are, however, tenacious, loyal, and dedicated. Unlike Cardinal signs they are slow to get started and will rarely push themselves unnecessarily but they will always finish whatever project they start. Each sign within this grouping tends to be fixed in a different manner.

TAURUS *Fixed Earth* Taureans are fixed in their attitudes toward materialistic and earthy matters. They accumulate wealth and possessions, do not let go easily, and prefer to concentrate on one thing at a time. Once they have deliberated over something, they will rarely be persuaded to change track.

LEFT Arians (Cardinal Fire) assert themselves physically and will push in oblivious of the needs of others.

LEO *Fixed Fire* Leo people are fixed in their enthusiasm and zest for life. Their fires burn brightly and constantly, long after the Cardinal and Mutable signs have given up. Their efforts to fight and make things work are admirable but often misguided, and they can eventually burn themselves out.

SCORPIO *Fixed Water* Scorpio subjects are fixed in their emotions. The deep, still waters of the lake are often stagnant and unmoving. Scorpions love and hate with all their heart but their ability to rigidly control their feelings makes them seem cold or ruthless.

AQUARIUS *Fixed Air* Aquarians are fixed in their mental attitudes to life. They absorb knowledge like a sponge and have wonderfully inventive minds. However, this sign's dogmatic and opinionated

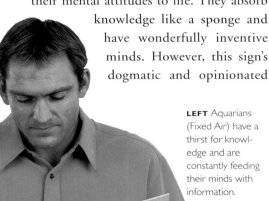

LEFT Aquarians (Fixed Air) have a thirst for knowledge and are constantly feeding their minds with information.

beliefs can easily alienate others who are less intellectual than themselves.

MUTABLE

Those born under the Mutable signs are changeable, moody, and adaptable people. They enjoy variety and often find themselves being pulled in several directions at the same time. They are dual-natured, complex people who can be inconstant or unstable. These signs tend to live for the moment and usually forgive and forget very easily.

GEMINI *Mutable Air* Gemini people have adaptable, changeable minds. They flit from one interest to another, rarely looking at anything deeply. Their wind is forever changing direction and they tend to chat incessantly about trivial matters.

VIRGO *Mutable Earth* Virgo people have adaptable, practical, and earthy skills. Their restless minds are forever seeking new and interesting ways to develop their talents. They can achieve a great deal in a short space of time providing the earth beneath their feet remains stable.

SAGITTARIUS *Mutable Fire* Sagittarians are adaptable and changeable in their enthusiasm and can happily indulge in many different activities at the same time. They love to explore and are always seeking adventure and excitement to spice up their lives.

PISCES *Mutable Water* Pisceans are adaptable and changeable in their emotions. Something that causes them great upset one day will be forgotten about the next. The rivers of Pisces are constantly flowing but they always return to the source to start the sequence all over again.

ABOVE Pisces (Mutable Water) has changeable emotions, and is up one minute and down the next.

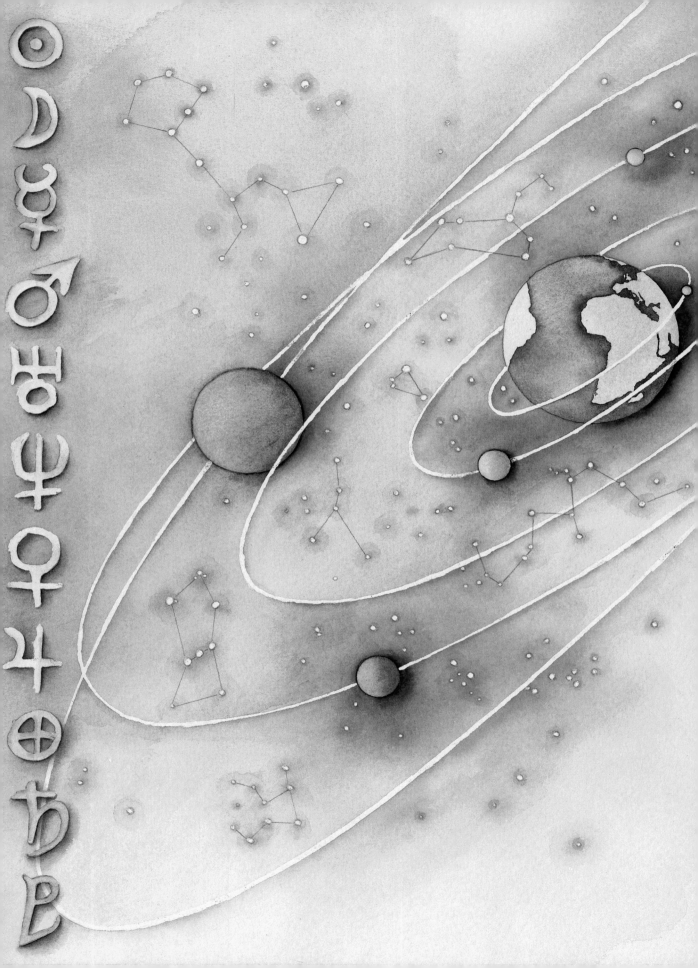

PART TWO

THE PLANETS

★ ★ ★ ★ ★

The eight major planets, plus the Sun and Moon, are the foundation for the study of astrology. We are affected by each of the planets in a different way and without their unique energies we would probably not exist. The planets of the solar system, among them the Earth, revolve around the Sun but for astrological purposes the Earth is seen as the central force of a personal birthchart and the other planets encircle us in their differing cyclic motions.

Ancient astrologers knew only seven "planets" – Sun, Moon, Mercury, Venus, Mars, Jupiter, and Saturn – upon which they based their delineations. During the last few centuries three more planets – Uranus, Neptune, and Pluto – have been discovered, enriching astrology

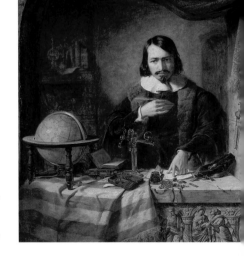

RIGHT The effect of other planets on our lives has fascinated astrologers for many centuries.

with their variable, vibrant energy. These discoveries have coincided with dramatic changes in our lifestyles and there are likely to be more planetary discoveries over the next few centuries which will change the course of our lives still further, perhaps solving the problem of matching ten planets with 12 signs of the Zodiac.

PLANETARY ENERGIES AND CYCLES

★★★★★★★★★★★★★★★★★★★★

ALL OF THE PLANETS possess their own unique cycles and can be divided roughly into three groups: *Personal, Middle,* and *Outer.* The personal planets, Sun, Moon, Mercury, Venus, and Mars, rotate swiftly around the Zodiac. The orbits of both the Sun and Moon are regular – 30 days (Sun) and 28 days (Moon) but Mercury, Venus, and Mars all possess slightly longer and more erratic orbits. Occasionally, however, Mercury will orbit extremely quickly in less time than the Moon's 28-day cycle. The middle planets, Jupiter and Saturn, move much more slowly than the personal planets – a year for Jupiter and two-and-a half years for Saturn – while the three most recently discovered outer planets, Uranus, Neptune, and Pluto, move even more slowly – Uranus seven years, Neptune 14 years, and Pluto's erratic orbit can be anything from eight to 33 years.

Each of the planets rules a particular sign of the Zodiac and it is this planetary energy which formulates the unique characteristics of each sign. For example, the energy of the Sun is hot, and therefore aptly attributed to the Fire sign Leo, whereas the energy of Saturn is cold, dry, and barren, and is usually associated with the character of Earth sign Capricorn. Until another two planets are discovered, Mercury and Venus will continue to govern two signs each – Mercury ruling both Gemini and Virgo, and Venus ruling Taurus and Libra. It is generally

> **PLANETARY GROUPINGS**
>
> **PERSONAL PLANETS**
> Sun, Moon, Mercury, Venus, Mars
>
> **MIDDLE PLANETS**
> Jupiter, Saturn
>
> **OUTER PLANETS**
> Uranus, Neptune, Pluto

considered that the lively, communicative skills of Mercury are appropriate to the sign of Gemini, whereas the serious, practical, literary talents of Mercury relate more to the sign of Virgo. The sensual, earthy, materialistic values of Venus seem appropriate to the sign of Taurus, while the love and relationship qualities projected by Venus are more fitting to the sign of Libra. A few astrologers argued when Pluto was first discovered that it ruled Aries rather than Scorpio – and there was certainly some evidence for this assumption as both signs had formerly been governed by Mars, but it quickly became clear that the intense, secretive, controlling powers of Pluto were better suited to the depths and fixity of Scorpio than the ardent, fiery qualities of Aries.

MAIN PICTURE
Each Sun sign is ruled by one of ten planets moving through the Zodiac in different orbits.

THE FIXED STARS There are millions of slow-moving fixed stars within the galaxy but most of them lie too far from us and are irrelevant to the study of astrology. However, some of the closer and well-known ones like Sirius, the Dog Star, are thousands of times larger than our own Sun and may well exert an influence upon the Earth. Certain stars are thought to be fortunate while others are variable or unlucky.

SOME FIXED STARS AND THEIR INFLUENCES

FORTUNATE	VARIABLE	UNFORTUNATE
Mirach	Canopus	Algol
Capella	Alphard	Castor
Sirius	Regulus	Pollux
Fomalhaut	Vega	Antares
Alphecca	Altair	Menkar

THE PLANETARY RULERSHIPS

PLANET	SYMBOL	SIGN RULERSHIP
Sun	☉	Leo
Moon	☽	Cancer
Mercury	☿	Gemini and Virgo
Venus	♀	Taurus and Libra
Mars	♂	Aries
Jupiter	♃	Sagittarius
Saturn	♄	Capricorn
Uranus	♅	Aquarius
Neptune	♆	Pisces
Pluto	♇	Scorpio

Prior to the discovery of Uranus, Neptune, and Pluto, Aquarius was ruled by Saturn, Pisces by Jupiter, and Scorpio by Mars.

CHIRON

With only ten planets to match the 12 signs of the Zodiac it has long been thought that there must be two more planets within our solar system yet to be discovered, which would take over the rulerships of Gemini or Virgo, and Taurus or Libra. Then, in 1977, a small planet (planetoid) orbiting between Saturn and Uranus was discovered. This planet was named Chiron – meaning "the key" – as it seemed to be a stepping stone or communicating link between the middle planets (Jupiter and Saturn) and the outer planets (Uranus, Neptune, and Pluto). There was uncertainty as to whether it ruled Sagittarius or Virgo – cogent arguments for both signs were presented – but during the 1980s astrologers decided after much research that Chiron is related to healing and the visionary new age and therefore more appropriate to the sign of Virgo. Although tiny (smaller than Pluto) and still relatively unknown, Chiron is being used increasingly in birthchart interpretation. Its discovery certainly assists Mercury in its dual rulership of Virgo, and now we eagerly anticipate discovery of a twelfth planet to relieve Venus of its dual governorship of Taurus and Libra.

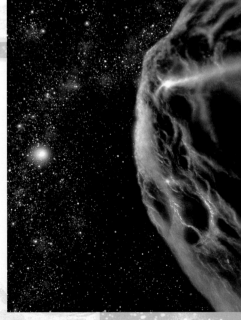

ABOVE Chiron, approaching the Sun in this illustration, has an orbit of 50.7 years.

SUN

It takes the Sun approximately 30 days to traverse one sign and a whole year to complete its journey through the Zodiac. The foundations of astrology, as printed in the Sun-sign columns in magazines and newspapers, are based on the predictable pattern of the Sun's movements (in reality the movement of the Earth around the Sun.)

The energy of the Sun relates to our individual egos and inner self. No matter how we may appear to others, we tend to view ourselves from the point of view of our Sun sign.

BELOW The influence of the Moon is frequently seen in children's birthcharts.

MOON

The fastest moving of the planets takes around two-and-a-half-days to travel through one sign and 28 days to complete the Zodiac. In some ancient systems of astrology the Moon sign is more important than the Sun sign. Certainly it tends to be more prominent within children's charts, but as we grow older, other planetary factors take precedence. Moon energy is emotional, responsive, and reactionary. It can sometimes be oversensitive and lacking in control.

MERCURY

The cycle of Mercury is short but variable, taking anything between 15 and 70 days to travel through one sign of the Zodiac. The energy Mercury directs toward us is restless and tends to come in short, sharp bursts. It governs all methods of human communication and is strongly associated with the more basic levels of the mind.

VENUS

The Venus cycle is also variable – occasionally taking as long as five months to traverse one sign. The energy of Venus is more balanced than that of Mercury. It projects slow, lingering, harmonious waves and is generally considered to govern everything that we esteem in life such as beauty, love, and peace, as well as relating to material values and earthly possessions.

MARS

Similar to the Venus cycle, but rarely taking less than six weeks to travel through a sign, and sometimes remaining for up to six months in one sign, Mars energy is vibrant and powerful and can easily (especially with men) override the energies of the other personal planets. Physical stamina, drive, aggression, and sexual needs all come under the vibrations of Mars.

JUPITER

The first of the slower-moving planets takes approximately a year to travel through one sign of the Zodiac, thus forming a 12-year cycle. The return of Jupiter to the position it occupied at your birth once every 12 years

ABOVE The harmonious energy of Venus is usually awakened when strong relationships are formed.

marks a very important development point. Jupiter energy is expansive but light. It is supposedly beneficial, but it can also be "a lot of hot air" with very little substance.

SATURN

This slower-moving planet takes two-and-a-half years to traverse one sign and approximately 28 years to complete a cycle. The Saturn return which occurs around the age of 28 is renowned for being a vital turning point in our lives, indicating major transformation. Compared with Jupiter, the energy of Saturn is repressive and dense but much longer-lasting. It governs our karmic responsibilities and our capacity to learn about life on every level.

URANUS

The nearest of the outer planets takes seven years to complete a sign, and 84 to finalize a cycle: those who do not survive to this age will not therefore experience the return of Uranus to the position it occupied in their birthchart. The half-return which occurs between the ages of 38 and 43 is usually a more dramatic period in most people's lives. Uranus energy is dynamic, bringing sudden change into our lives, which can be exciting, reckless, or catastrophic, but never boring.

NEPTUNE

This planet takes approximately 14 years to travel through one sign of the Zodiac and 84 years to complete a half-cycle. Neptune energy is slow and nebulous. It can shroud us in mystery, heighten our spiritual awareness, or drive us to the depths of despair.

Unlike the energies of the other planets, it is difficult to grasp or to understand. The enormous distance of Neptune from the earth could be one of the reasons for the dissipation of its energy.

PLUTO

Tiny Pluto has an erratic orbit – sometimes taking ten to 12 years to complete one sign of the Zodiac, as it has during the latter half of the 20th century, or at other times moving extremely slowly, way beyond the orbit of Neptune, and taking over 30 years to complete one sign. Despite its small size, its energy can be awesome. It governs complete transformation, death, the underworld, volcanoes, and deep spiritual matters.

ABOVE Pluto is linked to dramatic changes: World Wars and natural disasters such as volcano eruptions.

PLANETS IN SIGNS

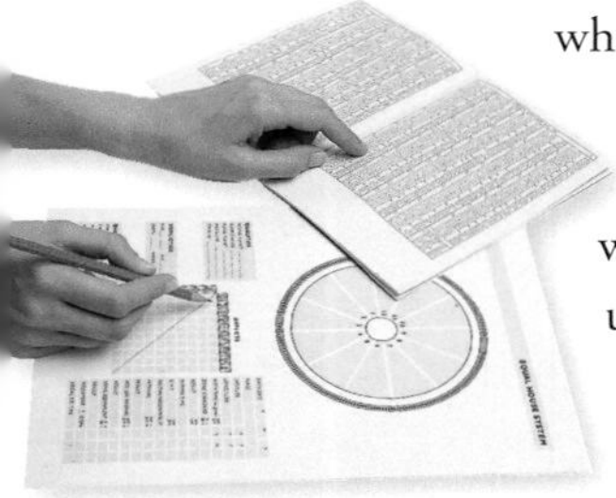

ABOVE You can plot your solar birthchart using the tables in planetary ephemerides.

ALL TEN PLANETS (11 if Chiron is included) form part of an individual's unique psyche which is bequeathed to them at the moment of birth. Planetary ephemerides give positions of the planets for every day within the 20th century and are available, usually to order, from your bookstore. Apart from the Moon, which may require minor adjustment, no calculation is needed to discover the positions of the planets, but a knowledge of the astrological symbols used for the signs and the planets will help you understand the tables much more easily. (See Further Reading on page 189 and example on pages 5 and 69.)

In a book of planetary ephemerides find the page for your month and year of birth, then check your planetary positions by locating your day of birth and reading across for each planet, starting with the Sun. The signs are listed at the top of the monthly section with the relevant degrees and sometimes down the column against another date when the planet moves into the next sign.

At this stage a solar birthchart can be erected on a birthchart (example on page 188) where the Sun sign and its degree are placed on the acute left angle of the chart with the remainder of the signs placed in chronological order at each consecutive 30-degree cusp, moving in an anticlockwise direction. The planets can then be placed in the relevant signs for the date of birth. The example on this page shows how the planets would be placed for someone born under the sign of Scorpio.

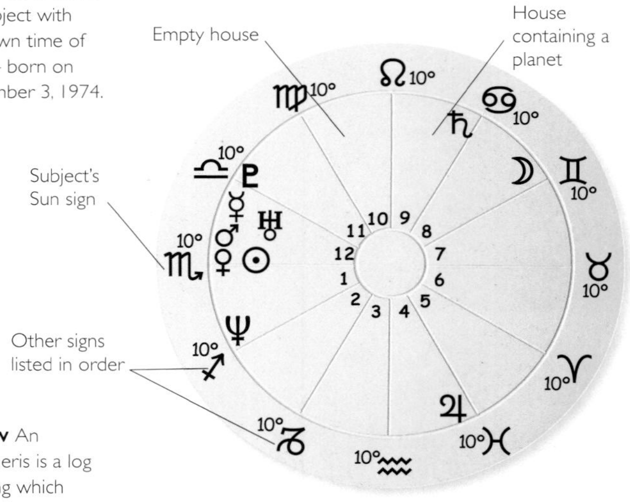

RIGHT Solar chart for subject with unknown time of birth – born on November 3, 1974.

RETROGRADE PLANETS

A capital "R" placed beside a certain planetary degree in the ephemeris stands for retrograde and means that the planet has changed its orbital direction from a forward to a backward motion as viewed from the Earth. Retrograde planets are thought to be weak in their effect, which may be true where the personal planets Mercury, Venus, and Mars are concerned, but is less likely with the outer planets which can stay in

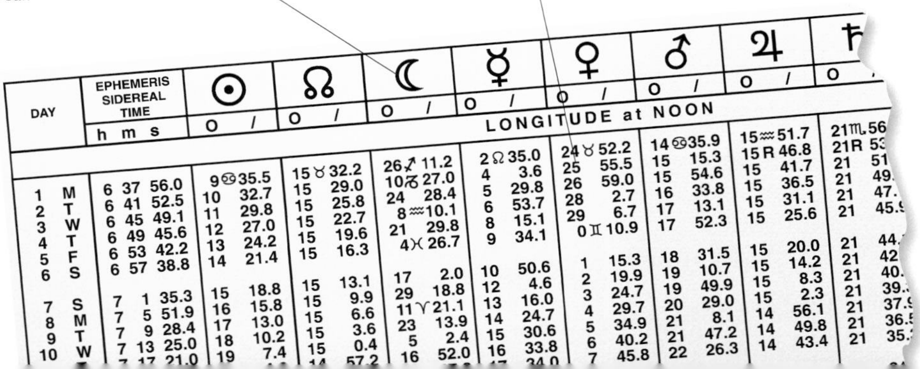

DAY		EPHEMERIS SIDEREAL TIME h m s	☉ ° ′	☊ ° ′	☽ ° ′	☿ ° ′	♀ ° ′	♂ ° ′	♃ ° ′	♄ ° ′
			LONGITUDE at NOON							
1	M	6 37 56.0	9♋35.5	15♉32.2	26♐11.2	2♌35.0	24♉52.2	14♋35.9	15♒51.7	21♏56
2	T	6 41 52.5	10 32.7	15 29.0	10♑27.0	4 3.6	25 55.5	15 15.3	15R 46.8	21R 53
3	W	6 45 49.1	11 29.8	15 25.8	24 28.4	5 29.8	26 59.0	15 54.6	15 41.7	21 51
4	T	6 49 45.6	12 27.0	15 22.7	8♒10.1	6 53.7	28 2.7	16 33.8	15 36.5	21 49.
5	F	6 53 42.2	13 24.2	15 19.6	21 29.8	8 15.1	29 6.7	17 13.1	15 31.1	21 47.
6	S	6 57 38.8	14 21.4	15 16.3	4♓26.7	9 34.1	0♊10.9	17 52.3	15 25.6	21 45.
7	S	7 1 35.3	15 18.8	15 13.1	17 2.0	10 50.6	1 15.3	18 31.5	15 20.0	21 44.
8	M	7 5 51.9	16 15.8	15 9.9	29 18.8	12 4.6	2 19.9	19 10.7	15 14.2	21 42
9	T	7 9 28.4	17 13.0	15 6.6	11♈21.1	13 16.0	3 24.7	19 49.9	15 8.3	21 40.
10	W	7 13 25.0	18 10.2	15 3.6	23 13.9	14 24.7	4 29.7	20 29.0	15 2.3	21 39.
		7 17 21.0	19 7.4	15 0.4	5 2.4	15 30.6	5 34.9	21 8.1	14 56.1	21 37.
				14 57.2	16 52.0	16 33.8	6 40.2	21 47.2	14 49.8	21 36.
						17 34.0	7 45.8	22 26.3	14 43.4	21 35.

BELOW An ephemeris is a log showing which planet is in which sign on a particular day of any year.

retrograde motion for up to six months of the year. People with Mercury retrograde in their birthchart do, however, often have some kind of communication problem, and those with Venus retrograde may find it difficult to give or receive love; Mars retrograde can have problems using physical energy. A capital "S" alongside the planetary degree in the ephemeris stands for the word stationary and will occur only when the planet is slowing down and has virtually stopped moving. The capital letter "D," which stands for direct, might also appear. This indicates that the planet is in direct motion and is written in when a planet changes from a backward direction (retrograde) to a forward direction (direct).

STELLIUMS *Satellitiums*

A stellium is a group of three or more planets occurring in one sign which place great emphasis on certain characteristics and developments in life. Although stelliums usually provide good powers of concentration, they are not always easy to handle. Stelliums occurring between Sun, Moon, Mercury, Venus, Mars, and Jupiter are usually beneficial and can be very positive, but when the outer planets and Saturn combine in a stellium with any of the personal planets (or Jupiter), difficulties can arise and various challenges in life need to be surmounted. Stelliums nearly always dominate the character of a person, whether they be beneficial or detrimental, but when channeled correctly the powerful influence of a stellium can create much success and determination to succeed.

LEFT Planets may be labeled in an ephemeris according to whether they are retrograde, stationary, or direct.

PLANETARY DIGNITIES

The planets are traditionally thought to be better placed in some signs than in others. Planets in exaltation are supposedly strongly placed but those in their "fall" are weakly placed. Planets in detriment are deemed to be badly positioned and difficult to express.

PLANET	EXALTED	FALL	DETRIMENT
SUN	Aries	Libra	Aquarius
MOON	Taurus	Scorpio	Capricorn
MERCURY	Virgo	Pisces	Sagittarius
VENUS	Pisces	Virgo	Aries
MARS	Capricorn	Cancer	Gemini
SATURN	Libra	Aries	Cancer
URANUS	Scorpio	Taurus	Leo
NEPTUNE	Cancer	Capricorn	Virgo
PLUTO	Pisces	Virgo	Taurus

PLANETS IN SIGNS INTERPRETATION

* * * * * * * * * * * * * * *

THE MOON

In Aries: Emotions and responses are expressed swiftly, enthusiastically, and bluntly, sometimes with irritation or aggression. Honest, childlike reactions.

In Taurus: Emotions and responses are expressed loyally, protectively, and practically. Tenacious, determined and highly sensual. Slow, sensible reactions.

In Gemini: Emotions and responses are expressed coolly and restlessly. Talkative about feelings but decries physical contact. Speedy, intellectual reactions.

In Cancer: Emotions and responses are expressed cautiously and shyly. Powerful nurturing instincts and need for emotional security. Protective, sensitive reactions.

In Leo: Emotions and responses are expressed flamboyantly with great feeling. Proud, but generous in displays of affection. Loud, habitual reactions.

In Virgo: Emotions and responses are expressed quietly, logically, and critically. Complex nature with undercurrents of sensuality. Puritanical and intelligent reactions.

In Libra: Emotions and responses are expressed with warmth and charm, but outwardly affectionate nature hides cool interior. Calm, polite reactions.

In Scorpio: Emotions and responses are expressed in secret with great passion. There is a tendency toward possessiveness and jealousy. Shrewd, obsessive reactions.

In Sagittarius: Emotions and responses are expressed freely with great warmth. Changeable and adventurous with feelings. Optimistic, humorous reactions.

In Capricorn: Emotions and responses inhibited but sensual when aroused. Hard outer shell is soft and amenable inside. Cautious, persevering reactions.

In Aquarius: Emotions and responses are expressed with detachment and reserve, in an unusual or overtly friendly manner. Dogmatic and committed reactions.

In Pisces: Emotions and responses are expressed in a wide variety of ways but always with sensitivity and adaptability. Tearful or sympathetic reactions.

MERCURY

In Aries: Speech and communication is bold, fearless, and sharp. Attention is easily ignited but concentration span is short. Can be hot-tempered.

In Taurus: Speech and communication is slow and deliberate. Practical mind with good head for finance. Ability to make something out of nothing.

In Gemini: Speech and communication is incessant, fast, and witty but sometimes unintelligible. Able to hear everything at once but quickly forget.

In Cancer: Speech and communication is limited but caustic and defensive when aroused. Imagination and thought processes highly evolved.

In Leo: Speech and communication is loud and bombastic. Slow to anger but violently abusive when temper erupts. Creative, artistic mind.

In Virgo: Speech and communication is quiet, logical, and organized. Can be extremely verbose and prattle on about minor details. Subjects can be critical of themselves and others.

In Libra: Speech and communication is polite and charming. Quick to learn but shy in childhood and not always able to communicate freely.

ABOVE Children with Moon in Aries can become difficult to handle and may be prone to tantrums.

ABOVE When the Moon is in Sagittarius, subjects express themselves warmly and are full of witticisms.

BELOW Subjects born with Mercury in Gemini may be extremely chatty and it can be hard to keep up with them.

In Scorpio: Speech and communication is quiet but purposeful. Intense thoughts and vivid imagination can either be anchored creatively or squandered in resentful attitudes.

In Sagittarius: Speech and communication is forthright and humorous. Love of relating adventures and telling stories. Can be outspoken or tactless.

In Capricorn: Speech and communication becomes ponderous but discerning. Ambitious thoughts are not easily converted into action. Serious-minded with retentive memory.

In Aquarius: Speech and communication is intellectualized, ingenious, and overtly friendly. Opinionated principles can cause antagonism.

In Pisces: Speech and communication can either be vague and disorganized or enigmatic and insightful. Powerful imagination and creative talents can be difficult to express.

ABOVE Venus in Cancer brings a need to give and receive affection and physical contact.

VENUS

In Aries: Loves ardently and recklessly and enjoys the chase but tires of routine relationships quickly. Appreciates speed and constant stimulation in most activities.

In Taurus: Loves with dedication and loyalty but can be dull or unromantic when settled in a relationship. Appreciates routine and being in touch with the earth.

In Gemini: Loves flirtatiously and likes variety. Communication is more important than sexual activity. Appreciates quick minds and intellectual rapport.

In Cancer: Loves with great sensitivity, loyalty, and thoughtfulness. Craves physical contact. Values material possessions and home life.

In Leo: Loves wholeheartedly with great pride and loyalty. Can be too possessive or dominant in relationships. Enjoys celebrations, pageantry, and dressing up.

In Virgo: Loves coolly and analytically but enjoys organized romance and intellectual debates. Appreciates hygiene, cleanliness, and practicality in others.

In Libra: Loves with sweetness and charm but is a perfectionist and will quickly disappear if partner does not come up to expectations. Enjoys taking part in the good things in life.

In Scorpio: Loves intensely, loyally, and passionately. Charismatic and highly sexed but attention-seeking. Values kindness, generosity, and hard work.

In Sagittarius: Loves freedom and variety, and finds it difficult to remain constant in love. Amorous, fun-loving, and adventurous. Enjoys gambling, sports, and animals.

In Capricorn: Loves seriously and cautiously. Cannot bear to be hurt and will hold back if feelings of insecurity arise. Appreciates loyalty, attention, and strong values.

In Aquarius: Loves with friendly detachment and remains loyal if allowed plenty of freedom. Difficult to understand but impossible to forget. Values uniqueness.

In Pisces: Loves with sensitivity and abandonment, but is also secretive. Romantic, escapist, and often addicted to love. Appreciates tenderness and artistic dispositions.

BELOW Subjects with Venus in Sagittarius love adventure and enjoy being with animals.

ABOVE When Mars is in Aries, physical sports can provide a healthy outlet for stress and tension.

RIGHT Jupiter in Sagittarius increases the need for excitement and prompts the search for bigger thrills.

MARS

In Aries: Physical and sexual energy is expressed assertively or aggressively. Sporting outlets release tension which could otherwise result in anger or violence.

In Taurus: Physical and sexual energy is expressed determinedly or lazily. Possesses great stamina and enjoys lengthy open-air activities.

In Gemini: Physical and sexual energy is expressed lightly or consigned to the realms of spectatorship. Satirical and highly verbose when communicating.

In Cancer: Physical and sexual energy is expressed with great feeling but oversensitivity to failure or rejection can cause vindictiveness or self-centered attitudes.

In Leo: Physical and sexual energy is vibrant and powerful. Enduring and successful when channeled correctly but angry or violent when misguided.

In Virgo: Physical and sexual energy is limited to short, sharp bursts. Tires easily and prefers to use brainpower. Subjects can be obsessive about cleanliness or minor details.

In Libra: Physical and sexual activity is enthusiastically undertaken in small doses but stamina is easily depleted. Can be verbally aggressive when roused.

In Scorpio: Physical and sexual energy is remarkably powerful and enduring but sometimes difficult to control. Left unused it can cause extreme bitterness, envy, or violence.

In Sagittarius: Physical and sexual energy is abundant but restless. Needs constant variety, stimulation, and movement. Adventurous but foolhardy.

In Capricorn: Physical and sexual energy improves with age and often leads to great achievements when others have failed. Can be cold, hard, or calculatingly aggressive.

In Aquarius: Physical and sexual energy are channeled toward the mind. Good concentration helps to produce a very commendable stamina, although a somewhat dogmatic approach.

In Pisces: Physical and sexual energy are easily released and just as easily dissipated. Creative and gifted but needs direction and containment to be successful.

JUPITER

In Aries: Expands assertiveness and encourages leadership qualities. Domineering, far-reaching, and confident attitudes. Lucky or optimistic about self.

In Taurus: Expands earthiness while adding stability and creativity. Loyal and tolerant. Lucky or optimistic about financial status.

In Gemini: The presence of Jupiter expands the mind and increases versatility. Mundane, daily routines can turn into great adventures. Lucky or optimistic about mental pursuits.

In Cancer: Expands and helps release the emotions in a caring, sympathetic manner. Adds authority and executive ability. Lucky or optimistic about home and family matters.

In Leo: Expands the Leonian need for fun, laughter and high drama. Ostentatious, regal, and demanding of respect. Lucky or optimistic about creativity and love affairs.

In Virgo: Increases ability to create something out of nothing. Practical, logical, and sensuous. Lucky or optimistic about health concerns and service received.

In Libra: Expands popularity. Believes in fair play. Excess of charm and intellectual talent can lead to great success. Lucky or optimistic about love and relationships.

In Scorpio: Expands depths of Scorpio's feelings, endurance, and perception. Generous but surprisingly shrewd in money matters. Lucky or optimistic about sexual relations and materialistic concerns.

RIGHT People with Mars in Virgo can become obsessive about cleansing and beauty regimes.

In Sagittarius: Expands humor and requirement of excitement and adventure. Popular, witty, and generally fortunate. Lucky or optimistic about travel and achieving success in life.

In Capricorn: Expands dedication, moral standards, and ability to succeed. Good for longevity, wisdom, and financial status. Lucky or optimistic about career prospects.

In Aquarius: Expands mental activity, producing oratory skills and genius. Leadership qualities and popularity in group activities. Lucky or optimistic with friends.

In Pisces: Expands sensitivity, creativity, and imagination but needs freedom. Lucky or optimistic with charities, religious concerns, and soul development.

ABOVE Those with Jupiter in Capricorn have the potential to succeed in their chosen career.

SATURN

In Aries: Limits or controls assertiveness, impulsiveness, and enthusiasm while teaching the subject how to exercise more tolerance and patience.

In Taurus: Limits or controls sensual and materialistic desires while teaching the subject how to be more practical and resourceful about their finances and possessions.

In Gemini: Limits or controls mental agility and restlessness while teaching the subject how to concentrate and use communicative skills in a practical and logical manner.

In Cancer: Limits or controls the emotions and hardens the outer shell while teaching the subject how to cope with feelings of inferiority and sensitivity.

In Leo: Limits or controls the garrulous, fun-loving qualities while teaching the subject how to take the responsibilities of power and leadership seriously.

In Virgo: Limits or controls the practical, analytical, restless nature while teaching the subject how to concentrate on one job at a time and complete it.

In Libra: Saturn limits or controls Librans' innate charm, politeness, and perfectionism while teaching the subject that actions speak louder than words.

In Scorpio: Limits or controls the deep turbulent emotional and sexual needs while teaching the subject that perseverance and tolerance make happy bed partners.

In Sagittarius: Limits or controls the desire for freedom and adventure while teaching the subject that the most exciting challenge is to be happy with what they have.

In Capricorn: Limits or controls the hard, ruthless qualities of its subjects while teaching them how to advance slowly and cautiously without fear of rejection.

In Aquarius: The presence of Saturn limits or controls the overt friendliness of Aquarians while teaching them how to absorb information more thoroughly and show leadership qualities.

In Pisces: Limits or controls the natural gullible and sensitive emotions while teaching the subject how to put on a brave face and show the world what they are really made of.

ABOVE Saturn in Gemini aids concentration and focuses mental agility.

URANUS, NEPTUNE, AND PLUTO

* * * * * * * * * * * * * * * *

Because the three outer planets take such a long time from a human viewpoint to travel through any one sign of the Zodiac, they are said to be "generational" in effect. When viewed on their own, therefore, they are less significant in personal chart interpretation than the other seven planets. They do, however, become more potent and individualistic by house position (see pages 92–103) and when forming aspects to the personal planets (see section on aspects, pages 109–129). They are also important for many kinds of predictive delineation.

The entrance of one of these outer planets into a new sign usually heralds major changes within the environmental world. Habits, lifestyles, and social structures are often irrevocably altered. Whether these changes are positive or negative depends upon the planet and sign involved and the attitudes of the people affected. A good

ABOVE The outer planets will have a different effect on the same Sun sign through the generations.

BELOW Military weapons programs are an example of Pluto's destructive influences when transiting Scorpio.

example of the effects of outer planetary movement upon the world at large occurred when Pluto moved from Libra into Scorpio in 1984 and remained there until the end of 1995. During this time there was an intense upsurge in such Plutonian activities as development of nuclear weaponry, destruction by landmines, crimes of sex and violence, and production of pornography. Pluto rules Scorpio and when passing through its own sign brought much of what was happening behind the scenes in these areas to light. As Pluto moved into Sagittarius in 1996 there will hopefully be a decline in these activities and an enhancement of the philosophical and religious attitudes commensurate with the positive side of Sagittarius.

URANUS

The seven-year cycle of Uranus heralds exciting or difficult changes…

In Aries: dynamism, assertiveness, self-absorption, fires. **In Taurus:** strength, dictatorship, structural damage. **In Gemini:** intellect, versatility, educational changes. **In Cancer:** detached emotions, unique family heritage. **In Leo:** great achievements, royal births, egomania. **In Virgo:** neurotic behavior, health changes, mental restlessness. **In Libra:** unique talent, coldness, superficiality. **In Scorpio:** sexual deviation, emotional coldness, cruelty. **In Sagittarius:** exploration, unique records, new discoveries. **In Capricorn:** ruthless power, insensitivity, new regulations. **In Aquarius:** inventions, rebellion, advanced space travel. **In Pisces:** unique talent, emotional chaos, tidal waves.

agricultural booms. **In Libra:** flower power, hallucinations, peace, beauty. **In Scorpio:** lack of control, addictions, healing power. **In Sagittarius:** restlessness, visions, religious fervor. **In Capricorn:** dissolution of laws, clouded principles. **In Aquarius:** intellectual depreciation, great visionaries. **In Pisces:** compassion, surrealism, spiritual awareness.

LEFT When Uranus is traveling through Aquarius, it heralds advances in space travel technology.

PLUTO

The cycle of Pluto brings major evolutionary changes to the physical structure of the whole world…

In Aries: sudden eruptions, nuclear wars. **In Taurus:** dedication, underground activity. **In Gemini:** advanced changes in communication, verbosity. **In Cancer:** family traumas, obsessions, ultrasensitivity. **In Leo:** changes in power and authority, magnetism. **In Virgo:** minor obsessions, earthquakes, ingenuity. **In Libra:** transforming legal changes, intense charm. **In Scorpio:** sexually transmitted diseases, alternative therapies. **In Sagittarius:** prophetic powers, extrasensory perception, extensive travel. **In Capricorn:** return to law and justice, earthly restrictions. **In Aquarius:** development of the new world, uniqueness, spiritual science. **In Pisces:** self-destruction, enlightenment, strengthening of the emotions.

NEPTUNE

The 14-year cycle of this planet introduces nebulous, spiritual, and far-reaching changes…

In Aries: dissolution of leadership, spiritual evolution. **In Taurus:** financial losses, gothic architecture. **In Gemini:** instability, openness to spiritual awareness. **In Cancer:** psychic development, oceanic changes. **In Leo:** theatrical talent, dissolution of royalty. **In Virgo:** floods, mental instability,

CHIRON

Like Pluto, the orbit of Chiron is extremely elliptical. At one extreme it remains in the signs Aquarius, Pisces, Aries, and Taurus for 30 years, but at the other it takes a mere eight years to travel through Leo, Virgo, Libra, and Scorpio; it is, however, more radical when occupying these last four signs. Used as a connecting bridge to the outer planets, it enables us to realize our subconscious and spiritual needs in different ways – forcefully if placed in Aries, for example, but with great

caution if placed in Capricorn. Most of the people born since 1940 have had either Chiron or Pluto placed in one of these radical signs, but those born between 1940 and 1948 have both of them. The roles these people are destined to play in the rapidly developing world are very important in both physical and spiritual dimensions for they are the pioneers who are endeavoring to show us how to cross that bridge safely and find a more rewarding world on the other side.

PART THREE

BIRTHCHART CALCULATION

Fifty years ago the complex mathematical calculations involved in drawing up a birthchart dissuaded many people from pursuing an interest in astrology. The advent of calculators and computers began to speed things up and now computer programs will do it all in a few minutes.

The practicalities of manually calculating and constructing a birthchart are infinitely simpler than putting all the information together to create an accurate interpretation. Anyone can learn basic mathematics but not everyone has the potential to interpret the entire birthchart.

In addition to Ephemerides (see page 72), you will need Tables of Houses for Northern and Southern Latitudes, an atlas listing longitudes and latitudes, and birthchart forms. In addition, you will need to know the time difference from Greenwich Mean Time for the time zone in which your subject was born. From your subject you will require the date, the place (town and country), and the precise time of their birth.

BELOW Advances in computer technology means that astrology is becoming more and more accessible.

CALCULATION

* * * * * * * * * * * * * * * *

THE MATHEMATICAL PROCESS of converting the date, time, and place of birth into a complete birthchart is a logical calculation as shown in the two examples – the first is for a birth occurring in Cyprus and the second for a birth in Great Britain. To begin with, you convert time of birth into Greenwich Mean Time (GMT), and then from GMT into Sidereal Time, which is the true or real time derived from the orbits of the planets.

After entering the birth details, write in the latitude and longitude of the town of birth: get these from an atlas or gazetteer. Enter the birth time as a.m. or p.m. from the 12-hour clock system rather than using the 24-hour clock and then convert it into Greenwich Mean Time. Zone Standard is used for births outside Great Britain and refers to the hours ahead or behind GMT which need to be added or subtracted to arrive at GMT (see the Cyprus birth in the example shown below). For instance, if your subject was born in San Francisco, you must subtract eight or nine hours (depending on current UK Summer Time) because the sun rises eight hours later on the west coast of the United States than it does in Greenwich,

BELOW An atlas, an ephemeris, and a calculator are the main items needed when calculating a birthchart.

An ephemeris will tell you the position of the planets on any given day.

This shows the conversion of Zone Standard, Longitude, and Latitude into Greenwich Mean Time and local sidereal time.

The Ascendant in this case is 17 degrees of Cancer with the Midheaven at 2 degrees of Aries.

RIGHT Calculation for subject born at 4:00 a.m. in Cyprus on July 22, 1927.

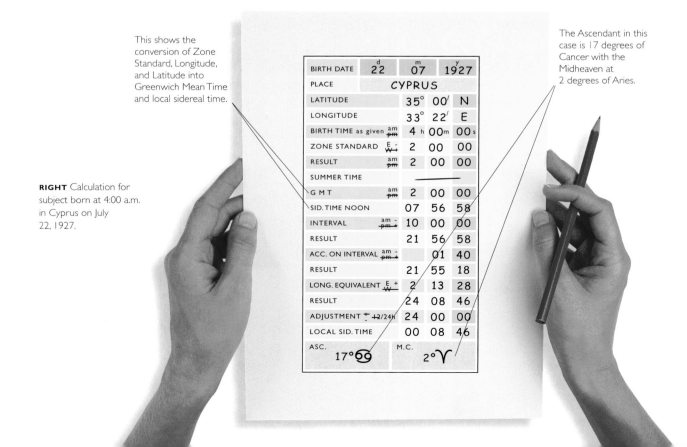

	d	m	y
BIRTH DATE	22	07	1927
PLACE	CYPRUS		
LATITUDE	35°	00′	N
LONGITUDE	33°	22′	E
BIRTH TIME as given am/pm	4 h	00 m	00 s
ZONE STANDARD E:/W:	2	00	00
RESULT am/pm	2	00	00
SUMMER TIME	—		
G M T am/pm	2	00	00
SID. TIME NOON	07	56	58
INTERVAL am:/pm:	10	00	00
RESULT	21	56	58
ACC. ON INTERVAL am:/pm:		01	40
RESULT	21	55	18
LONG. EQUIVALENT E+/W-	2	13	28
RESULT	24	08	46
ADJUSTMENT + -12/24h	24	00	00
LOCAL SID. TIME	00	08	46
ASC. 17°♋	M.C. 2°♈		

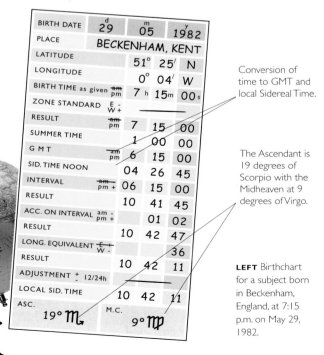

The position of the sun by sign and degree.

The position of the Moon by sign and degree.

ABOVE Small section of typical ephemeris page showing the days of the month.

London. If the birth occurred during Summer Time in Great Britain, the relevant hours are deducted to arrive at the actual time of birth at GMT.

The next stage is to find the Sidereal Time at noon from the relevant ephemeris which you write in after the GMT time of birth. The amount of time *before* noon or *past* noon then has to be worked out. For instance, someone born at 3:20 a.m. GMT has an interval *before or to* noon of eight hours 40 minutes, whereas someone born at 7:25 p.m. has an interval *after or from* noon of seven hours and 25 minutes. The interval is added (p.m. births) or subtracted (a.m. births) to the Sidereal Time at noon to form a new Sidereal Time.

One more slight adjustment called *acceleration on the interval* is required because Sidereal Time is actually four minutes per day faster than GMT. This is calculated by adding (p.m. birth) or subtracting (a.m. birth) ten seconds for every hour of difference so that a person born at 1:30 a.m. (ten and a half hours *to* noon) will require a deduction of 105 seconds (S), that is one minute 45 seconds, whereas a birth occurring at 9:00 p.m. (nine hours *from* noon) requires an addition of 90 seconds – one minute 30 seconds. This minor adjustment gives the correct Sidereal Time at Greenwich at birth.

The final process is to find the Local Sidereal Time for all births outside the 0-degree Greenwich longitude. This is called

the longitude equivalent and necessitates the multiplication of the longitude figure by 4. For example: longitude for Manchester, Great Britain, is 2 degrees 15 minutes west x 4 = 9 minutes (M) to be *deducted* from Sidereal Time. Longitude for Tokyo is 139 degrees 45 minutes east x 4 = 9 hours (H), 19 minutes to be *added* to Sidereal Time.

If the figure is above 24 hours, (e.g. H.M.S. 29 16 48) then 24 hours (24 00 00) needs to be deducted to arrive at a local Sidereal Time of 5 16 48.

BIRTH DATE	d 29	m 05	y 1982
PLACE	BECKENHAM, KENT		
LATITUDE		51° 25'	N
LONGITUDE		0° 04'	W
BIRTH TIME as given am/pm	7 h	15 m	00 s
ZONE STANDARD E/W +			—
RESULT am/pm	7	15	00
SUMMER TIME	1	00	00
GMT am	6	15	00
SID. TIME NOON	04	26	45
INTERVAL am/pm +	06	15	00
RESULT	10	41	45
ACC. ON INTERVAL am/pm +		01	02
RESULT	10	42	47
LONG. EQUIVALENT E/W +			36
RESULT	10	42	11
ADJUSTMENT + 12/24h			
LOCAL SID. TIME	10	42	11
ASC.	19° ♏	M.C.	9° ♍

Conversion of time to GMT and local Sidereal Time.

The Ascendant is 19 degrees of Scorpio with the Midheaven at 9 degrees of Virgo.

LEFT Birthchart for a subject born in Beckenham, England, at 7:15 p.m. on May 29, 1982.

BIRTHCHART CONSTRUCTION

✦ ✦ ✦ ✦ ✦ ✦ ✦ ✦ ✦ ✦ ✦ ✦ ✦ ✦ ✦ ✦

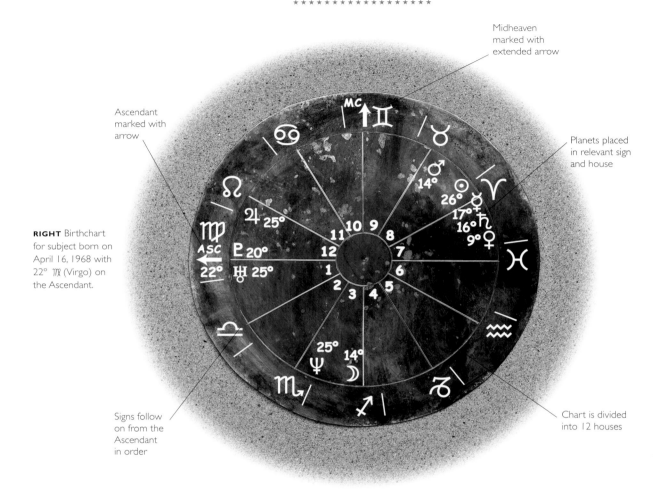

Midheaven marked with extended arrow

Ascendant marked with arrow

Planets placed in relevant sign and house

RIGHT Birthchart for subject born on April 16, 1968 with 22° ♍ (Virgo) on the Ascendant.

Signs follow on from the Ascendant in order

Chart is divided into 12 houses

1 The Table of Houses for your subject's latitude of birth now enables you to start constructing a personal birthchart. Find the nearest Sidereal Time (first column) to that of the local Sidereal Time at birth, and check across the column marked "Ascen" to find the sign and degree of the Ascendant. For example, in the table of houses for latitude 52 degrees 28 minutes north (Birmingham), the nearest Sidereal Time to 5 16 48 is 5 16 29 which, reading across, provides an Ascendant of 22 degrees 26 minutes of Virgo. The sign and degree of the Ascendant are marked on the left-hand side of the chart

form with an extended arrow as shown in the example above.

2 The birthchart form is divided into 12 equal segments of 30 degrees called houses (see pages 92 to 103 for interpretations.) The remaining 11 signs following on from the sign on the Ascendant are written in at each segment in an anticlockwise direction. For example, in the illustration here Libra follows on from Virgo, so therefore the second 30-degree dividing line, which represents the start (cusp) of the second house, is marked at 22 degrees of Libra and the next dividing line, representing the start of the

third house, is 22 degrees of Scorpio, and so on until the last line, which represents the 12th house and the sign of Leo.

3 Once the signs have been written in, the positions of the planets can be placed in their relevant sign and house. Referring back to the ephemeris for the day of birth, the planets can be read from left to right starting with the Sun. Because ephemerides are based upon the position of the planets at noon (or midnight), some minor adjustments to the personal planets (Sun, Moon, Mercury, Venus, and Mars) may need to be made according to the time of birth. Births occurring within an hour of noon do not require any planetary adjustment.

The Sun moves one degree per day (30 minutes every 12 hours, 15 minutes every six hours, and so on) and needs to be adjusted only if the degree changes; for example, someone born at 11:30 p.m. with the Sun at noon positioned at 28 degrees 50 minutes will have the Sun positioned at approximately 29 degrees 19 minutes (an adjustment of 29 minutes for the addition of 11 hours and 30 minutes from noon). Obviously the minutes would need to be deducted for an a.m. birth.

The Moon moves approximately one degree every two hours and usually needs adjusting from the noon position. Someone born at 4:00 a.m. with the Moon at 20 degrees at noon would, therefore, require an adjustment of minus eight hours which equals four degrees of Moon movement, thereby giving a Moon position at birth of 16 degrees. Mercury, Venus, and Mars move more erratically and will often need no adjustment, but when moving very fast they need to be checked for minor adjustments.

4 Reading across the ephemeris from left to right, ignoring for the moment the column marked between the Sun and Moon which is the Moon's north node (see page 133), after making the necessary adjustments for the time of birth all the planets from the Sun to Pluto should be entered in the birthchart in their relevant position as shown in the example. It should be remembered that each section (house) contains 30 degrees and unless the Ascendant and corresponding house cusps are at exactly 0 degrees they will always run from one sign to the next (22 degrees of one sign to 22 degrees of the next sign in our example).

5 The position of the Midheaven (MC) (see page 132) can be placed in the chart with an extended arrow, as in the example, by referring back to the table of houses and looking down from the column marked "10" to the relevant Sidereal Time and noting the sign and degree therein. When the Ascendant is at 22 degrees Virgo, the MC is listed as 20 degrees Gemini and should be placed in the chart at this position. The opposite point to the MC is called the Nadir (IC) and this can be placed in the chart if desired.

6 At this point the section of the chart form marked "Qualities" can be filled in by counting the number of planets placed in the polarities, elements, and quadruplicities and noting the ruling planet (the planet which rules the sign on the Ascendant), ruler's house and any rising or angular planets (explained fully on page 132).

PART FOUR

THE HOUSES

★ ★ ★ ★ ★

When you have calculated the Ascendant and Midheaven, draw up the birthchart using one of the various house systems devised by astrologers throughout the history of astrology. The houses are, in fact, the division of the 360-degree Zodiacal circle into 12 segments. The three most common house systems today are The Equal House System, The Koch System, *and* The Placidus System. *The Equal House System is most frequently used and the*

ABOVE This illustration by Metz in 1840 portrays Belgian astrologer Mathieu Lansberg, famed for his astrological predictions.

one which students of astrology are advised to start with. It is one of the oldest and was favored by the ancient Egyptians. It is also the simplest – the 12 houses being divided into 12 equal segments of 30 degrees.

The Koch System, popular in the USA and used increasingly world-wide, differs slightly as not all the houses are equal in degrees. The Placidus System, which grew in popularity during the 19th century and remained the most popular until recently, is based on different concepts – the size of the houses can vary enormously and in latitudes greater than 66 degrees only a limited birthchart with a few house cusps can be erected.

THE HOUSES: INTERPRETATION

* * * * * * * * * * * * * * * * *

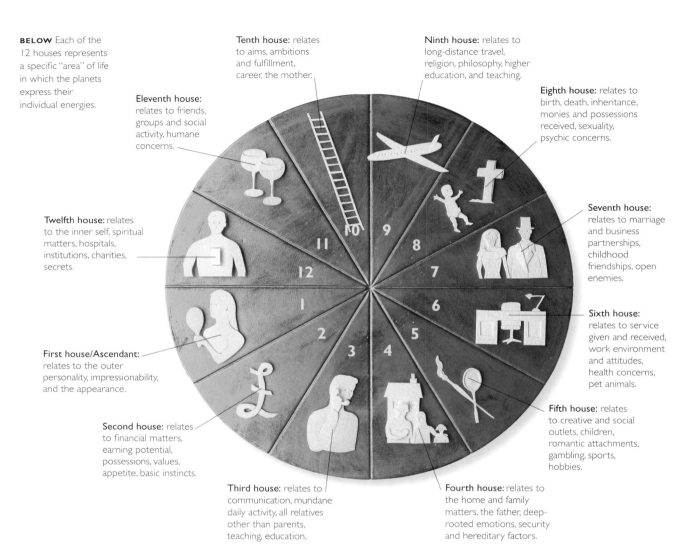

BELOW Each of the 12 houses represents a specific "area" of life in which the planets express their individual energies.

Tenth house: relates to aims, ambitions and fulfillment, career, the mother.

Ninth house: relates to long-distance travel, religion, philosophy, higher education, and teaching.

Eleventh house: relates to friends, groups and social activity, humane concerns.

Eighth house: relates to birth, death, inheritance, monies and possessions received, sexuality, psychic concerns.

Twelfth house: relates to the inner self, spiritual matters, hospitals, institutions, charities, secrets.

Seventh house: relates to marriage and business partnerships, childhood friendships, open enemies.

First house/Ascendant: relates to the outer personality, impressionability, and the appearance.

Sixth house: relates to service given and received, work environment and attitudes, health concerns, pet animals.

Second house: relates to financial matters, earning potential, possessions, values, appetite, basic instincts.

Fifth house: relates to creative and social outlets, children, romantic attachments, gambling, sports, hobbies.

Third house: relates to communication, mundane daily activity, all relatives other than parents, teaching, education.

Fourth house: relates to the home and family matters, the father, deep-rooted emotions, security and hereditary factors.

QUADRANTS

FIRST QUADRANT
Houses 1–3 relate to ages 0-9, 36-45

These three houses are highly personalized and self-absorbed. People with most of their planets in this section have difficulty understanding the feelings or motives of others. There is a certain naiveté in their appearance but they apply themselves well and are happy to work alone. The most important word in their vocabulary is "I" which makes them seem extremely self-centered.

SECOND QUADRANT
Houses 4–6 relate to ages 9-18, 45-54

People with most of their planets in this sector desire social outlets and one-to-one communication. Work, play, and creativity are important aspects of their development, but they can also be weak and dependent on others for personal satisfaction.

THIRD QUADRANT
Houses 7–9 relate to ages 18-27, 54-63

People with most of their planets in this sector are sociable and dependent upon the company of others. They do not like to be alone and can only realize their true potential when supported. These people are eager to advance into the big wide world but need someone to hold their hand in the process. They may appear altruistic or self-denying in their eagerness to please.

FOURTH QUADRANT
Houses 10–12 relate to ages 27-36, 63-72

The final quadrant relates to the world on a spiritual, humane level. People with most of their planets in this sector are often worldly wise and may appear detached from the personal traumas of the physical world. They can be highly ambitious but their innate attunement to the spiritual well-being of the world and the realization that they alone cannot change its self-destructive course can make them sad, lonely, or depressed.

QUALITIES

ANGULAR HOUSES
1st, 4th, 7th and 10th

Planets in Angular houses are said to be prominently placed. When situated within an eight-degree orb of either side of the cusp, planets become extremely important and may even dominate the birthchart – see the chart on page 84 where the planets Pluto and Uranus are placed on either side of the Ascendant in angular positions. When most of the planets are positioned in Angular houses, the subject's character is forceful, enterprising, and dynamic.

SUCCEDENT HOUSES
2nd, 5th, 8th and 11th

Succedent houses follow on from Angular houses. The area of life which they depict is, in part, a continuation of the Angular house's representation; for example, the eighth house signifies the deeper sexual and emotional qualities of a relationship engendered in the seventh house. People with most of their planets in Succedent houses are rarely dynamic or assertive, but they are strong, fixated, and creative.

CADENT HOUSES
3rd, 6th, 9th and 12th

Cadent houses are considered to be weaker than Angular and Fixed houses. They represent communication, adaptability, and movement. People with most of their planets in these houses are highly talented but very restless and need excitement and variety.

THE ASCENDANT

★ ★ ★ ★ ★ ★ ★ ★ ★ ★ ★ ★ ★ ★

THE ASCENDANT (or Rising Sign) is calculated from the time of birth and is placed on the left side of the birthchart. It is always the sign on the cusp of the first house and is the most important factor in astrological divination – without the Ascendant a true birthchart cannot be erected.

The Rising Sign and its ruling planet provide most of the information about our outer personality and appearance. They indicate how we are perceived by others, our immediate, conscious reactions, and the general impact we make within our lives. In order to reveal what is happening in the other areas (houses) of the birthchart, the outer layers of the Ascendant must first be peeled away. The ease of this depends on the strength of the Ascendant and the number of planets in the first house which also affect the personality and appearance, especially when they are close to the Ascendant, that is, within an eight-degree orb.

ABOVE The Fire ascending person on the left has a strong ego and is able to exert power over the more sensitive Water ascending person on the right.

When late degrees of a sign are rising, most of the first house is situated within the sign that follows it. For example, an Ascendant of 26 degrees of Scorpio would contain four degrees of Scorpio and 26 degrees of Sagittarius. Planets placed in these 26 degrees of Sagittarius would play an important role in the nature of the personality but it is still the sign of Scorpio (and its ruler, Pluto) which hold the most power.

Each of the 12 signs form an individual Rising Sign Personality when placed on the Ascendant. (See the box opposite for a Libra ascending personality.) Fire and Air signs usually project a more confident, extrovert exterior than Earth and Water signs who tend to exude a quiet, introspective image. However, the outer personality as projected by the Ascendant may not have any bearing on the true character beneath. The more planets that are situated in the Ascendant (first house), the more likely the individual's true self will be similar to their Ascendant.

For example, a person born with three planets, including the ruler, around a Sagittarian Ascendant is more likely to act in a typically Sagittarian manner than someone who has Sagittarius rising, no planets in the first house, and the ruler, Jupiter, placed in the passive sign of Scorpio. People are constantly judged by their Ascendant which is like judging a book by its cover – the book needs to be read in order to discover its worth. Similarly, the astrologer searches beyond the Ascendant to try and discover what the inner person is like.

ABOVE Fire ascending personality born December 6, 1969 with a Sagittarian Ascendant and two planets in Sagittarius in the first house, showing a strong and fiery, but friendly personality with much confidence and a powerful ego.

ABOVE Water ascending personality born December 3, 1962 in the USA with a Cancerian Ascendant and Mars in Cancer in the 1st house, depicting a shy, vulnerable personality even though the ruler of the chart (Moon) is placed in lively Sagittarius.

LIBRA ASCENDING PERSONALITY

Each of the 12 signs when placed on the Ascendant forms a Rising Sign Personality

First house cusp – Libra: charming, intelligent, peace-loving exterior

Second house cusp – Scorpio: shrewd, fixed attitudes toward money and possessions

Third house cusp – Sagittarius: expansive and free-ranging ideas about relatives, education, communication, and short-distance travel

Fourth house cusp – Capricorn: rigid, disciplinary, and serious about home matters

Fifth house cusp – Aquarius: unusual, eccentric, and sometimes ingenious regarding romantic attachments, creative outlets, children, and hobbies

Sixth house cusp – Pisces: sensitive, quiet, and emotional within a working environment. Intuitively tuned-in to personal health concerns

Seventh house cusp – Aries: dominant, enterprising, leadership qualities projected into partnerships and relationships

Eighth house cusp – Taurus: sensual and earthy within relationships. Practical and materialistic about the monetary concerns of others

Ninth house cusp – Gemini: restless, lively, and adaptable regarding traveling and higher learning

Tenth house cusp – Cancer: quietly ambitious, but sensitive and protective of personal aims

Eleventh house cusp – Leo: loyal, demanding, and fun-loving within group situations and friendships

Twelfth house cusp - Virgo: practical, critical, and detailed about spiritual matters, inner personal development, charities, and large institutions

RIGHT This is the chart of a strong Libra ascending personality (note that the ruler of Libra (Venus) is also placed on the Ascendant).

FAR RIGHT Social groups relate well to Leo on the eleventh house cusp.

All 12 Sun signs appear on the eastern (Ascending) horizon throughout the course of each 24 hours. Some signs, however, appear for a longer period of time than others – hence there are signs of long ascension such as Virgo, Libra, and Scorpio, which take up to three hours to move across the horizon, and signs of short ascension such as Aquarius, Pisces, and Aries, which can take as little as one hour to cross the horizon and complete their cycle.

CROSSING THE HORIZON

SIGNS OF LONG ASCENSION	SIGNS OF SHORT ASCENSION
Northern Latitudes	*Northern Latitudes*
Cancer, Leo, Virgo	Capricorn, Aquarius, Pisces
Libra, Scorpio, Sagittarius	Aries, Taurus, Gemini
Southern Latitudes	*Southern Latitudes*
Capricorn, Aquarius, Pisces	Cancer, Leo, Virgo,
Aries, Taurus, Gemini	Libra, Scorpio, Sagittarius

PLANETS IN HOUSES

* * * * * * * * * * * * * * * * * *

SUN

The Sun embodies our true inner self and spiritual pathway. It represents the ego and how we perceive ourselves. The house in which the Sun is placed depicts the area of life in which we project these qualities.

In the 1st House: the ego and perception of self are centered around the personality and projection of image, usually bestowing a strong, egocentric or narcissistic attitude.

In the 2nd House: the ego and perception of self are directed toward basic material and earthly instincts, achieving financial security and possessions, and upholding strong values.

In the 3rd House: the ego and perception of self are motivated by communication, education, relatives, and mundane daily activity. Restlessness, liveliness, individuality.

In the 4th House: the ego and perception of self are focused on home and family matters, emotions, and domestic attachments. Strong father figure can suppress the individuality.

In the 5th House: the ego and perception of self are expressed through creative outlets, hobbies, romantic attachments, children, and socializing.

In the 6th House: the ego and perception of self are channeled into work and organization, health concerns, and pet animals. Gives good service and expects the same in return.

In the 7th House: the ego and perception of self are centered around partnerships and committed friendships. The true self can be expressed only through involvement with others.

In the 8th House: the ego and perception of self are fixated upon the gratification of emotions, passions, and financial resources through others. Deep concerns about birth and death.

In the 9th House: the ego and perception of self are motivated by higher learning, long-distance travel, religion, and philosophy. Both mind and body need to be constantly exercised.

In the 10th House: ego and perception of self are gratified by ambition and prominence in career. Strives for fulfillment and influenced by mother.

In the 11th House: the ego and perception of self are channeled into strong lasting friendships and harmonious group activities where the subject is a figure of authority.

In the 12th House: the ego and perception of self are often inhibited and confused. Activity within hospitals, institutions, or charities usually generates confidence and self-satisfaction.

MOON

The house in which the Moon is placed is the area of life in which we tend to express our emotional needs and wish to give and receive support. It can be a very reactive and sensitive area of the birthchart.

ABOVE Mothers -to-be with the Sun in the 8th house can become pre-occupied about the welfare of their baby and the birth.

BELOW People with the Sun in the 1st house can be preoccupied with admiring their appearance.

In the 1st House: the emotions and responses are outwardly projected with keen attention to the needs of self, enhancement of appearance, and public image.

In the 2nd House: the emotions and responses are intensified by materialistic and personal concerns. Needs plenty of security and backup to feel appreciated.

In the 3rd House: the emotions and responses are expressed during mundane daily activities, communication, and short-distance travel. Good rapport with female relatives.

In the 4th House: the emotions and responses are directed toward home matters, hereditary factors, and parents. Appreciates privacy and is usually intuitive.

In the 5th House: the emotions and responses are channeled into creative outlets, romantic attachments, and social pleasures. Enjoys the company of children.

In the 6th House: the emotions and responses are very apparent within a working environment or when dealing with health matters. Need of demonstrative interaction with colleagues at work and pet animals.

LEFT People with the Moon in their 1st house need to feel accepted on a personal level.

In the 7th House: the emotions and responses are overtly expressed within relationships. Subject needs to give or receive emotional support on a one-to-one basis.

In the 8th House: the emotions and responses are expressed on a deep, sexual level within partnerships. Accrues wealth and possessions from others. Psychic ability.

In the 9th House: the emotions and responses are directed toward higher learning, foreign concerns, and philosophy. The subject tends to feel happier in foreign lands.

In the 10th House: the emotions and responses are channeled into career aims and fulfillment. Tendency to be in the public eye in some way. Close connections with mother.

In the 11th House: the emotions and responses are sensitive to the reactions of friends. Needs to feel wanted and part of a social group.

In the 12th House: the emotions and responses are hidden and subjects find it difficult to express themselves. They can feel lonely or misunderstood but need solitude and space to search within themselves.

BELOW When the Moon is in the 5th house, subjects enjoy social pleasures and are happy in the company of children.

MERCURY

The house placement of Mercury at birth is the area in life in which we need to express ourselves through communication with others — usually in verbal or written form. It also indicates an important sector of our lives which we contemplate and involve in our daily activity. The form of communication is shown by the sign Mercury occupies.

In the 1st House: communication is centered around the self, either enhancing or undermining the popularity of the subject. Adds liveliness, wit, or sparkle to the personality.

In the 2nd House: communication skills are focused toward material concerns. Enjoys handling and earning money. Adds versatility and livens the mind toward practical earthly matters.

In the 3rd House: communication is vital within mundane daily activity. Good for writing, educational matters, and connecting with relatives. Enjoys constant movement.

In the 4th House: communication is propelled into home or family matters. Confident and chatty in private, subjects can appear insecure or shy in public.

In the 5th House: communication is creatively expressed within social, artistic, or sporting activities. Enjoys mental activity, talking with children, and romantic liaisons.

In the 6th House: communication is important within the working environment. Enjoys studying and talking about health matters, pet animals, and work activities.

In the 7th House: communication is important within relationships. A chatty, lively disposition when involved in close partnerships but can be too dependent upon others for mental stimulation.

In the 8th House: communication is directed toward deeper aspects of life and relationships and the financial concerns of others. Good at verbalizing emotional or physical needs.

In the 9th House: communication is channeled into higher learning, overseas matters, religion, and philosophy. Knowledgeable and well-traveled.

In the 10th House: communication skills are centered around career and ambitions. Needs to be listened to and is capable of inspiring the crowd. Restless, lively mother.

In the 11th House: communication is important within group activities. Enjoys debates and informal discussions and has a wide variety of friends.

In the 12th House: communication is inhibited but the imagination is powerful. Activity within hospitals, charities, institutions, or spiritual retreats helps to develop latent communicative urges.

ABOVE Subjects with Mercury in the 12th house may find caring for others helps develop their communication skills.

VENUS

The house which Venus occupies at birth is the part of life where we like to relax and feel at peace – often a place we consider beautiful and value highly. It is usually that part of our life where we can be seen to be at our best and most attractive. It can also represent an area of laziness or extreme materialism. The manner in which the desire for love, peace, and harmony are projected is revealed by the sign in which Venus is placed.

In the 1st House: harmony, peace, and love are projected into a mild, easy-going, well-liked attitude. Appearance is softened and can be very attractive.

In the 2nd House: harmony, peace, and love are channeled into money, possessions, and eating. Strong appreciation for the good things in life but can be lazy with a tendency to put on weight.

In the 3rd House: harmony, peace, and love are directed toward relatives, education, writing, and short journeys. Benign, popular image.

In the 4th House: harmony, peace, and love are important within the home environment. Appreciates home comforts. Good rapport with one of the parents.

In the 5th House: harmony, peace, and love are projected into social, creative, and romantic pursuits. Enjoys the company of children but can be too easy-going with others.

In the 6th House: harmony, peace, and love are channeled into work and health matters. Affinity with animals. General good health and popular with work colleagues.

In the 7th House: harmony, peace, and love are focused into partnerships. This person loves being in love and rarely needs to struggle to make it work.

In the 8th House: harmony, peace, and love are channeled into meaningful partnerships and physical passion. Acquisitive and fortunate when dealing with other people's financial concerns.

In the 9th House: harmony, peace, and love are channeled into foreign matters, higher learning, religion, and philosophy. Loves traveling in luxury. Attracted to foreigners.

In the 10th House: harmony, peace, and love are directed toward work and ambitions. Popular and artistic within career. Attachment to mother.

In the 11th House: harmony, peace, and love are focused upon group activities, humane outlets, and friendships. Good fortune through affluent and loving friends.

In the 12th House: harmony, peace, and love are initiated quietly and secretively. Enjoys seclusion and clandestine love affairs. In touch with nature and the spiritual realms.

LEFT Subjects with Venus in the 2nd house appreciate good food and wine and may suffer weight gain.

MARS

The house position of Mars at birth is the area of life where we possess and expend a great deal of physical energy — whether the outlet is sport, leisure, sex, domestic chores, or something else depends on the house and the sign. Mars energy is naturally assertive, demanding, and selfish. When used negatively it can also be aggressive, irritable, hot-headed, or violent. The area in which it is placed is often a sector of life over which we have little control and usually do what we want to do regardless of the consequences.

BELOW When Mars is in the 1st house, subjects are more in touch with their masculine side and are a force to be reckoned with.

ABOVE Mars in the 6th house lends a control over and affinity with animals.

In the 1st House: assertiveness or aggression is directed outward in the personality. Strong features combined with a macho image make for a formidable exterior.

In the 2nd House: assertiveness or aggression is motivated by financial and personal concerns. Subjects display a good capacity to accumulate wealth but can become avaricious.

In the 3rd House: assertiveness or aggression is expressed by verbal or written communication. Exudes power and confidence. Can be argumentative, especially with relatives.

In the 4th House: assertiveness or aggression is exhibited mainly within the home environment, sometimes toward one of the parents. Dominant and unrelenting in private.

In the 5th House: assertiveness or aggression is openly channeled into creative outlets, romantic attachments, and sporting activities. Children are dealt with firmly by these subjects.

In the 6th House: assertiveness or aggression is manifested within the work environment or with colleagues. These subjects are driven by health matters and can also assert good control over animals.

In the 7th House: assertiveness or aggression is directed toward relationships. Likes to dominate or be dominated by partner. Appreciates decisiveness in others.

In the 8th House: assertiveness or aggression is usually controlled and expressed passionately within relationships and acquisitions, but care must be exercised as it can erupt dangerously and damage everything in its path.

In the 9th House: assertiveness or aggression is channeled into higher learning, overseas travel, and adventure. Good subject for religious study or spiritual leadership.

In the 10th House: assertiveness or aggression is focused on career objectives and prominence in vocation. Dominant mother and tendency toward military regimes.

In the 11th House: assertiveness or aggression is directed toward improving friendships and enjoying group activities. Enjoys leading within organizations or inciting frenzied riots.

In the 12th House: assertiveness or aggression is inhibited or released emotionally in private. Activity in hospitals, institutions, or charities is beneficial. Secret sex life.

JUPITER

The house in which Jupiter appears at our birth is considered to be a fortunate, highly productive, and expansive area of life. We feel happy and optimistic about the area represented and find it hard to believe that anything bad could happen to us. Sometimes, however, the luck and benefits attributed to this planet are expanded beyond proportion and can occur more in the mind than as actual physical manifestations.

In the 1st House: expansiveness and optimism are projected openly within the personality and often onto the physical body which can balloon in later years. Usually well-liked.

In the 2nd House: expansiveness and optimism are focused on monetary and personal matters. Excellent ability to accumulate through earnings. A hearty appetite can cause weight problems.

In the 3rd House: expansiveness and optimism are channeled into communication, especially with regard to relatives, short journeys, and educational matters. Thinks big.

In the 4th House: expansiveness and optimism are expressed mainly in private. Needs a large home with plenty of space. Beneficial or free-range upbringing.

In the 5th House: expansiveness and optimism are directed toward children, romantic attachments, and creative outlets. Good sporting ability and lucky when taking chances.

In the 6th House: expansiveness and optimism are exhibited within the working environment and in health concerns. Success through work and with colleagues and has good recuperative powers.

In the 7th House: expansiveness and optimism are experienced within relationships. Lucky or benign marriage with elevated or wealthy partner. Good for business connections.

In the 8th House: expansiveness and optimism are focused on the resources, emotions, and passions of others. Lucky in acquiring money and possessions, especially through inheritance and competitions.

In the 9th House: expansiveness and optimism are channeled into long interesting journeys, exciting adventures, higher learning, and religious beliefs. Subjects have an open, exploring mind with a need for physical freedom.

In the 10th House: expansiveness and optimism are directed into ambitions and career. Subjects are likely to be successful or achieve recognition through vocation. Generous upbringing.

In the 11th House: expansiveness and optimism are generated within group activities and friendships. Popular, influential and lucky with friends.

In the 12th House: expansiveness and optimism are kept hidden and are relegated to a fantasy world. Subjects would dearly love to be popular but are unable to open up. Works tirelessly and generously behind the scenes.

ABOVE Jupiter in the 9th house spells a need for physical freedom which may be satisfied by travel.

LEFT When Jupiter is in the 5th house, subjects tend to be good at sports and may be lucky in competitions.

BELOW Subjects with Saturn in the 2nd house often have a poor appetite.

SATURN

The house which Saturn occupies at birth is an area of life which is often quite difficult. Labeled "the hard taskmaster," Saturn is considered to be responsible for many of the limitations, frustrations, and fears which beset our lives. But Saturn is also the Lord of Karma and consequently rules a part of our lives in which we need to learn many lessons. Treated with insight and patience, however, the obstacles which Saturn represents can be overcome and bestow rewards and success during the latter half of life.

In the 1st House: limitations, fears, and inhibitions are projected into the personality. The natural energy of the ascending sign is repressed. Slim frame with dark Saturnine features.

In the 2nd House: limitations, fears, and inhibitions are expressed regarding money and possessions. Subjects have an ability to hold onto resources. Works tirelessly to accumulate wealth. Poor appetite. Rigid values.

In the 3rd House: limitations, fears, and inhibitions are experienced within communication, education, and mundane daily routines. Restrictive, older relatives. Officious manner.

In the 4th House: limitations, fears, and inhibitions are expressed in private. Restrictive attachment to the father. Stark or disorderly home environment. Prone to emotional depression.

In the 5th House: limitations, fears, and inhibitions are revealed in creative works, romantic attachments, and sporting activities. Subjects struggle with bringing up children or giving birth. Serious attitudes.

In the 6th House: limitations, fears, and inhibitions are expressed within the working environment. Subjects may be a workaholic or shun work altogether. Chronic health problems. Fear of animals.

RIGHT People born with Saturn in the 6th house can be obsessed with work and climbing the career ladder.

In the 7th House: limitations, fears, and inhibitions are projected into relationships. Attracted to much older or much younger partners. Marriage late in life. Can become too attached.

In the 8th House: limitations, fears, and inhibitions are experienced in emotional and sexual relationships. Attachment to financial resources of others. Fear of death. Delays in acquisitions.

In the 9th House: limitations, fears, and inhibitions are demonstrated in religious beliefs, philosophies, and overseas travel. Serious and slow in learning, but dedicated in later years.

In the 10th House: limitations, fears, and inhibitions are suffered within the career. Needs responsibility, respect, and position of authority. Reliable. Dominant or severe mother.

In the 11th House: limitations, fears, and inhibitions are experienced in group activities, debates, and friendships. Subjects are loyal to friends, who are loyal back. Thrives on responsibility in big organizations.

In the 12th House: limitations, fears, and inhibitions are deeply ingrained but rarely expressed. Subjects have strong karmic reactions and enjoy offering care to the elderly, or institutionalized people.

URANUS

The house in which Uranus is placed at birth is an area of life which demands recognition, change, and excitement. Uranus can be even more selfish in its actions than Mars and more destructive in its approach. When this area of life is not allowed freedom of expression, Uranus rebels, causing havoc and disruption. When the energy of Uranus is acknowledged, it produces important changes, great talent, inventiveness, and dynamic results.

In the 1st House: dynamic, disruptive individuality is projected into the personality. May appear self-centered or eccentric. Unusual, striking appearance.

In the 2nd House: dynamic, disruptive individuality is expressed in personal matters. Subjects often have unusual attitudes toward money, possessions, values, eating, and sex.

In the 3rd House: dynamic, disruptive individuality is channeled into daily communication, educational concerns, and dealings with relatives. Unique approach. Unusual journeys.

In the 4th House: dynamic, disruptive individuality is expressed in the home environment which is often very unusual. Detached, unemotional father. Rebellious, irritating habits.

In the 5th House: dynamic, disruptive individuality is encountered with offspring and in love affairs. Sociable but detached. Creatively gifted. Enjoys exercising the mind.

In the 6th House: dynamic, disruptive individuality is exercised within the work environment and in health concerns. Unusual attitude toward animals. Does not enjoy routine work.

In the 7th House: dynamic, disruptive individuality is apparent in relationships. Subject (or partner) will be self-willed, dominant, and need freedom but also innately loyal.

In the 8th House: dynamic, disruptive individuality is controlled but channeled into the emotional, physical, and financial needs of relationships. Unusual spiritual attitudes and sexual desires.

In the 9th House: the dynamic, disruptive individuality of subjects is expressed in religious beliefs, higher learning, and foreign concerns. Can be magnetically forceful when communicating with the public.

In the 10th House: dynamic, disruptive individuality is channeled into the career, which is often unusual. Subjects need space and freedom to follow ambitions and make unique or dictatorial mothers.

In the 11th House: dynamic, disruptive individuality is expressed in group situations. Unusual, eccentric, loyal friends. Sociable but guarded and sometimes supercilious in attitude.

In the 12th House: dynamic, disruptive individuality is deeply ingrained but difficult to express. Problems with the nervous system. Unrecognized talents. Unique karma.

LEFT
People born with Uranus in the 9th house can give powerful public addresses which capture attention.

BELOW
People born with Uranus in the 5th house often have unusually creative talent.

NEPTUNE

The house in which Neptune is positioned at birth relates to an area of life which is intangible or obscure. Neptune is often shrouded in a veil of mystery and nothing is quite as it appears. This gentle planet can cause chaos just by being there. Sensitivity, confusion, illusion, disillusion, and escapism are typical characteristics which can occur under the influence of Neptune.

In the 1st House: intangibility and sensitivity are overtly expressed in the personality. Magnetic, mystical aura. Something soft, gentle, and unattainable about the appearance.

In the 2nd House: intangibility and sensitivity are apparent in financial and personal matters. Subjects find it easy to gain and lose money. Weak values. Addiction to food or drink.

In the 3rd House: intangibility and sensitivity occur during communication, mundane travel, and education. Artistic dreamer. Easily loses direction. Strange connections with relatives.

In the 4th House: intangibility and sensitivity arise in the home. Disillusion with or idealization of father. Impractical and chaotic in domestic matters. Losses in the home.

In the 5th House: intangibility and sensitivity are expressed in creative endeavors, love affairs, and social outlets. Loving but undisciplined with children. Artistic or musical talent.

In the 6th House: intangibility and sensitivity arise in the workplace. Seeks perfection through work but easily disillusioned. Loves animals. Often suffers undiagnosable health problems.

In the 7th House: intangibility and sensitivity occur within relationships. Idealizes or sacrifices self to partner. Attracted to weak, deceptive characters. Yearns for spiritual fulfillment in partnerships.

In the 8th House: intangibility and sensitivity are expressed within the emotional and sexual needs of a relationship. Subject or partner prone to financial loss. Spiritual attunement.

In the 9th House: intangibility and sensitivity inhibit the subject from expressing beliefs. Religious or worldly wise. Enjoys long journeys by sea and traveling into the unknown.

In the 10th House: intangibility and sensitivity are channeled into career. Artistically or musically gifted. May not be able to handle responsibility for fame or fortune. Weak mother.

In the 11th House: intangibility and sensitivity are directed toward groups and friendships. Vulnerable and easily led. Spiritual, religious, or charitable groups can boost confidence.

In the 12th House: intangibility and sensitivity are so deeply rooted that only the subject is aware of their existence. Vivid dreams. Chaotic karma. Spiritually insightful.

ABOVE A woman who is born with Neptune in the 4th house may idolize her father.

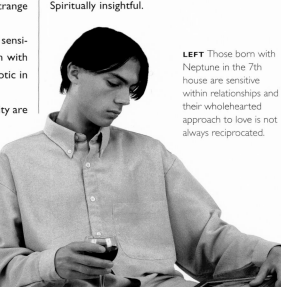

LEFT Those born with Neptune in the 7th house are sensitive within relationships and their wholehearted approach to love is not always reciprocated.

PLUTO

The energy of tiny Pluto is generally passive but remarkably powerful when aroused. The house in which it falls can be a very important area of life, especially when placed in an angular position. The need to express this area can be a dominant, obsessive, or controlling factor in life. Transformations, eruptions, and matters of life and death may all become highly pertinent when Pluto is activated in the area it occupies at birth.

In the 1st House: power, control, and authority ooze from the personality. The subject gives out little but gains much from others. They often have intense eyes, firm mouth, and determined expression.

ABOVE People born with Pluto in the 1st house have a determined look.

In the 2nd House: power, control, and authority are manifested in monetary and personal matters. Rarely lets go and is capable of great wealth. Strong values and sexual magnetism.

In the 3rd House: power, control, and authority are exerted within communication. Enjoys repetitive short journeys. Intense contact with relatives.

In the 4th House: power, control, and authority are expressed privately. Can be a tyrant at home. Emotional depths. Rejuvenated by transformations of home environment.

In the 5th House: power, control, and authority are exerted in social matters, romantic attachments, and creativity. Obsessive or overindulgent with offspring. Has creative talent which can be self-destructive if not correctly channeled.

In the 6th House: power, control, and authority are revealed in the workplace. Excels in positions of authority. Workaholic. Obsessive about health regimes. Good recuperative powers.

In the 7th House: power, control, and authority are projected into relationships. Subject or partner extremely dominant or overbearing. Does not let go easily. Prone to loss of partner.

In the 8th House: power, control, and authority are shrewdly exercised with close partners. Sexually magnetic and intense. Excels in handling other's finances and delving into private lives.

In the 9th House: power, control, and authority are expressed in higher learning and overseas concerns. Could become religiously fanatic. Powerful mind with excellent retentive qualities.

In the 10th House: power, control, and authority are maximized within the career. Well-respected and often feared. Can be arrogant or demanding. Domineering mother.

In the 11th House: power, control, and authority are exercised within group activities and friendships. Loyal, dedicated, and desirous of taking control in large organizations.

In the 12th House: power, control, and authority are experienced in the mind. Karma decrees that this person must relinquish control. Needs to be involved with hospitals or institutions.

BELOW Subjects born with Pluto in the 6th house can be obsessive about the need to be fit and healthy.

EMPTY HOUSES

★ ★ ★ ★ ★ ★ ★ ★ ★ ★ ★ ★ ★ ★

AN EMPTY HOUSE is one that is not occupied by a planet at the time of birth, but this does not necessarily mean that this specific area of life is unimportant to us. We know that planets in the houses signify areas of influence, good and bad, but a lack of planets indicates an area that does not require our attention until some later point in our lives when it is visited by a transiting planet. (See page 144.)

Empty houses can uncover almost as much about a person as occupied houses. Someone with an unoccupied second house, for example, is usually less concerned about material matters than someone who has planets in this area. An unoccupied 11th house is more likely to indicate the need for a few close friends rather than a fondness for group activities with lots of people.

When interpreting the effect of an empty house it is essential to find out where the ruler of the sign on the cusp is placed in order to discover how the activities of the empty area are encompassed into the person's lifestyle. If the sign of Taurus, for example, is placed on the cusp of an empty fourth house, the planet Venus (ruler of Taurus) must be found in order to assess where the concerns of the fourth house (home, family, father) tend to become more important. If, in this case, Venus was in the tenth it could signify that home and

ABOVE A person with an empty 2nd house and the ruler in the 9th house would find it easy to set off on a trip leaving most of their belongings behind them.

RIGHT Empty houses in a birthchart suggest areas of life which do not require much attention from the subject. The box opposite gives a detailed interpretation of the empty houses.

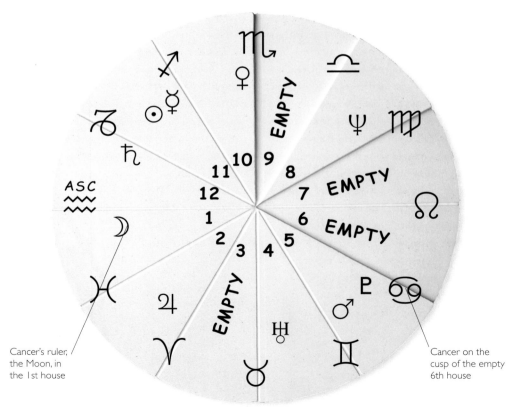

Cancer's ruler, the Moon, in the 1st house

Cancer on the cusp of the empty 6th house

domestic concerns (the fourth) become important components of the career (the tenth). Such a connection might suggest that the subject would be happy in an occupation that is linked to domestic situations or home environments, such as selling real estate or running a hotel business.

Empty houses also relate to "easy" or "latent" karma, suggesting that the area of life represented is not a required lesson within the present lifetime. Lots of empty houses in a birthchart indicate an old soul who has returned to earth in order to concentrate on one or two specific areas of life; this would reveal itself as the area where most of the planets are situated.

ABOVE A good hotelier might have an empty 4th house with the ruler in the 10th house.

INTERPRETATION OF THE EMPTY HOUSES CHART

EMPTY THIRD HOUSE

Aries on Cusp – Ruler Mars placed in 5th house
communication, short-distance travel, and dealings with relatives (third house) are undertaken enthusiastically and impulsively (Aries on cusp) within social gatherings, outings, and creative outlets. (Mars, ruler in fifth house.)

EMPTY SIXTH HOUSE

Cancer on Cusp – Ruler Moon placed in 1st house
work and health concerns (sixth house) are treated with sensitivity and protectiveness (Cancer on cusp) when the

RIGHT Someone with an empty 6th house and the ruler in the 1st house may work in an environment related to appearance such as that of a model.

personality and appearance are affected. This could imply that the subject is happiest working as a fashion model or hairstylist. (Moon, ruler in first house.)

EMPTY SEVENTH HOUSE

Leo on Cusp – Ruler Sun placed in 11th house
partnerships and relationships are not vital (empty seventh) but become important and are treated with pride, loyalty, and attachment (Leo on cusp) when formed within group activities or long-lasting friendships. (Sun, ruler in eleventh house.)

EMPTY NINTH HOUSE

Libra on Cusp – Ruler Venus placed in 10th house
long-distance travel, foreign concerns, religion, and philosophy (ninth house) are viewed with harmony and intelligence, (Libra on cusp), with regard to career or vocation. Subject will tend to travel and enjoy overseas or religious concerns only when career enhancement is involved. (Venus, ruler in tenth house.)

ABOVE A subject with an empty 9th house and the ruler in the 10th house would enjoy traveling on business.

CHART SHAPING

★ ★ ★ ★ ★ ★ ★ ★ ★ ★ ★ ★ ★ ★ ★ ★

THE FIRST GLANCE at a birthchart will instantly reveal important snippets of information about the subject. For example, planets scattered at fairly equal distances around the chart will create a pattern of behavior entirely different from that generated when the planets are all clustered together in a small area.

The system of dividing the Zodiacal circle into distinct shapings was originally devised by Marc Edmund Jones for his book *The Guide to Horoscope Interpretation* published in the 1940s and has since become an integral part of astrological interpretation. Jones describes seven common shapings. These are called *Bundle, Bowl, Bucket, Locomotive, Seesaw, Splash,* and *Splay.*

Sometimes a chart will not fit any of these patterns and some astrologers have described additional shapings they have called *Fan* and *Undefined.*

BUNDLE SHAPING

Bundle shaping occurs when all planets are contained within an arc of 120 degrees. This intense concentration of planets in such a small area indicates a determined, single-minded person who has difficulty adapting to change. When the bundle is situated in the lower half of the chart, such people enjoy privacy and are usually quiet but egocentered. When it is in the upper section, they are objective and relish public life though may be unable to cope with personal commitments.

ABOVE A very private, self-pleasing nature may indicate a bundle shaping in the lower half of the person's birthchart.

BOWL SHAPING

Bowl shaping occurs when all planets are contained within 180 degrees. The bowl is a confined chart shaping which, like the bundle, allows no access into the other half of the birthchart. When placed in houses 1-6, the subject may be introverted or shy but in houses 7-12 the subject oozes confidence but may lack empathy or imagination. If situated on the ascending side of the chart (houses 10-3), they are selfcontained and independent but in houses 4-9 on the opposite side, they are sociable but dependent on the dictates of others.

LEFT A child who is clingy and shy may have bowl shaping in houses 1-6.

planets are contained within 180 degrees

BUCKET SHAPING

one planet is situated in the opposite sphere of the chart —

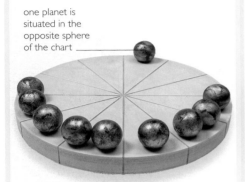

Bucket shaping occurs when one planet is situated in the opposite sphere of the chart which forms a "handle" allowing access to the "other side." Unlike the bundle and bowl person, the bucket person does not possess an isolated outlook and can adapt to changes in lifestyle. The singleton planet (the handle) is always an important planet and may even dominate the chart. The subject often desires to give expression to the area of life in which this planet is situated before

moving on to the rest of the chart; for example, someone with nine planets in the lower half of their birthchart and a handle in the tenth house (career) may be excessively ambitious.

LEFT A bucket person with their handle in the 9th house (further education) may crowd their diary with study dates.

LOCOMOTIVE SHAPING

four consecutive unoccupied houses

all the planets are sited within a 240 degrees arc

BELOW Assuming the planet pulling this locomotive is Venus, the subject would project peace and harmony.

This shaping occurs when all the planets are sited within a wide arc of 240 degrees leaving four consecutive unoccupied houses. This person usually possesses a self-driving personality. The planet leading (pulling) the group in a clockwise direction za need for peace, harmony, and love. The planet at the rear end of the locomotive can, however, be just as important, especially if it is a dominant planet such as the Sun, Mars, or Uranus.

ABOVE A see-saw person rarely follows a smooth path through life and is constantly in a quandary over which way to turn.

SEE-SAW SHAPING

See-saw shaping occurs when planets are divided into two even groups on opposite sides of the chart. As the name implies, this shaping produces a see-saw or up-and-down effect on the subject who is constantly striving for perfection and balance. This is rarely achieved, unfortunately, as the see-saw is unable to remain in a balanced position for more than a few seconds. Such subjects have complicated personalities, therefore, and are often moody and indecisive.

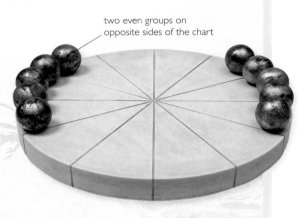

two even groups on opposite sides of the chart

SPLASH SHAPING

planets are scattered evenly around the chart

only a few empty spaces

Splash shaping occurs when the planets are scattered evenly around the chart with only a few empty spaces. Such people are creative and knowledgeable and have broad interests, but unless many of the planets are in Fixed signs, they may lack concentration or reliability and be good at most tasks but master of none.

RIGHT Splash-shaping types like to express their creative talents, but find it difficult to focus on the task in hand.

several irregular groupings of planets

SPLAY SHAPING

Splay shaping occurs when there are several groupings of planets – similar to the splash but more irregular. The subject is likely to be a nonconformist and may be unique, willful, eccentric, or in some way unusual. Highly gifted people but they are often unable to channel energy in a constructive manner.

LEFT The planets in a splay shaping are situated in a pattern similar to splash but more irregular.

FAN SHAPING

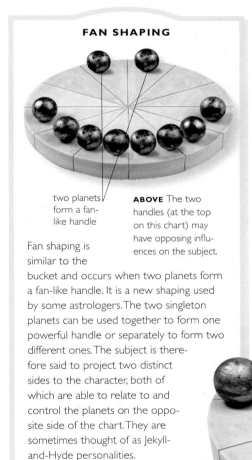

two planets form a fan-like handle

ABOVE The two handles (at the top on this chart) may have opposing influences on the subject.

Fan shaping is similar to the bucket and occurs when two planets form a fan-like handle. It is a new shaping used by some astrologers. The two singleton planets can be used together to form one powerful handle or separately to form two different ones. The subject is therefore said to project two distinct sides to the character, both of which are able to relate to and control the planets on the opposite side of the chart. They are sometimes thought of as Jekyll-and-Hyde personalities.

UNDEFINED SHAPING

Undefined shaping occurs when all the planets are situated within 210 degrees of the chart with a largely empty area of 150 degrees. They are too widely spaced to be regarded as a bowl but do not reach out far enough to be called a locomotive. This shaping has become more common since the 1960s and occurs in the charts of those who need to make many adjustments to their lives in order to "fit in." A difficult or unusual childhood may have upset their equilibrium and left them discontented or lacking direction.

BELOW People with an undefined shaping often lack direction or drive and may feel like they are outsiders.

largely empty area of 150 degrees

all the planets are situated within 210 degrees

PART FIVE

ASPECTS

★ ★ ★ ★ ★

Now that the birthchart has been erected, the planets placed into position,

and the sign groupings and chart shaping noted, it is time to look at the

aspects formed between the planets.

   The 360 degrees of the Zodiacal circle automatically fall into twelve 30-

degree sections and most astrologers concentrate on the

seven major aspects which are divisible by 30. But there

are numerous minor aspects, a few of which are also felt

to be important.

   Aspects usually evoke an "easy" or "difficult" response. The semi-

sextile, sextile, trine, and sometimes the conjunction are thought

to be "easy" whereas the square, quincunx, opposition, and some-

times the conjunction are labeled "difficult."

ABOVE The aspects are formed by the exact positioning of the planets in relation to one another.

   Aspects supply the finishing touches to the birthchart analysis and can be

vital factors in the formation of someone's character. For example, Venus in

Libra in the first house represents charm, attractiveness, and popularity, but

if Venus makes several difficult aspects from this position, the outlook is not

so rosy and may even present a taciturn, narcissistic, or unpopular image.

ASPECTS

★ ★ ★ ★ ★ ★ ★ ★ ★ ★ ★ ★ ★ ★ ★

THE SEVEN MAJOR ASPECTS

CONJUNCTION ☌ Two or more planets positioned together within an eight-degree orb of each other.

SEMI-SEXTILE ⚺ Two or more planets positioned 30 degrees apart with an allowable orb of two degrees in either direction.

SEXTILE ✶ Two or more planets positioned 60 degrees apart with an allowable orb of four degrees in either direction.

SQUARE □ Two or more planets positioned 90 degrees apart with an allowable orb of eight degrees in either direction.

TRINE △ Two or more planets positioned 120 degrees apart with an allowable orb of eight degrees in either direction.

QUINCUNX ⚻ Two or more planets positioned 150 degrees apart with an allowable orb of two degrees in either direction.

OPPOSITION ☍ Two or more planets positioned 180 degrees apart with an allowable orb of eight degrees in either direction.

RIGHT Four of the seven major planetary aspects.

B = Semi-sextile

E = Trine

C = Sextile

D = Square

a Venus-Moon conjunction, for instance, is beneficial whereas a Saturn-Mars conjunction is thought to be stressful.

SEMI-SEXTILE These aspects are usually placed in consecutive signs 28 to 32 degrees apart (30 degrees with a two-degree orb) – for example, Mars at 12 degrees of Aquarius is semi-sextile to planets at 13 degrees of Pisces and 11 degrees of Capricorn. This is reckoned to be mildly favorable with the planets working well together.

SEXTILE Sextile aspects are usually placed in compatible signs 56 to 64 degrees apart (60 degrees with a four-degree orb). For example,

CALCULATION

CONJUNCTION Two or more planets grouped together form a conjunction as long as they are no more than eight degrees apart – for example, planets at ten and 14 degrees of Libra form a conjunction but they do not do so when placed at ten and 21 degrees. The conjunction is a powerful aspect which combines the energies of two planets to create a singular force regarded as "easy" or "difficult" according to the planets involved:

Venus at four degrees of Aries is sextile to planets at six degrees of Gemini and one degree of Aquarius. This is considered a very benign aspect indicative of talent, confidence, and popularity.

SQUARE This is a highly potent and stressful aspect. The planets involved are 82 to 98 degrees apart (90 degrees with an eight-degree orb) and placed in incompatible signs within the same quadruplicity – Mars placed at 14 degrees of Aquarius is square to planets

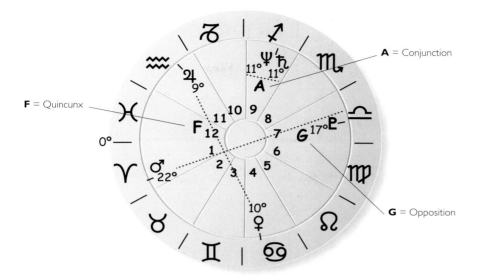

A = Conjunction

LEFT Three of
the seven major
planetary aspects.

F = Quincunx

G = Opposition

placed at 20 degrees of Taurus and 15 degrees of Scorpio. Planets in square to one another clash, each planet vying for supremacy over the other and thereby causing tension. In order for the aspect to achieve a benign potential, the subject needs to learn how to blend the energies of their planets.

TRINE This is considered highly beneficial for a trine involves two or more planets placed 112 to 128 degrees apart (120 degrees with an eight-degree orb) in compatible signs and elements. For example, a planet at nine degrees of Leo is trine to planets at 12 degrees of Sagittarius and four degrees of Aries. The trine heralds natural talent and good fortune but is easily overlooked in a birthchart comprising mainly difficult aspects.

QUINCUNX The aspect has a similar effect to semi-sextile but it is regarded as slightly stressful. The planets are placed 148 to 152 degrees apart (150 degrees with a two-degree orb) in signs which have

nothing in common and thus require an adjustment of energy to relate compatibly. For instance, Mercury at 15 degrees of Gemini is quincunx to planets at 15 degrees of Capricorn and 14 degrees of Scorpio. Provided the necessary adjustments are made, quincunxes can bestow multi-faceted abilities and unusual talents.

OPPOSITION This aspect involves planets in direct opposition (180 degrees apart with an orb of eight degrees) in incompatible signs of the same quadruplicity. The energy of the planets operates separately and needs delicate handling to keep the planets balanced. Oppositions can manifest as mood swings. The subject finds it difficult to remain satisfied with one side of the opposition and is always seeking an exit to the other side. An opposition in Taurus–Scorpio in the fourth–tenth houses, for instance, could mean that the subject is always torn between home (4th) and career (10th).

MINOR ASPECTS

SEMI-SQUARE ∟
45 degrees (one degree orb).
Half a square. Stressful.

SESQUIQUADRATE ⌐
135 degrees (no orb) Square,
plus half a square. Slight difficulty.

QUINTILE Q
72 degrees (no orb) Division
of the circle by five. Said to
produce an active mind.

BI-QUINTILE BQ
144 degrees (no orb)
Possibly beneficial.

MAJOR PLANETARY CONFIGURATIONS

* * * * * * * * * * * * * * * * *

F OUR PLANETARY CONFIGURATIONS – *The T-Square, The Grand Trine, The Grand Cross,* and *The Yod* – are a combination of the major aspects with the exclusion of the semi-sextile. They represent a powerful energy force which can be advantageous or detrimental according to the aspects involved.

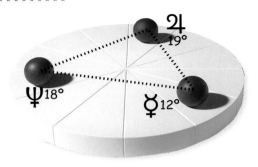

ABOVE
The Grand Trine configuration.

THE GRAND TRINE

△ Less common than the T-square but much more beneficial in its effects, this configuration involves a combination of three trines which are usually placed in the same element. It can bestow creativity and good fortune which are the reward of well-used talents from past lifetimes. However, because there is no challenge to achieve good results, inertia or acceptance can arise and this can weaken the otherwise bounteous effects of this configuration.

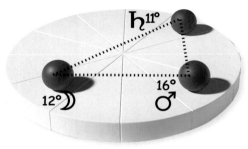

ABOVE
The T-square configuration.

BELOW Subjects with a T-square may suffer from stress, often caused by deep-rooted lack of confidence.

THE T-SQUARE

☍⊥ The commonest of the four configurations, this involves a combination of two squares and one opposition. The two planets which form the opposition are both square to the third planet which forms a T-shape.

Because both aspects are stressful, the T-square can be highly problematical in its expression according to the signs and houses it occupies, and can cause stress and tension, lack of confidence, aggression, and general disharmony. Much hard work is required by the subject in order to render this configuration harmonious and productive, but it is achievable.

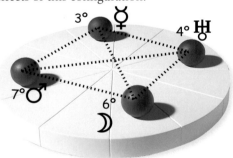

ABOVE
The Grand Cross configuration.

THE GRAND CROSS

✛ An uncommon but extremely powerful configuration of four planets in a combination of four squares and two oppositions – double the trouble of the T-square! The shape formed by this configuration is that of a cross and, true to its title, those who possess a Grand Cross certainly do have a cross to bear, or many crosses, within their lifetime. Six difficult aspects brought together in one major aspect are almost insurmountable and although subjects try hard to structure their lives positively, inevitably they fail as the strength of the configuration overwhelms them. They tend to make the same mistakes over and over and may become aggressive, obsessed, depressed, escapist, or highly stressed, according to the planets, signs, and houses involved. However, there is nothing that cannot be achieved if they learn to harness the tremendous powers of this configuration.

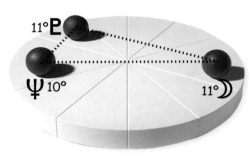

ABOVE
The Yod configuration.

THE YOD

Also referred to as the Finger of God or Finger of Fate, this is an uncommon configuration which combines two quincunxes and one sextile to form a pointing finger. The benefits of the sextile aspect are merged into the energies of the two quincunxes with the focal planet placed at the point. This planet is particularly significant because it represents the culmination of talent which is achievable when the adversity of the quincunxes has been channeled into

positive creativity. The configuration is usually troublesome and difficult to handle during childhood but can develop into an ingenious force in later years. It is often found in the charts of highly developed or spiritual individuals.

ABOVE Also called the Finger of God, the Yod configuration is often found in the charts of highly spiritual people.

DISASSOCIATED ASPECTS

When planets are placed at the very beginning or the very end of a sign, they sometimes form aspects which do not adhere to the specific formula of compatible or incompatible signs. Venus at 29 degrees of Leo, for example, is trine to Mars at three degrees of Capricorn even though they are not in the same element, because they are placed 124 degrees apart. Another example would be Jupiter at 26 degrees of Scorpio square to the Moon at two degrees of Pisces even though they are not incompatible signs, because they are 96 degrees apart.

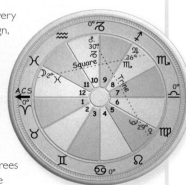

ABOVE Planets placed at the extreme edges of signs can form disassociated aspects.

ASPECTS TO THE SUN

★ ★ ★ ★ ★ ★ ★ ★ ★ ★ ★ ★ ★ ★ ★ ★

THE SUN IS OFTEN the most important planet in the birthchart and must always be studied carefully in regard to the aspects. Any aspects to the Sun deeply affect our individual psyches. The Sun's energy is naturally warm, ardent, and egocentered. Easy aspects encourage these qualities in a generous, confident, likeable manner, but difficult aspects may produce too much ego, pride, and overconfidence; conversely, when planets like Saturn are involved, this can lead to a lack of confidence. An excess of difficult aspects to the Sun encourages tension and may lead to over wilfulness or depressions. A person with no difficult aspects to the Sun but plenty of Sun trines is usually pleasant and popular but may lack drive or self-confidence.

ABOVE People with a lot of difficult aspects to the Sun can suffer from stress and bouts of depression.

ABOVE The planet Sun is represented in astrology by the Greek sun-god Apollo – patron of poetry, music, medicine, and archery.

BELOW Sun conjunct Venus people often display strong artistic qualities.

MOON

EASY ☌ ⚺ ✳ △ The inner self (Sun) is at ease with the emotional expression (Moon). Good relationship between parents and harmonious upbringing.

DIFFICULT □ ☍ ⊼ Discord or tension is experienced through emotional expression, lack of confidence, or feelings of insecurity linked to upbringing. Rifts between parents.

MERCURY

As the Sun and Mercury are never more than 28 degrees apart, only the conjunction aspect can occur between them. The conjunction is extremely common occurring in about one in three birthcharts. Traditionally regarded as a difficult aspect incurring an inability to separate communicative urges (Mercury) from personal ego (Sun), further studies suggest that although this aspect does engender a serious need to talk about the self, it does not in any way detract from the mentality of the subject which is often well above average.

VENUS

As the Sun and Venus are never more than 48 degrees apart, only the conjunction, semi-sextile and the semi-square can occur. Of these, the conjunction is by far the most important. Nowhere near as common as the Mercury–Sun conjunction – occurring in about one in eight birthcharts – it is an extremely fortunate connection. It serves as a protector against challenges and tension when it occurs in a chart with otherwise difficult aspects. Sun conjunct Venus people are often charming and always possess redeemable, likeable qualities. In general, it adds harmony, artistic ability, and good fortune.

MARS

EASY ♂ ⊻ ✳ △ The Sun and Mars are highly energetic, assertive planets and combine well in an easy aspect to produce great enthusiasm, qualities of leadership, physical strength, and a forceful but likeable manner.
DIFFICULT □ ⊼ ♂° The qualities of the easy aspect still apply but the mannerisms may be aggressive, irritating, or domineering. The ego can be inflated and the physical strength directed in negative ways.

JUPITER

EASY ♂ ⊻ ✳ △ A powerful combination which promotes good luck, success, and popularity, apparently bestowed without any effort from the subject. Optimistic and adventurous.
DIFFICULT □ ⊼ ♂° The power and vitality of this combination may be abused which results in a desire to dominate regardless of the consequences. Can be overoptimistic and bombastic. Success can be achieved if the exaggerative tendencies are modified.

SATURN

EASY ⊻ ✳ △ Although the character is quiet and seems repressed, the Sun with Saturn in easy aspect means the subject is a responsible, reliable citizen who recognizes their value and achieves much through hard work, especially later in life.
DIFFICULT ♂ □ ⊼ ♂° Saturn represses the individuality and self-expression of the Sun which can produce insecurity, shyness, stilted mannerisms, and an apparent lack of warmth or empathy.

URANUS

EASY ♂ ⊻ ✳ △ A dynamic, magnetic combination which can produce genius or great talent. The subject is friendly and often eccentric but insistent and able to achieve results.
DIFFICULT □ ⊼ ♂° Dynamism, eccentricity, and magnetism are still apparent but here promoted with great self-interest and flagrant stubbornness. Prone to dictatorship and indifferent to the feelings of others.

NEPTUNE

EASY ⊻ ✳ △ The dreamy, passive qualities of Neptune weaken the Sun to produce an easy-going, idealistic, and kindly nature with great psychic abilities or spiritual attunement.
DIFFICULT ♂ □ ⊼ ♂° The passive, idealistic qualities here become manifest in confusion, escapism, and an unrealistic outlook. The subject cannot see the wood for the trees and often lives in a muddled dreamworld.

PLUTO

EASY ⊻ ✳ △ The Sun with Pluto in easy aspect is a powerful, mesmeric combination which gives tenacity, physical strength, and the ability to lead. Major transformations will occur several times throughout the life.
DIFFICULT ♂ □ ⊼ ♂° Power and the desire to lead can, however, override everything else to produce bigotry, obsession, or violence. This could produce sexual deviances and/or callous behavior. Subjects are prone to traumatic losses.

LEFT Subjects with a Sun–Jupiter conjunction often breeze through life finding success easily where others have to work hard.

ABOVE When the Sun combines with Pluto it encourages physical strength.

ASPECTS TO THE MOON

★ ★ ★ ★ ★ ★ ★ ★ ★ ★ ★ ★ ★ ★ ★ ★

ABOVE Diana, the moon-goddess is representative of chastity and hunting.

BELOW The siting of the Moon reveals how subjects relate to their mother and can have opposing effects.

THE MOON is the most reactionary, sensitive, and gullible planet in the birthchart and all aspects to it affect the way in which we express our emotions. Whether we reveal them outwardly for all the world to see, or inwardly in private, depends on the house and sign position of the Moon. Moon reactions can be childish, tearful, wilful, and illogical. Harmonious aspects, however, encourage the nurturing, protective, and caring qualities of the planet to be activated. The Moon (along with the tenth-fourth house axis) is one of the main representations of the Mother in the birthchart. Any aspects it makes will, therefore, have great importance on the subject's relationship with their mother. Difficult aspects often produce distance, coldness, dislike, or anger toward or from the mother, while easy aspects engender caring, loving, maternal feelings. Aspects to the Moon in a child's chart, however, will show the feelings expe-

rienced by the child, but difficult aspects will not necessarily indicate that the mother's character is negative or wholly to blame for any tense maternal situation – karma, environmental situations, and many other factors must be taken into account. Children of the same family may experience the mother in totally different ways – Moon square Saturn in the chart of one of them may find the mother cold and indifferent, but Moon conjunct Venus in their brother's or sister's chart may suggest the mother is wonderfully warm and caring. In general, children with Moon in a difficult aspect experience traumatic childhoods, the effects of which often reach into adult years.

ABOVE People born with the Moon in easy aspect to Venus often have a lasting, harmonious link with their mother.

MERCURY

EASY ⊻ ✳ △ When the Moon and Mercury are in easy aspect the emotions and the intellect are in accord. The subject is able to communicate with sympathy and sensitivity, is popular with women, and has good rapport with mother.

DIFFICULT ☌ □ ⊼ ☍ The emotions and intellect are expressed inharmoniously with verbal outbursts and oversensitivity to the responses of others. Discord with mother.

VENUS

EASY ☌ ⊻ ✳ △ Emotions are expressed in a charming, easy-going manner. The subject is friendly, communicative, loving, and popular. Good rapport with women and harmonious relationship with mother.

DIFFICULT □ ⊼ ☍ The innate charm is tempered by lack of ease and a tension in expressing emotions. The subject wants to communicate lovingly but finds it difficult, possibly due to an interfering mother.

MARS

EASY ⊻ ✳ △ Strong emotions expressed enthusiastically and demonstratively are a sign of the Moon in easy aspect to Mars. The subject loves to touch and be touched. Assertive and protective toward those they care about and has a forceful but loving mother.

DIFFICULT ♂ □ ⊼ ☍ Emotions are hard to express and tend to manifest in anger, irritability, or impatience. The contrasting energies of these planets may result in stomach problems if not handled carefully.

JUPITER

EASY ⊻ ✳ △ Jupiter in benign aspect with the Moon expands the emotions beneficially to produce much hospitality, geniality, and kindness of attitude toward others. Good upbringing with helpful mother.

DIFFICULT ♂ □ ⊼ ☍ Emotions may become effusive or difficult to control and the subject may tend to kill with kindness. Overly protective or overbearing mother.

SATURN

EASY ⊻ ✳ △ The emotions are stabilized and held in check with this combination but the subject is at ease with himself and is respected for clear-headed functioning and dutiful ways.

DIFFICULT ♂ □ ⊼ ☍ The emotions are repressed and difficult to express. The subject tends to feel unloved, especially by the mother who may be cold or strict.

URANUS

EASY ⊻ ✳ △ These people are lively and emotionally expressive, especially when verbalizing their feelings. They are uniquely talented and able to blend successfully the bizarre with a happy home life.

DIFFICULT ♂ □ ⊼ ☍ Dynamic and unique but can be emotionally unstable, self-absorbed, and prone to hysterical outbursts. Unusual, cold, or detached mother.

NEPTUNE

EASY ♂ ⊻ ✳ △ Spiritual, versatile, artistic, and quietly magnetic, subjects with Moon in easy aspect to Neptune is able to be all things to all people. Love the sea and have usually had a congenial upbringing.

DIFFICULT □ ⊼ ☍ Unproblematical, but the subject may feel vague or confused deep inside and lack direction in life. Easily tempted into escapist or addictive activity.

PLUTO

EASY ♂ ⊻ ✳ △ The subject expresses emotions with great intensity and sensitivity when the Moon is in easy aspect to Pluto. They need to give or receive nurturing. Capable of great compassion and self-sacrifice.

DIFFICULT □ ⊼ ☍ Emotions are intense and hard to release and may manifest in anger, violence, or obsessive behavior. Overpowering attachment to, or from, mother.

BELOW Subjects with the Moon in aspect to Neptune have a deep love of the sea.

ASPECTS TO MERCURY

* * * * * * * * * * * * * * * *

ABOVE
Messenger of the gods, Mercury was linked to merchandise, theft, and eloquence.

MERCURY WAS TRADITIONALLY the messenger of Zeus and aspects to the planet Mercury therefore affect the manner in which we communicate – how we talk, the topics we talk about, our effect on others, how we write, the way we deal with travel arrangements and mundane daily activity. For example, Mercury–Saturn aspects slow down and stabilize all forms of communication but Mercury-Mars contacts speed up and energize them. Mercury on its own is adaptable, androgynous, and likeable but it takes on the energies of other planets directly it makes contact with them. Easy aspects can produce remarkable skills in speech, writing, or communication when opportunities for them are readily at hand, but it is the difficult aspects which are often more inspiring to Mercury and propel it into action, especially when connections involve masculine planets such as the Sun, Mars, Jupiter, and Uranus. However, challenging aspects always demand a price and the skills and talents of Mercury in difficult aspect seldom achieve the success and recognition they deserve. Difficult aspects fight back, often to their own detriment, and hard Mercury aspects often produce aggression, rudeness, quarreling, and verbal or written abuse. These people cannot stop themselves once they are challenged and are often their own worst enemy,

BELOW Difficult Mercury aspects can lead subjects to be verbally abusive. Subjects won't back down even if they are in the wrong.

ABOVE Benign Mercury–Venus aspects can increase physical appeal.

whereas those who possess only beneficial aspects to Mercury rarely utter a wrong word. Difficult aspects to Mercury need to be controlled so that the abilities they engender can be used to the subject's best advantage. (See pages 114 to 116 for Mercury aspects to Sun and Moon.)

VENUS

EASY ☌ ⚺ ✶ △ Subject is able to express love and appreciation in an endearing manner when Mercury is in easy aspect to Venus. Good sense of humor and physically attractive.

DIFFICULT □ ⚻ ☍ The subject endeavors to communicate in a loving, kindly manner but often gets it wrong and causes irritation and tension instead of harmony and peace.

MARS

EASY ⚺ ✶ △ Benign aspects between these planets produces good debating skills which combine with an assertive but kindly nature. They excel in sports or games which require a sharp mind or skillful communication.

DIFFICULT ☌ □ ⚻ ☍ The voice and manner of communication here may be aggressive or irritating. The subject speaks their mind without thought of the consequences. Good mental and physical stamina but a tendency to be too competitive.

JUPITER

EASY ⚺ ✶ △ The subject possesses a loud or distinctive, congenial voice which conveys

optimism or jollity. Good writing or oratory skills are apparent combined with a direct, lively sense of humor.

DIFFICULT ♂ □ ⊼ ♂° Voice loud, verbose, or overly expressive. Writing or oratory skills may be challenged, stilted, or hard to express. An arrogant attitude during communication can lead to their downfall.

SATURN

EASY ⊻ ✳ △ Beneficial aspects between Saturn and Mercury provide stability, fortitude, and a responsible attitude combine with a slow deliberate method of communication and make the subject serious-minded but successful at speech or writing.

DIFFICULT ♂ □ ⊼ ♂° Speech impediments, problems in communicating, excruciating shyness, and seriousness of attitude are all common with the difficult aspects and may make the subject appear slow or dimwitted though, in fact, the reverse is true.

URANUS

EASY ♂ ⊻ ✳ △ These planets combine well in easy aspect to create a brilliant mind and a lively magnetism which often bestows success and popularity upon the subject in the areas where the planets are situated.

DIFFICULT □ ⊼ ♂° However, the same brilliant mind may go over the top when difficult aspects are involved. The subject is often highly strung and lives on nervous energy. Health problems relating to the brain and mental faculties can occur.

NEPTUNE

EASY ⊻ ✳ △ Mercury in easy aspect with Neptune leads to a vivid imagination and highly attuned spirituality that produces a visionary or saintly person who is able to put others first. The subject is attracted to artistic pursuits such as poetry, drama, and dancing, and is usually very impressionable.

DIFFICULT ♂ □ ⊼ ♂° The imagination can become overactive, turning inward, and becoming destructive. A multitude of talents may be suppressed by shyness, escapism, and feelings of persecution.

PLUTO

EASY ⊻ ✳ △ Speech and communication is slow, intense, and compelling when Mercury forms benign aspects with Pluto. The subject makes a verbal point and sticks to it, thereby gaining a reputation for loyalty, strength, determination, and courage.

DIFFICULT ♂ □ ⊼ ♂° The manner of communication may be dogmatic or ruthless. The hypnotic sway is still very much apparent but there is more of a tendency for these subjects to use it for negative purposes. May be prone to violent, verbal eruptions.

ASPECTS TO VENUS

* * * * * * * * * * * * * * * *

ABOVE Venus, the Greek goddess of love, possessed an alluring grace and beauty.

VENUS ASPECTS, TRADITIONALLY associated with love and beauty, enhance the fortunes of all but the most difficult birthcharts. Venus softens, beautifies, charms, and lightens even in difficult aspect, but the easy aspects are more natural and readily accepted by those who come into contact with them. All aspects to Venus represent love in its many guises, and sometimes materialistic concerns as well. But the expression of Venus in a birthchart always requires careful study because both facets of this planet will often manifest at the same time; for instance, a person with a beneficial Venus–Jupiter contact is likely to be expansive in displays of love and affection and readily attract the attention of others, but may also enjoy spending money and acquiring the luxuries that money can provide. Difficult Venus aspects are always harder to manifest on a positive level. Charm and good fortune are there, but not for the taking – challenging aspects have to work twice as hard to achieve half the results. With the difficult aspects, the beneficial charm of Venus may be falsified or less easy to manifest and subjects may find material wealth harder to acquire. Venus is a planet which enjoys the harmony of easy aspects but struggles to find equilibrium when thrown into difficult contact with powerful masculine planets like Mars, Jupiter, and Uranus. (See pages 114 to 118 Venus contacts with Sun, Moon, and Mercury.)

ABOVE People with a positive Venus–Jupiter contact enjoy accumulating wealth.

RIGHT Jupiter in easy aspect with Venus increases natural qualities of love and happiness.

MARS

EASY ⊻ ✳ △ The beneficial combination of the masculine and feminine principles of Venus with Mars produces masses of charm, confidence, and sex appeal. The subject is able to relate well to both sexes and is always in demand.

DIFFICULT ♂ □ ⊼ ⚹ The sex appeal and charm are still apparent but are tinged with tension and an inability to accept that the characteristics of both genders require equal expression. As a result the subject may completely deny the energies of one planet and favor the other, manifesting aggressive, forceful qualities (Mars) or overly passive, gentle qualities (Venus).

JUPITER

EASY ♂ ⊻ ✳ △ The loving, appreciative qualities of Venus are expanded when forming benign aspects with Jupiter, rendering the subject confident, attractive,

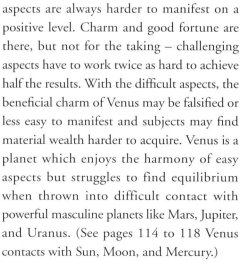

and extremely popular. This person is capable of selfless love when the right person comes along.

DIFFICULT □ ⊼ ♂ With difficult aspects the subject is still loving and popular but expects a great deal back. Excess of optimism, vanity, and narcissism may also arise.

ABOVE Subjects with Venus in difficult aspect to Jupiter can be prone to an unbecoming vanity.

SATURN

EASY ⊻ ✳ △ Venus and Saturn in easy aspect creates loyal, stable, and reliable subjects with the ability to love and give of themselves in a quiet and unpretentious manner. Relationships are often enduring.

DIFFICULT ♂ □ ⊼ ♂ The subject wants to project all the positive qualities of the easy aspects but is unable to do so through fear, lack of confidence, and possibly a difficult upbringing. They may, therefore, appear self-centered and grasping in their relationships.

URANUS

EASY ⊻ ✳ △ The easy aspects of Uranus with Venus give masses of magnetism and sex appeal which can be projected in a benign manner. The subject is regarded as "unique," has many ardent followers, and is highly creative or artistic.

DIFFICULT ♂ □ ⊼ ♂ The subject is still magnetic and attractive but may appear to be detached, self-centered, or indifferent to the feelings of others. The tension engendered by the difficult aspects causes Uranus to rebel and perhaps seek excitement within the arms of different lovers.

NEPTUNE

EASY ♂ ⊻ ✳ △ The easy aspects of Neptune with Venus are soft, gentle, and harmonious, producing a person who is kind and passive within relationships but very gullible and sensitive. Artistic, creative, and psychic abilities manifest in abundance but may not be put to positive use as these people tend to be happy in the background or living in a fantasy world.

DIFFICULT □ ⊼ ♂ The subject is a perfectionist who loves deeply and longs to meet a soulmate. Many disappointments can occur that often manifest as depression, self-destruction, or escapism. Psychic abilities may be present and if these can be channeled into spiritual or charitable activity, then much can be achieved.

PLUTO

EASY ⊻ ✳ △ Benign contacts between Venus and Pluto show that the subject loves deeply, and usually manages to command respect, loyalty, and devotion from loved ones. Physically demonstrative and very passionate.

DIFFICULT ♂ □ ⊼ ♂ The depth of love experienced is often so great that the subject is unable to let go, even when divorce or death of the partner occurs. The subject may be relentless or obsessive in pursuit of love and will rarely take "no" for an answer.

ABOVE Individuals born with benign Venus–Uranus aspects are charismatic and creatively talented.

ASPECTS TO MARS AND JUPITER

✦ ✦ ✦ ✦ ✦ ✦ ✦ ✦ ✦ ✦ ✦ ✦ ✦ ✦ ✦ ✦ ✦ ✦

M ARS WAS THE GOD of war to the Ancient Greeks but to astrologers it represents pure physical energy which needs to be channeled constructively by forming contacts with other planets. Unfortunately, the energy of Mars is also raw, uncontrolled, and headstrong and although easy aspects help to refine this energy, difficult aspects can act as a spur for Mars to plunge headlong into disaster and warfare. Difficult Mars contacts to Sun, Jupiter, Uranus, and Pluto create superb physical energy which can burst forth as temper, aggression, or violence, manifested either outwardly by the subject or assimilated in projected form from other people by actually attracting violence. Sporting activity is a good way to expend excessive Mars energy and beneficial aspects to Mars usually infer great strength, a drive to succeed, and athletic prowess. (See pages 115 to 120) Mars aspects to Sun, Moon, Mercury, and Venus.)

ABOVE Mars was labeled by the ancient Greeks the god of war and represents great physical strength.

ABOVE Difficult aspects between Mars and Saturn can cause problems or repression in sexual activity.

DIFFICULT □ ⊼ ☍ Excess of energy is used competitively, aggressively, or sexually. The subject can present a bombastic attitude which makes them hard to respect.

SATURN

EASY ⊻ ✳ △ When benign aspects occur, the serious, responsible attitudes of Saturn tone down the raw power of Mars to produce a person who can control and sublimate energy into practical achievement.

DIFFICULT ☌ □ ⊼ ☍ Frustration and anger may occur. The subject feels helpless and lacks energy when they need it most. Can cause physical or sexual imbalances.

JUPITER

EASY ☌ ⊻ ✳ △ Beneficial aspects between Mars and Jupiter provide lots of energy, physical stamina, and sex appeal which can be used productively. The subject likes to lead or dominate but does so in an unaffected or friendly manner.

URANUS

EASY ☌ ⊻ ✳ △ Mars and Uranus in easy aspect give the subject dynamic energy, magnetism, and unique talents, with a positive approach and a desire to get things done quickly and efficiently.

DIFFICULT □ ⊼ ☍ Although highly independent and talented, the subject may be thoughtless and brash, causing blunders and upsets which are blamed on the inefficiency of others.

BELOW Aspects from Mars to Jupiter usually generate physical energy often channeled into sports.

NEPTUNE

EASY ⊻ ⚹ △ The nebulous energy of Neptune can be channeled into a more solid foundation in this highly artistic combination with Mars. The subject often possesses powerful psychic abilities.

DIFFICULT ♂ ☐ ⊼ ♂° The creative and physical energy is depleted. The subject possesses great ability but is unable to harness it successfully. Tendency to escape into a physical, hero-centered dreamworld.

PLUTO

EASY ⊻ ⚹ △ When Mars forms benign aspects to Pluto, there is intense, powerful energy which can be channeled constructively. The subject is attracted to the armed forces or rigid, disciplinary, uniformed occupations.

DIFFICULT ♂ ☐ ⊼ ♂° The subject has masses of energy which are hard to control unless directed into sports or arduous physical regimes. May be aggressive or fascinated with war and violence.

J UPITER IS THE planet of expansion and optimism with the beneficial aspects generating much good fortune, but the difficult aspects may cause overoptimism, overconfidence, and bombastic attitudes; for instance, Jupiter–Mercury never knows when to shut up, Jupiter–Mars never knows when to give up, and Jupiter–Saturn finds it hard to recognize boundaries. Generally, however, Jupiter has a lovely benign influence which, when easily aspected, helps to protect and bring good luck. (See pages 115 to 122 Jupiter aspects to Sun, Moon, Mercury, Venus, and Mars.)

SATURN

EASY ⊻ ⚹ △ When forming benign aspects the expansive qualities of Jupiter combine reasonably well with the restrictive qualities of Saturn to allow the subject to manage without going to extremes.

DIFFICULT ♂ ☐ ⊼ ♂° The expansion–restriction principle is not easily accepted. The subject is angry at being held back but, when given the opportunities, lack of confidence inhibits their capabilities.

URANUS

EASY ♂ ⊻ ⚹ △ Jupiter and Uranus in easy aspect form a powerful, confident combination which can produce great talent and the ability to get things done. The subject is a natural leader.

DIFFICULT ☐ ⊼ ♂° Subjects may be self-opinionated, arrogant, or eccentric.

NEPTUNE

EASY ⊻ ⚹ △ Benign contacts between Neptune and Jupiter are excellent for psychic, spiritual, or religious matters. The subject has an affinity for music, art, or drama.

DIFFICULT ♂ ☐ ⊼ ♂° The subject may overdramatize everything and be too confident about their abilities. Could be prone to religious bigotry or false claims of talent.

PLUTO

EASY ⊻ ⚹ △ Easy aspects between Jupiter and Pluto increase physical energy and concentration.

DIFFICULT ♂ ☐ ⊼ ♂° Stressful energy and enforced concentration can cause obsessions and religious or philosophical fanaticism.

ABOVE Jupiter was the counterpart to Zeus, the greatest of the Greek gods.

ASPECTS BETWEEN SATURN, URANUS, NEPTUNE, AND PLUTO

★ ★ ★ ★ ★ ★ ★ ★ ★ ★ ★ ★ ★ ★ ★ ★

ANY ASPECT between these planets is long-lasting and, depending on the degree of orb used, can take generations to work through when the major aspects are involved. The lesser aspects – semi-sextile, sextile, and quincunx – rarely seem to produce any obvious effect, whereas the square, opposition, and trine are mildly effective. The conjunction, however, can be awesome in its effect and dominate the whole chart. Neptune and Pluto aspects arise only once every few hundred years and when they do occur, they usually herald an important event, milestone, or catastrophe somewhere on the earth.

ABOVE
Neptune–Pluto aspects are thought to be connected with disasters like volcanic eruptions.

ABOVE Saturn was the ancient Roman god of agriculture who became identified with Kronos, the supreme god of the Greeks.

SATURN

All planets which aspect Saturn will be limited, slowed-down, and muted in their effect, but not necessarily weakened. Saturn can teach us much about life. It is capable of restraining an over-exuberant Mars, of controlling an oversensitive Moon, or stabilizing a chaotic Neptune. Beneficial aspects are readily accepted and integrated into the subject's lifestyle but difficult aspects often cause irritation and resentment at

RIGHT People with a Saturn–Neptune aspect can appear vague and often do not say what they actually mean.

Saturn's disciplinary influence. (See pages 115 to 123 for Saturn aspects to Sun, Moon, Mercury, Venus, Mars, and Jupiter.)

SATURN–URANUS Responsibility and restriction combine with freedom and excitement. The conjunction of these two planets can be very frustrating. Freedom is inhibited, thereby causing rebellion and a stubborn determination that life should be exciting or different. The subject is constantly trying to break free from routines of their own making.

SATURN–NEPTUNE Responsibility and restriction combine with nebulosity and a desire to escape from reality. People with this aspect often say "yes" when they mean "no" or the other way round. Seriousness and upright

principles predominate, but the subject often opts out just when things are going well and can even become a bit of a recluse.

SATURN–PLUTO Responsibility and restriction combine with dedication, intensity, and passion to produce a strong-minded person who knows what they want and how to get it. This person is highly magnetic but can also be dogmatic and obsessive.

URANUS

Uranus strengthens and gives individuality to every planet it comes into contact with. Its over-riding influence easily magnetizes the personal planets but detrimental aspects can be disastrous. There is heavy warfare when it comes into contact with other outer planets, and it will stop at nothing to seek out self-fulfillment. (See pages 115 to 124 for Uranus aspects to Sun, Moon, Mercury, Venus, Mars, Jupiter, and Saturn.)

URANUS–NEPTUNE Last seen during the first half of the 1990s, this dynamic combination is capable of creating havoc around the world and within a natal birthchart it often has the same effect. Wherever it falls in the chart, the subject will struggle to find equilibrium. Personal disasters occur frequently. The subject may feel they have no control over a certain area of their life. However, when the influence is harnessed into creative or spiritual endeavors, it can produce brilliance or genius.

URANUS–PLUTO More destructive and powerful than Uranus–Neptune. Last seen

ABOVE
The ancient Greek God Uranus was father of Kronos (Saturn).

in the 1960s, it created a new world of freedom (Uranus) combined with sexuality (Pluto). Children born in the 1960s who have this aspect in their chart have grown up with the vital energy of this combination causing continual disturbance somewhere in their life. It can manifest in sudden (Uranus) violent (Pluto) eruptions and cause extreme mental (Uranus) or physical (Pluto) distress.

NEPTUNE

Difficult aspects to Neptune weaken, confuse, and disorientate the planets it makes contact with, but beneficial aspects soften, spiritualize, and inspire the subject into greater achievements. (See pages 115 to 125 for Neptune aspects to Sun, Moon, Mercury, Venus, Mars, Jupiter, Saturn, and Uranus.)

NEPTUNE–PLUTO Occurs very rarely (last seen in the early 1890s in the sign of Gemini.) Not cruelly destructive like Uranus–Pluto but causes gradual disintegration of outdated earthly patterns and personal lifestyles in order to transform and bring in the new. Both planets are feminine by nature and rule Water signs (Pisces and Scorpio) and are therefore fairly compatible.

PLUTO

Pluto's influence when aspecting other planets is often indiscernible until it strikes with such volcanic force that the subject's whole world can be transformed forever. Such power should never be underestimated or overlooked. Many famous unforgettable people possess highly aspected or strongly positioned Plutos in their charts. (See pages 115 to 125 for individual Pluto aspects.)

ABOVE Neptune was the Roman sea god, linked to Poseidon, the Greek water god. This planet rules Pisces.

ABOVE Pluto was the Greek god of the underworld. The force of this planet should not be underestimated.

UNASPECTED PLANETS

★ ★ ★ ★ ★ ★ ★ ★ ★ ★ ★ ★ ★ ★ ★ ★ ★

APLANET that does not form any of the major seven aspects with another planet is said to be "unaspected" and therefore operates on a level of pure energy. When a planet makes an aspect with another planet, their combined energies blend if it is an easy aspect, or are forced into combat if it is a difficult one and thus form a new composite energy. Unaspected planets do not form new combined energies and can therefore manifest freely. Such energy is like that of a wild animal that roams at will, hunts and eats as nature intended, and has no contact with humans. The abundance of natural energy relating to a specific unaspected planet often dominates the birthchart.

therefore become "almost unaspected." Although much of the planetary energy will go into the weak aspect, the energy flow of the planet as a whole is strengthened and it may react as if it were unaspected.

Unaspected planets are nearly always overtly expressed in a person's nature and they often appear to dominate a chart. My father possessed a somewhat rare unaspected Venus in the sign of Virgo and he was always smiling – he was a popular man, charming, generous, and extremely easy-going, despite a challenging Mars–Saturn conjunction and a badly aspected Sun in Scorpio. Unaspected Sun occurs most frequently among the personal planets (Queen Elizabeth II of

ABOVE The abundance of energy manifested by unaspected planets can be likened to the natural energy of a wild animal.

Unaspected planets are not common and if one took account of the various minor aspects, the Ascendant and Midheaven and all the energy points of the birthchart through which planets make contact, they would probably not exist at all. But, in my experience, a planet reacts as unaspected when it has no contact with any other planet while using the seven major aspects within their suggested orbs. It is also quite common for a planet to form only one weak, minor aspect such as a quincunx or semi-sextile and

England and King Louis XIV of France are good examples), while unaspected Venus is six times less common. When unaspected planets occur in a birthchart, they should always be noted and observed closely as they are capable of changing the apparent structure of an individual's psyche.

SUN UNASPECTED

The effect of an unaspected Sun can be brilliant and dazzling or egocentered and selfish, but over 50 percent of subjects with this

well to women. They are overtly responsive and friendly but need to retreat once in a while into another, darker world in order to recharge their batteries, thus enabling them to reflect both the light and the dark sides of the Moon. It is not easy to control the abundant, free-flowing emotions of the Moon but these people tend to manage remarkably well and usually develop a kindly, nurturing nature.

MERCURY UNASPECTED

Restless, volatile, androgynous Mercury can find it difficult to maintain stability when unaspected. People with this placement tend to be likeable, intelligent, and adaptable, but forever flitting from one thing to another as they seek a permanent outlet for Mercury's talents. The weak energy of Mercury usually takes on the form of its aspects and its free-flowing energy can feel very lost when placed on its own, stage-center. To offset this, a veneer of confidence, humor, and sociability is often adopted that makes subjects with this placing highly popular.

ABOVE Chart for Mahatma Gandhi born October 2, 1869 with an unaspected Mercury in the sign of Scorpio in the 1st house.

configuration become successful or famous. Children with this placement are usually wilful, hot-headed, and demanding, but as they grow older they learn to command respect and exploit the pure energy of the Sun for their own glorification. King Louis XIV of France was known as the "Sun King" (his Sun was placed in Virgo) and possessed an unaspected Sun, as did Vincent Van Gogh (Sun in Aries) who was obsessed by the sun and painted it boldly in his "Sunflowers."

MOON UNASPECTED

The passive, sensitive qualities of the Moon are highly emphasized when unaspected. People with this placement – men in particular – tend to possess many feminine qualities and relate

ABOVE Chart for Louis Pasteur born December 27, 1822, France, showing an unaspected Gemini Moon in the 8th house.

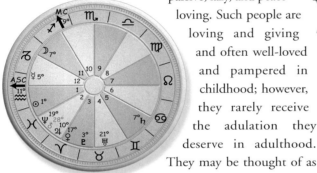

VENUS UNASPECTED

The unadulterated energy of Venus is not common – about one and a half percent of people have unaspected Venus and very few of them become famous or successful, which is not surprising as Venus energy is basically passive, lazy, and peace-loving. Such people are loving and giving and often well-loved and pampered in childhood; however, they rarely receive the adulation they deserve in adulthood. They may be thought of as weak and may even be derided rather than praised for their generous open natures, even though they are liked for their attractive appearance and polite charm. Those people with this placement are usually very old souls who have returned to Earth to give help to the rest of us and must expect little in return; however, they should take care not to allow the materialistic side of Venus precedence over the loving element.

MARS UNASPECTED

The vital, raw energy of Mars when unaspected is capable both of great physical achievement and destruction. Fortunately, most unaspected

planets in their pure form tend to operate on a positive level and Mars is no exception. The Englishman, Lord Baden Powell, founder of the Boy Scout movement, was a forceful character with an unaspected Mars which he used beneficially. The excess of energy provided by Mars when unaspected can sometimes produce great athletic ability and deeds of bravery. War heroes and high-ranking military officers often have Mars prominent or unaspected in their charts.

JUPITER UNASPECTED

The lucky few who have Jupiter unaspected possess a large share of optimism and good fortune. The expansive, beneficent qualities of the planet in its unadulterated form provide a good buffer against any difficulties in the birthchart. Unaspected Jupiter will shine through no matter what the rest of the chart is like and give the subject a good sense of humor and an innate sense of self-confidence. These people are invariably likeable and what to others may seem like misfortune, to them quickly becomes the "luck of the gods."

SATURN UNASPECTED

The restrictions, fears, and inhibitions which regularly occur when Saturn is aspected do not seem to manifest themselves when it is unaspected. Instead, the positive qualities of seriousness, conformity, practicality, and responsibility are projected to produce an upright pillar of society who, although not overly charming or popular, is usually well-trusted and respected.

URANUS UNASPECTED

As with all the outer planets and their lengthy cycles, it is difficult to find a completely unaspected Uranus but evidence suggests that weak generational aspects between the outer planets (semi-sextiles, quincunxes, and sextiles) do not operate on a personal level and can therefore be disregarded when looking for unaspected planets.

Many people would possess an otherwise unaspected outer planet if it were not for these aspects. When Uranus is unaspected (or almost unaspected), it does not seem to engender the same dynamic, rebellious, or eccentric qualities which are often apparent when aspects do occur. Unaspected Uranus is quietly unique, strongly gifted, and subtly independent. It is less excitable and more stable than an aspected Uranus.

NEPTUNE UNASPECTED

The vagaries and nebulosity of aspected Neptune are far less apparent when Neptune is unaspected. This enables the subject to consolidate talents and intuitive abilities while leading a constructive life, unlike other strongly Neptunian people – those for instance, who have Neptune Angular or powerfully aspected. Neptune can manifest on many different levels – from the highest spiritual attunement to the depths of depravity, but unaspected Neptune does not have to face the challenges of difficult aspects and is therefore allowed more freedom to utilize imagination and inspiration.

PLUTO UNASPECTED

A completely unaspected Pluto is very uncommon but those who do have this rare placement are usually intense, well-balanced people who lack the usual Plutonian need to exert power over others. They are magnetic and forceful without being overbearing. When Pluto is virtually unaspected (one minor aspect between Pluto and another outer planet), the effect can, however, be remarkably different. The energy becomes much more difficult to harness and in extreme cases seems to attract violence or destruction to its owner – as with President John F. Kennedy whose virtually unaspected Pluto helped give him power and control over the United States but also brought him the violence that caused his death. Powerful people often possess dominant Plutos – Queen Elizabeth II of England (Angular), actress and pop star Madonna (conjunct Ascendant), and the German composer Beethoven (conjunct Midheaven) are but a few. So great is their impact on human life that these people are often remembered for years, perhaps centuries, after their passing. Pure, unaspected Pluto also possesses this remarkable capacity for fame or infamy but it is weakened and thus made easier to control.

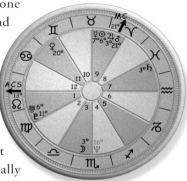

ABOVE Chart for female born on December 6, 1969 with an unaspected Uranus in Libra on the cusp of the 11th house.

ABOVE Chart for subject born on April 26, 1964 in Glasgow, Scotland with a very rare unaspected Neptune in Scorpio in the 4th house.

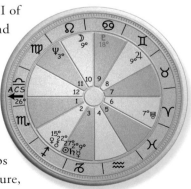

ABOVE Chart for male subject born on December 19, 1929 with an unaspected Pluto in the sign of Cancer in the 9th house.

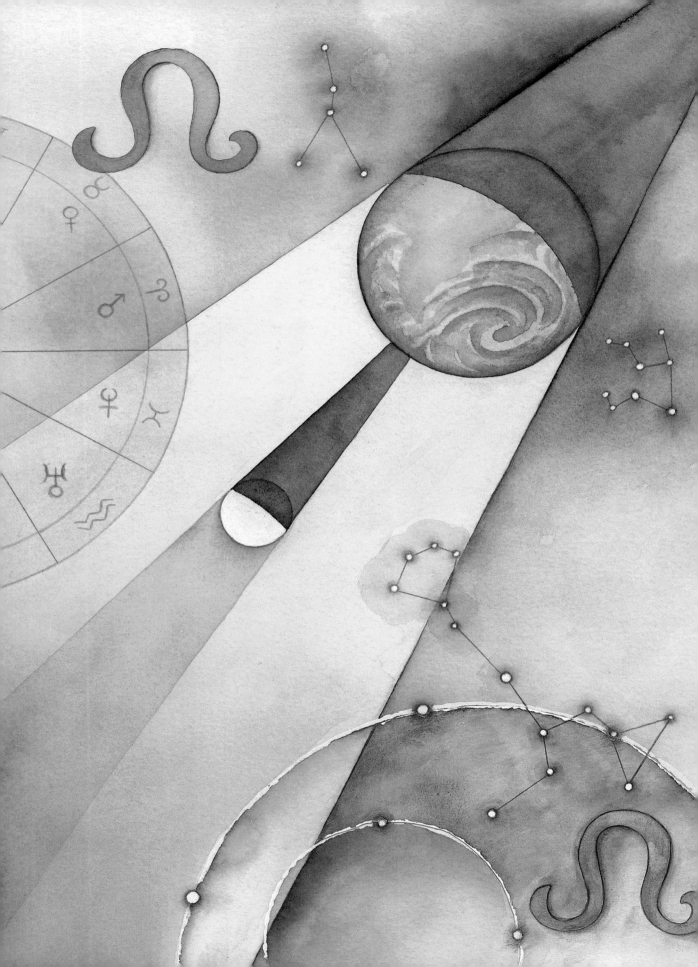

PART SIX

OTHER FACTORS

★ ★ ★ ★ ★

Although the signs of the Zodiac and the planetary energies as they relate to the houses of the chart wheel are the most important factors in modern astrology, there are other minor points and systems of division which manifest their own unique energies that we need to consider. Hypothetical points such as the Moon's Nodes and the Arabian Parts have been used as additional sources of information for thousands of years. Some astrologers believe that the Moon's Nodes are extremely important, especially in health matters, and the Arabian Parts are used extensively in Horary Astrology, a branch of predictive astrology. No minor factor should ever be ignored or discarded, because study of these same factors will sometimes reveal why a person does something unusual or reacts in a certain way. From my own personal experience I have found that Ruling Planets and Decanates can be particularly revealing.

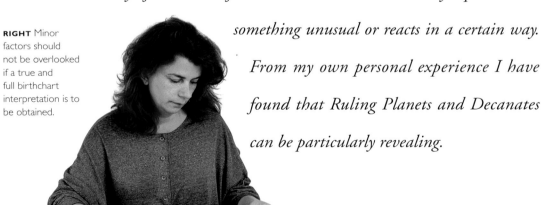

RIGHT Minor factors should not be overlooked if a true and full birthchart interpretation is to be obtained.

MINOR POINTS AND DIVISIONS

* * * * * * * * * * * * * * * *

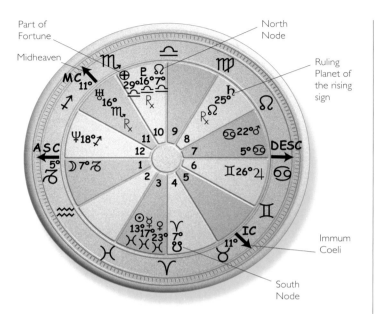

Part of Fortune

Midheaven

North Node

Ruling Planet of the rising sign

Immum Coeli

South Node

ABOVE There are several minor points on the birthchart which the astrologer will need to take into account in assessing the subject.

RIGHT Success of a project such as a new novel can be heralded when the Arabian Part of Fortune is placed in Gemini or Virgo in the 10th house.

THE MIDHEAVEN (MC) This important point is the actual "zenith" (highest point) of the birthchart and must fall between the eighth and 11th houses when using the Equal House System of division. However, it is more commonly found in the ninth or tenth houses. With Placidus and other methods of division the Midheaven always forms the cusp of the tenth house. It is regarded as the pinnacle of the chart wherever it falls – an area where great achievement, satisfaction, or fulfillment can be recognized. Any planets forming a conjunction to the MC are vitally important and should be viewed as "Angular."

IMMUM COELI (IC) This point is always in exact opposition (180 degrees) to the MC; if, for example, the MC were at 15 degrees of Cancer, the IC would be placed at 15 degrees of Capricorn. It is

therefore regarded as the "nadir" (lowest part) of the birthchart and can fall anywhere between the second and fifth houses in the Equal House System. It usually represents the quietest, most subjective point of the chart. Any planets forming a conjunction to the IC are important but are not considered Angular unless within an eight-degree orb of the cusp of the fourth house.

THE DESCENDANT This point refers to the cusp of the seventh house in all house systems. It is the exact opposite point to the Ascendant and tends to relate to others rather than the self. Any planets conjuncting the Descendant show an important requirement for companionship within relationships.

RULING PLANETS Ruling planets are those which rule the sign on any given house cusp, the most important being the Ruling Planet of the rising sign (Ascendant) which is regarded as the Ruling Planet of the whole birthchart. The house and sign in which the Ruling Planet(s) is placed are extremely important areas. A person will sometimes look more like the sign in which the ruling planet of the Ascendant is placed than the ascending sign itself – for instance, if Cancer was rising and the Moon placed in Sagittarius, the subject may look and act more like a typical Sagittarian.

THE ARABIAN PARTS There are many of these hypothetical, mathematically calculated points which refer to different categories such as the Part of Death, the Part of Marriage, and the Part of Children. The only one in common use today, however, is *The Part of Fortune* which is thought to be a beneficial point in which the sign and house occupied can bring good fortune through expression of the qualities represented. For example, the Part of Fortune placed in Leo in the tenth house augurs well for fame and honor within that person's career. The Part of Fortune can be calculated by using the formula *Ascendant plus Moon minus Sun*. The example below shows the calculation for a subject born with the Ascendant at 12 degrees of Capricorn, the Moon at 23 degrees of Pisces, and the Sun at two degrees of Leo, using the Table of Zodiacal degrees.

TABLE OF ZODIACAL DEGREES

0° Aries	=	0°	0° Libra	=	180°
0° Taurus	=	30°	0° Scorpio	=	210°
0° Gemini	=	60°	0° Sagittarius	=	240°
0° Cancer	=	90°	0° Capricorn	=	270°
0° Leo	=	120°	0° Aquarius	=	300°
0° Virgo	=	150°	0° Pisces	=	330°

PART OF FORTUNE CALCULATION

**Ascendant 12 degrees Capricorn
(270 + 12) = 282 degrees**

**plus Moon 23 degrees Pisces
(330 + 23) = 353 degrees**

Total = 635 degrees

**minus Sun 2 degrees in Leo
(120 + 02) = 122 degrees Leo**

Total = 513 degrees

**When total exceeds the 360 degree circle,
subtract 360 degrees = 153 degrees**

*153 degrees represents 3 degrees of Virgo on the tables
so the Part of Fortune is placed in the chart at this point.*

THE NODES Nodes are astronomical points within a planetary orbit as it crosses the ecliptic from South to North (forming the North Node) and from North to South (forming the South Node). All the planets form nodes but only the Moon's are consid-

ered significant enough to be inserted into the birthchart. The Moon's Nodes are particularly relevant within spiritual matters, relationships, and the arising of karma.

MOON'S NODES North Node: traditionally known as the Dragon's Head. The house and sign in which this is placed correspond to the main area of life in which we should be aspiring to learn and gain knowledge and success in this lifetime. We should look to the North Node for the solutions to problems and the development of benign karma. South Node: traditionally known as the Dragon's Tail. The house and sign in which these are placed corresponds to the main area of life where our past-life talents and abilities are easily utilized but often abused. This is the area where we feel "comfortable" and where we go in times of stress.

BELOW The Moon's Nodes are known as the Dragon's Head and the Dragon's Tail.

DECANATES

★ ★ ★ ★ ★ ★ ★ ★ ★ ★ ★ ★ ★ ★ ★ ★ ★

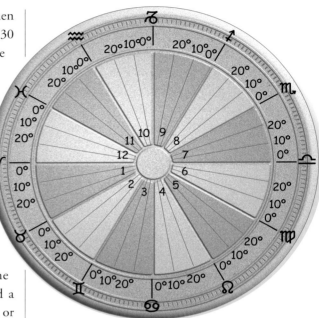

ACH SIGN OF THE ZODIAC (or house when using the Equal House Method) contains 30 degrees which can be divided into three groups of ten degrees: zero to nine, ten to 19 and 20 to 29. These divisions are called Decanates. The first ten degrees (zero to nine) of any sign are called the First Decanate, the second ten degrees (ten to 19) the Second Decanate, and the third ten degrees (20 to 29) the Third Decanate. When a degree reaches 29 degrees 59 minutes, it has completed its cycle and moves on to zero degrees. In reality, 30 degrees and zero degrees are the same degree, combining an ending (30) and a beginning (0). People born with the Sun or other planets around this degree are highly complex in character.

RIGHT Each sign is divided into three decanates which have their own qualities.

Decanates are used mainly in Sun-sign interpretation but can be successfully applied to all planetary positions within the signs and houses of the birthchart. At this level, they are an extensive and highly rewarding method of character delineation.

RIGHT People born with planets at 29 or zero degrees can be complex characters.

The first decanate of any sign always corresponds to the sign being studied so that the first decanate of Aries will relate to Aries. The second decanate of any sign takes on the characteristics of the next sign in the same element so that here the second decanate of Aries will relate to Leo. The third decanate of any sign represents the last sequential sign within the same element so that the third decanate of Aries will therefore relate to Sagittarius. If Sagittarius were the sign being studied, the first decanate would be Sagittarius, the second Aries, and the third Leo. A person born when the Sun was at 12 degrees of Pisces (around 2 March) would be placed in the second decanate of this sign which is the Cancerian decanate.

Each decanate within a sign adopts some of the qualities of the sign ruling the decanate. The first decanate is usually the strongest as it corresponds to a double energy of that particular sign, whereas a person born during the second and third decanates will be less typical of the sign in question. Someone whose birthday falls on June 18, for example, is a Gemini subject, born during the last ten degrees of the sign, which is the third decanate relating to the sign of Aquarius. They are then more likely to project some fixated qualities of Aquarius and be less restless than a typical Gemini.

TABLE OF DECANATES

	1ST DECANATE	2ND DECANATE	3RD DECANATE
ARIES	Aries	Leo	Sagittarius
TAURUS	Taurus	Virgo	Capricorn
GEMINI	Gemini	Libra	Aquarius
CANCER	Cancer	Scorpio	Pisces
LEO	Leo	Sagittarius	Aries
VIRGO	Virgo	Capricorn	Taurus
LIBRA	Libra	Aquarius	Gemini
SCORPIO	Scorpio	Pisces	Cancer
SAGITTARIUS	Sagittarius	Aries	Leo
CAPRICORN	Capricorn	Taurus	Virgo
AQUARIUS	Aquarius	Gemini	Libra
PISCES	Pisces	Cancer	Scorpio

MIND, BODY, AND SPIRIT

The decanates can also be interpreted from an esoteric point of view wherein they relate to *Mind, Body,* and *Spirit.*
Degrees zero to nine are physical and relate to the *Body.* Those with many planets placed at physical degrees in their birthchart are generally practical, materialistic, and sensible with a strong sense of self and their own earthly requirements. Degrees "0" and "9" are the most powerful: "0" indicates new beginnings and "9" represents endings and powerful physical sensations.
Degrees ten to 19 are mental and relate to the *Mind.* When most of the planets are placed in mental degrees, the subject is usually highly intelligent with a need to communicate and is also able to concentrate upon mind activities. These people are the logical thinkers who are well-informed about the latest scientific and technological discoveries. Degrees "10" and "19" are the most powerful with "10" representing new pursuits and "19" the peak in mental activity.
Degrees 20 to 29 are the spiritual degrees and relate to the *Spirit.* When many planets are placed in these degrees, the subject is spiritually creative and capable of great karmic development. These degrees are, however, difficult to handle and can cause problems such as addiction, escapism, and self-destruction. Degrees "20" and "29" are the most powerful, with "29" relating to the pinnacle of spiritual attunement. Many people with this degree potent within their chart are psychically gifted.

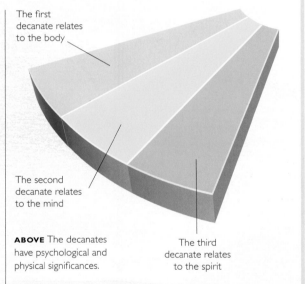

The first decanate relates to the body

The second decanate relates to the mind

The third decanate relates to the spirit

ABOVE The decanates have psychological and physical significances.

Degrees "0" and "29" are thought to be "critical." The extreme spiritual sensitivity of "29" can make it hard for the subject to adapt to earthly conditions, whereas a "0" is just beginning to adapt. People with planets at 29 degrees rarely lead mundane lives. Trauma often besets them, creating escapism in many forms and especially accidents or suicide; but those who use their gifts positively are able to reach iconic status within their chosen field.

PART SEVEN

PREDICTIVE ASTROLOGY

★ ★ ★ ★ ★

There are many forms of divination used in astrology — a few are very simple and others are quite complex. Some of the methods use the daily movements of the planets and their effect on the natal birthchart, on specific events, or on miscellaneous topics. Other methods require questions to be asked of the subject before referring to the planetary movement, while others involve further mathematical calculations. All that is needed is the date, place, and time of the birth, event, or question, and the relevant astronomical data as listed in the chapter on Chart Calculation on pages 82–83.

A solar chart is erected when the time of birth is unknown — or to create Sun-sign columns of the sort that appear in magazines and newspapers. The Sun-sign is placed on the left of the birthchart in the normal Ascendant position with the rest of the Zodiac following in a natural sequence around the circle in an anticlockwise direction. The chart is then treated as a birthchart with the natal positions entered for personal readings or the transiting planets written in when working out Sun-sign predictions.

ABOVE Before you can predict events in a person's life, you first need to ask a few questions to create an accurate birthchart.

CLASSIFICATIONS USED IN PREDICTIVE ASTROLOGY

* * * * * * * * * * * * * * * *

EVENT CHARTS

Event Charts are common in astrology and can be set up for almost any event – personal, political, or practical. They are especially relevant for special occasions such as weddings, moving house, new relationships, new jobs, or political elections.

It is important when erecting an event chart to note the time of the commencement

ABOVE You will need to draw up an event chart to predict how successful an important occasion, such as a wedding, will be.

of the occasion and treat it just like a person's birthtime. Planned events such as weddings have a definite start time but others – like house moves – have less easily definable moments of birth. Is it the point when legal paperwork reaches completion or is it when you physically walk through the door? In such situations you could erect a chart for both but the action of entering the premises is likely to be more decisive.

Pointers to look for when analyzing event charts are Fixed angles (fixed signs on the cusps of the first, fourth, seventh, and tenth houses) which denote permanence and reliability. Look, too, for nicely aspected planets,

which produce a benign effect, and planets falling in the same position as the subject's personal birthchart which show that the occasion is important to them. With weddings, the seventh house of relationships is the most relevant, whereas a house move requires study of the fourth house. Events relating to money can be revealed through the second house, and so on. In general, an easy chart with Fixed angles should produce a beneficial effect and a difficult chart with Mutable angles could lead to problems.

SOLAR AND LUNAR RETURNS

This is a fairly new method of astrological prediction. A solar return (Sun-sign) represents a yearly forecast and a lunar return (Moon-sign) yields a monthly forecast. For any given year erect a new chart using the date and time when the Sun or Moon have returned to the exact position (degrees and minutes) that they occupied at birth and the latitude and longitude of the subject's current residence. It is vital that the degrees and minutes of the planetary position are used in order to make the reading credible. Interpretation is based on the usual planetary positions, aspects, and configurations, just as if you were reading from a birthchart, but it is valid only for a year or a month. For instance, if a solar return showed three or more planets in one house, the relevant area of life would be emphasized throughout that year. If the chart has difficult aspects, the subject might expect a challenging year with regard to the areas and signs represented by the planets concerned. An assertive approach to the year can be expected when most of the planets appear in positive signs but when the planets are in negative signs, then the trend may be more subjective.

PLACE CHARTS

A chart can be set up for any city, town, or country in the world but the main problem lies in trying to assess just when the actual place was inaugurated, named, or "born." Strictly speaking, this is not predictive astrology but you can use it to define the direction of developments within countries and how they will be perceived by other countries. Challenges looming on the horizon can be predicted by an astrologer once the current planetary movement is inserted into these charts. Most countries and major cities have already been allocated a date and time of "birth" and a chart erected for them, from which their birth sign or grouping can be identified. This can also give an indication of the future outlook – for instance, a country ruled by Aries will move faster and be more assertive in its attitudes than a country ruled by Taurus. Fire-sign countries will be more active in the world than most Water- or Earth-sign countries, and Water-sign countries may be renowned for their "water" content whereas Air-sign countries or towns may be "windy" places.

ZODIACAL RULERSHIPS FOR CITIES AND COUNTRIES

ARIES: Birmingham, Marseilles, Naples. England, Germany, Japan

TAURUS: Palermo, Rhodes, St. Louis. Cyprus, Greece, Ireland

GEMINI: London, Melbourne, San Francisco. Corsica, Egypt, United States

CANCER: Berne, Cadiz, Istanbul. Holland, Mauritius, Paraguay

LEO: Blackpool, Chicago, Los Angeles. France, Italy, Romania

VIRGO: Boston, Jerusalem, Paris. Brazil, Crete, Switzerland

LIBRA: Copenhagen, Frankfurt, Lisbon, Burma (Myanmar)

SCORPIO: Dover, New Orleans, Washington. Canada, Norway

SAGITTARIUS: Cologne, Oregon, Toronto. Australia, Hungary, Spain

CAPRICORN: Orkney Islands, Port Said. Afghanistan, Albania, Bulgaria

AQUARIUS: Bremen, Brighton, Hamburg. Lithuania, Russia

PISCES: Alexandria, Seville, Venice. India, Philippines

BELOW The city of Chicago is ruled by the Fire sign Leo.

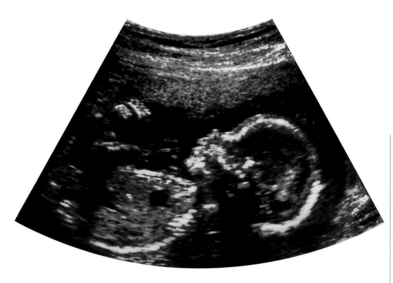

ABOVE The Prenatal Epoch system was used in the 20th century to predict the sex of an unborn baby.

THE PRENATAL EPOCH

The system of using the time of conception to predict the sex of an unborn baby was pioneered by E. H. Bailey, President of the British Astrological Society, during the early part of the 20th century but is rarely used today. The main disadvantage is the extreme difficulty in pinpointing the moment of conception, as well as the need to be completely accurate with the time of birth. The system seems to work remarkably well when these factors are known.

HORARY ASTROLOGY

The word horary means "relating to hours." Horary astrology is an ancient branch of predictive astrology centered around the notion of time and is specifically concerned with questions and answers. Almost any question can be answered using the horary system of prediction. The position of the planets at the precise moment a question takes shape, either in the mind or expressed verbally, will usually give the correct answer, though this depends, of course, on the skill of the interpreter. Horary astrology is a complex study in its own right and can take years to perfect but the general formula is quite simple. Immediately a question is asked, you should note down the time and the question itself and erect a chart using the latitude and longitude of the area in which the questioner is located at the time, thus producing the "birth" of a question. Erect the chart in exactly the same way as a birthchart but remember that there are many rules and conditions which must be adhered to. The most basic principles are covered in the box (see top right).

BELOW Conception Chart: the conception occurred around midday in London on November 9, 1998. Because the Ascendant and the Moon were both in feminine signs at this time, it is highly likely that the baby would be a girl.

BASIC PRINCIPLES OF THE PRENATAL EPOCH

The position of the Moon at conception depicts the Ascendant, Descendant, or Moon position at birth, depending on whether the Moon is increasing or decreasing in light – and also the sex of the baby at birth. When placed in a masculine sign (Aries, Gemini, Leo, Libra, Sagittarius, or Aquarius), the baby will be a boy, but when placed in a feminine sign (Taurus, Cancer, Virgo, Scorpio, Capricorn, or Pisces), the baby will be a girl.

What sex is my baby?

HORARY QUESTIONS

The querent (questioner) and their significator (you) are represented by the Ascendant and its ruler. The person or subject under scrutiny is represented by the relevant house: for example, a marital or business partner would be depicted by the seventh house and its ruler, but a friend or group would be the 11th house and ruler. If the question concerns career, the tenth house and its ruler would be the significators, whereas questions concerning children or creative outlets would relate to the fifth house and ruler. When the two rulers relating to the querent and the subject matter do not aspect one another, the position of the Moon becomes an important significator. Various degrees such as zero, 15, and 29 are critical.

RIGHT Questions about careers, for instance the outcome of a job interview, can be answered through reference to the tenth house and its ruler.

WEATHER PREDICTIONS

You can predict general weather patterns throughout the world at any specific time merely by observing the movements of the four outermost planets, Saturn, Uranus, Neptune, and Pluto. If these planets are grouped together in one sign or element, the weather will be extreme – hotter than usual in Fire signs, wetter than average in Water signs, unexpected high winds or hurricanes in Air signs, and the possibility of earthquakes or landslides in Earth signs. Through the 1990s Saturn was in Aries (Cardinal Fire), Uranus was in Aquarius (Fixed Air), Neptune was in Aquarius (Fixed Air), and Pluto was in Sagittarius (Mutable Fire), all of which are active signs. The emphasis on Air and Fire suggests that soaring temper-

atures, hurricanes, and strong winds have dominated the world's weather for a while. Saturn in Aries means long-raging fires, while Pluto in Sagittarius indicates fires caused by explosions or volcanic eruptions. Uranus and Neptune will both occupy Aquarius until well into the 21st century and indicate sustained devastation (Uranus) and disintegration (Neptune) caused by sudden, unexpected hurricanes. Floods (Neptune) could also occur as a side effect of the winds.

BELOW The position of the outer planets dictates that the current pattern of extreme weather conditions is set to continue.

PROGRESSIONS

* * * * * * * * * * * * * * * *

THE CALCULATION

This is a method of prediction which progresses the personal planets – Sun, Moon, Mercury, Venus, and Mars – one day for each year in the ephemeris. Popular during the early part of the 20th century before the outer planets Uranus, Neptune, and Pluto came into vogue, the system is used less often these days – astrologers prefer transits and solar-lunar returns which tend to produce more dramatic results. Progressed planets remain in the same sign and house for a long time, thus moderating small shifts in energy and producing subtle, psychological influences. When they do move, however, major changes in lifestyle and character can occur.

The most useful planet in progressions is the Moon which takes only two and a half years to travel through one house or sign, creating a 28-year cycle to complete the 360 degrees of the Zodiacal birthchart. The Sun's normal 30-day cycle is lengthened to 30 years when progressed, while Mercury, Venus, and Mars are variable according to their speed of orbit and whether or not they move retrograde. (See chart construction, pages 84 and 85.)

CALCULATING PROGRESSIONS

There is an easy formula for calculating progressions. You will need an ephemeris for the year of birth.
Open the ephemeris. Count down from your subject's date of birth the number of days equal to the number of years of their age. This gives you a new date with new planetary positions. Applying the subject's GMT time at birth, calculate the exact positions of the progressed Sun to Mars from this new date in the same manner as the natal chart (see the sections on chart calculation and erection on pages 82 to 85). Bear in mind that the ephemeris positions are for those at noon (or midnight) and may need slight adjustment to the time of birth. Enter the new planetary positions into the birthchart to interpret the effect of their movements.

INTERPRETATION

When a progressed planet moves into a new sign or house, its influence on the character and lifestyle can be quite potent, though rarely dramatic. Any of the planets moving from a positive sign into a negative sign (especially Sun and Mars) will slowly instill into the subject a need for more subjective or introspective thought and action, particularly when relating to the area (house) of life in which the planet is moving. A typical extrovert might become much quieter and more thoughtful. Likewise, a change from negative to positive can force a normally introverted, quiet person to become more assertive and positive.

When progressed Sun, Mercury, Venus, or Mars enter an unoccupied sign or house, characteristics of the sign and area of life represented by that house become important for the rest of that person's life. The Moon's effect is more transient (two and a half years in any sign or house) but important when examining emotional cycles – the Moon entering passive Water and Earth signs represents a two-and-a-half-year cycle of sensitive emotions and deep feelings (Water) or materialistic, practical needs (Earth). On the other hand, if it enters positive Air and Fire signs, the emotions will become more objective and rationalized (Air) or impulsive and outgoing (Fire).

If Mercury, Venus, or Mars turn retrograde, they remain in one sign or house longer than usual – Mars, especially, can occupy a sign for up to six months. When this happens, the planets may not progress beyond their natural birth positions during the lifetime of the subject. When they do move on, however, the subject will find that their usual expression of qualities such as communication (Mercury), love, appreciation, and materialistic values (Venus), and assertiveness and physical stamina (Mars) may alter quite considerably. The change is always slow and rarely drastic but is usually noticed by other people. Planets in retrograde motion during years of progression are usually inhibited in some way, but the year they turn direct (noted by a capital "D" beside the planetary degrees in the ephemeris), then restrictions must be removed and their natural energy allowed to flow freely.

Most of us have an average life expectancy of about 75 years and in that time the Moon will progress completely around our birthchart – completing one cycle at the age of 28, the second at 56, and a third at 84 – if we are fortunate. These ages also coincide with important Saturn, Uranus, and Neptune movements and should therefore always be considered as vital turning points within a lifetime.

Progressions are responsible for many of the profound adjustments which take place infrequently during our lifetimes and, where possible, should always be considered when analyzing the future potential of a birthchart.

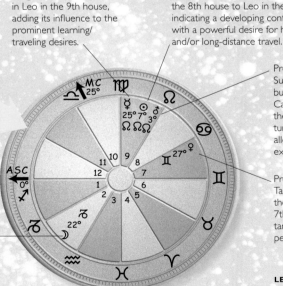

Progressed Mercury is still in Leo in the 9th house, adding its influence to the prominent learning/traveling desires.

Progressed Sun has moved from Cancer in the 8th house to Leo in the 9th house indicating a developing confidence and ego with a powerful desire for higher learning and/or long-distance travel.

Progressed Mars is still conjuncting the Sun (physical strength and self-assertion) but has moved from the sensitive sign of Cancer and the secretive 8th house to the open sign of Leo and the adventurous expansive 9th house, thereby allowing the subject to exhibit more extrovert characteristics.

Progressed Venus has moved from Taurus to Gemini and is nearing the end of its journey through the 7th house, which refers to important changes in love matters and permanent relationships.

ABOVE Chart details for subject born on July 2, 1985, 6:00pm GMT, London.

Progressed Moon has completed its 28-year cycle through the signs and has returned to its birth position in the sign of Capricorn in the 2nd house indicating an important learning time regarding money and possessions.

LEFT Chart showing the progressed positions of the Sun to Mars for the subject at the age of 28.

TRANSITS

★ ★ ★ ★ ★ ★ ★ ★ ★ ★ ★ ★ ★ ★ ★

THE EASIEST and most popular method of astrological prediction is the one that uses the continuous orbits, transits, of the planets. The positions of the planets for any given day can be checked in an ephemeris or planetary movement guide. Transits are used for almost all types of astrological chart, including the Sun-sign horoscopes that appear in magazines and newspapers. They are much more dynamic in effect than progressed planets, but not everyone responds to transiting planetary energies in the same way. Some people are hardly aware of their motion while others are immediately sensitive to movement or change.

RIGHT AND BELOW Some people are hardly aware of transits while others sense change immediately.

The five personal planets (Sun, Moon, Mercury, Venus, and Mars) are used all the time for daily or weekly predictions of an everyday or mundane nature but the five outermost planets (Jupiter, Saturn, Uranus, Neptune, and Pluto) are more important for major events and monthly or yearly analysis. Place transiting planets on your chart wheel close to the center or draw them in a different color in order not to confuse them with the permanent planetary positions.

Transits are analyzed in much the same way as natal planetary positions. The planets are most potent when changing sign or house or when forming major aspects to planets in the birthchart. Aspects from outer planets must be exact (one degree orb) for accurate interpretation. Take note of any planet returning to the position it occupied at birth as this always indicates an important or eventful time. Remember that Jupiter returns every 12 years, Saturn takes 28 years, and Uranus 84 years. Because of their slow movements, Neptune and Pluto cannot return to their natal position but they do sometimes reach focal points, as when forming sextiles, trines, squares, and oppositions to those natal positions.

When planets go retrograde, they sometimes retreat into the previous sign or house, or form recurring aspects during the course of a year – sometimes longer if Neptune or Pluto are involved. The first formation of the aspect usually bears the most impact, but occasionally the final confrontation is the strongest. Conjunctions are far more powerful in transit than the other major aspects, while the three minor aspects (semi-sextile, sextile, and quincunx) often seem to have little effect.

The signs occupied by the transiting planets are less important but, in general, planets that are moving through positive signs help to cultivate action, communication, and assertiveness, while planets in negative signs tend to encourage subjectivity, imagination, and sensitivity.

The passage of the planets of the solar system as they orbit the sun is closely linked to astrological prediction; the inner band of planets is used to predict the day-to-day course of our lives, while the outer band tell us about significant events in our lives.

TRANSITS IN ACTION: Female born July 31, 1979

RIGHT Taking note of where planets are moving, or transiting, through a birth-chart on a particular day will further refine predictions.

PLUTO	℞	7 degrees Sagittarius in the 6th house
NEPTUNE	℞	2 degrees Aquarius in the 8th house
URANUS	℞	15 degrees Aquarius in the 9th house
SATURN		16 degrees Taurus in the 12th house
JUPITER		4 degrees Taurus in the 11th house
MARS		11 degrees Scorpio in the 5th-6th houses
VENUS	℞	5 degrees Virgo in the 3rd house
MERCURY	℞	0 degrees Leo in the 2nd house
SUN		7 degrees Leo in the 2nd house
MOON		6-20 degrees Pisces in the 9th-10th houses

Here, five of the planets are transiting through unoccupied houses in the upper portion of the chart which indicates a period of major expansion and communication with objective, worldly concerns. The subject is usually introspective and can sometimes be shy (nine planets in the lower half of the birthchart) but the transits are giving her the freedom to explore new areas of life and become more assertive.

Transiting Pluto in the sixth house of work and health is trining her natal Sun in the second house, depicting a time of good working relationships, improved monetary concerns, and transformations in health matters. Transiting Neptune in the empty eighth house gives scope for imagination, sexual exploration, psychic matters, and deeply creative studies, but it might also indicate disillusion within relationships and financial concerns and thoughts of escapism. Uranus is moving through Aquarius, the sign it rules. Both are indicative of rebellion, sudden changes, and a need for excitement and change. In the ninth house this could relate to foreign travel or higher learning. Saturn traveling through the 12th in the stoical sign of Taurus could indicate secret burdens or responsibilities, possibly concerning older people. It is in opposition to natal Uranus in the sixth house, and may therefore cause depression, anxiety, or ill-health in work matters. Transiting Jupiter in the 11th is excellent for expansion, popularity, friendships, and group activities.

Mars is about to move from the fifth to the sixth house, changing the emphasis of physical energy from social and romantic concerns (fifth) to work and health matters (sixth). Venus is moving slowly in retrograde motion in the third house, creating harmonious short-distance travel and communication, especially with family.

The birthday itself should be a relatively good one, with Mercury (communication) conjuncting Venus in the second — good for money and presents — and the Sun returning to its natal position. The Moon moves from six to 20 degrees of Pisces throughout the day, changing from the ninth to the tenth house in the process and indicating emotional fulfillment in the evening.

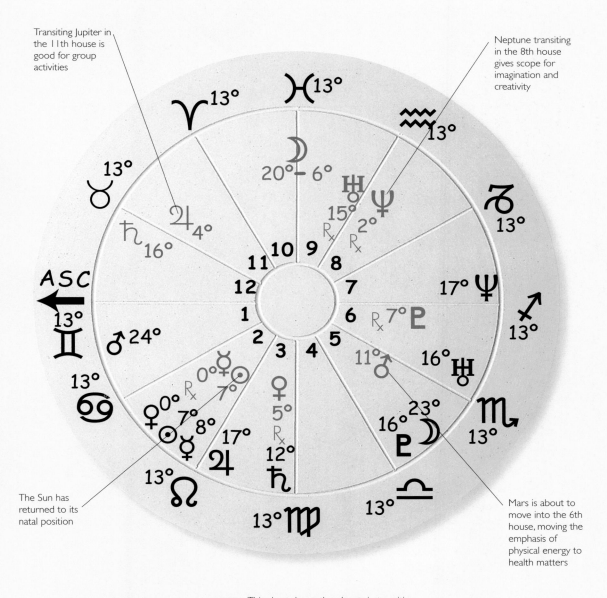

Transiting Jupiter in the 11th house is good for group activities

Neptune transiting in the 8th house gives scope for imagination and creativity

The Sun has returned to its natal position

Mars is about to move into the 6th house, moving the emphasis of physical energy to health matters

ABOVE This chart shows the planets in transition (colored red) on the subject's 20th birthday, July 31, 1999.

PART EIGHT

SYNASTRY

★ ★ ★ ★ ★

The compatible or incompatible energy vibrations between the planets contained in our birthcharts reflect the chemistry within human relationships and most of the mysteries generated by them can be answered through the study of synastry — the art of comparing the birthcharts of two people.

Once you know the origin of a certain situation, it is usually easier to understand or amend it. Synastry tells us whether a relationship is worth working at and how to make the best of a difficult situation by concentrating on the harmonious resonances between two or more birthcharts. It is rare for two people to like one another or be drawn together romantically when difficult energy vibrations predominate, but situations — usually karmic in origin — often place us with people with whom we are totally incompatible. We have all experienced poor relationships between teacher and pupil, boss and employee, doctor and patient. This is when synastry can usually be of great help by telling us if the relationship is based on active karma* and whether or not to proceed with it.

BELOW Whether our relationships on a personal and everyday level are positive or negative can be explained by Synastry.

* Active karma is the energy of cause and effect brought forward from our previous lives that is being objectified and enacted, positively or negatively, within the present lifetime.

SYNASTRY IN ACTION: STAGE 1

★ ★ ★ ★ ★ ★ ★ ★ ★ ★ ★ ★ ★ ★ ★ ★

THE FOUR MAJOR stages of synastric interpretation are like climbing a ladder – the more
rungs you climb, the higher your investiga-
tion. The first step introduces us to basic
Sun-sign compatibility, the second deals with
House Comparison, the third with Aspect
Comparison, and the final rung takes a look
at Composite Charts. Stages two and three
can be listed on a Comparison Chart Form
like the example of the synastry analysis
between John and Jackie Kennedy on pages
151 and 152.

THE FOUR STAGES OF SYNASTRY

1 SUN-SIGN COMPARISON A basic look
at how the Sun-signs relate to each
other through the polarities, elements,
and quadruplicities.

2 HOUSE COMPARISON The placing of one
person's natal chart positions into another
person's chart to locate those areas of life
where the first person has most influence
over the second.

3 ASPECT COMPARISON The comparing of
aspects between one person's natal chart
planetary positions and another's to see
whether their energies blend with each
other or are antagonistic.

4 COMPOSITE CHARTS The process of
taking the midpoint degree position
between like planets (Sun–Sun,
Moon–Moon, etc.) from two people's
birthcharts to create one complete chart
which shows how they will relate to each
other as a combined entity.

BELOW A Taurus
has conflicting
needs to an
Aquarius and such
a coupling may not
be successful.

RIGHT An
Aquarius–Sagittarius
coupling is likely to be
happy and long-lasting.

SUN SIGN INTERACTION – COMPATIBILITY

SIGN		COMPATIBLE	INCOMPATIBLE	VARIABLE
ARIES		Leo, Sagittarius, Gemini, Aquarius	Taurus, Cancer, Virgo, Scorpio, Capricorn, Pisces	Aries, Libra
TAURUS		Virgo, Capricorn, Cancer, Pisces	Gemini, Leo, Libra, Sagittarius, Aquarius, Aries	Taurus, Scorpio
GEMINI		Libra, Aquarius, Leo, Aries	Cancer, Virgo, Scorpio, Capricorn Pisces, Taurus	Gemini, Sagittarius
CANCER		Scorpio, Pisces, Virgo, Taurus	Leo, Sagittarius, Libra, Aquarius, Aries, Gemini	Cancer, Capricorn
LEO		Sagittarius, Aries, Gemini, Libra	Virgo, Scorpio, Capricorn, Pisces, Taurus, Cancer	Leo, Aquarius
VIRGO		Capricorn, Taurus, Scorpio, Cancer	Libra, Sagittarius, Aquarius, Aries, Gemini, Leo	Virgo, Pisces
LIBRA		Aquarius, Gemini, Leo, Sagittarius	Scorpio, Capricorn, Pisces, Taurus, Cancer, Virgo	Libra, Aries
SCORPIO		Pisces, Cancer, Virgo, Capricorn	Sagittarius, Aries, Aquarius, Gemini, Leo, Libra	Scorpio, Taurus
SAGITTARIUS		Aries, Leo, Libra, Aquarius	Capricorn, Pisces, Taurus, Cancer, Virgo, Scorpio	Sagittarius, Gemini
CAPRICORN		Taurus, Virgo, Scorpio, Pisces	Aquarius, Aries, Gemini, Libra, Leo, Sagittarius	Capricorn, Cancer
AQUARIUS		Gemini, Libra, Aries, Sagittarius	Pisces, Taurus, Cancer, Virgo, Scorpio, Capricorn	Aquarius, Leo
PISCES		Cancer, Scorpio, Taurus, Capricorn	Aries, Gemini, Leo, Sagittarius, Libra, Aquarius	Pisces, Virgo

SYNASTRY IN ACTION: STAGE 2

★ ★ ★ ★ ★ ★ ★ ★ ★ ★ ★ ★ ★ ★ ★ ★

HOUSE COMPARISON

House Comparison is the second stage of synastry. This assesses the level of vibrations of the "visiting" or other person's planets in the areas of life (houses) in which they are placed. In order to progress beyond Sun-sign compatibility into House Comparison, two accurate birthcharts must be available. I have here used the charts of President John F. Kennedy and his wife Jackie where partner's planetary placements are illustrated nearest to the center of the chart in red. The houses in which the other person's planets fall indicate the areas which are most important within the basic structure of the relationship. Houses that are unoccupied by the partner's planets will not be focal points of the relationship even though

they may remain highly significant for either subject on an individual level. Note here that Jackie's Saturn, Uranus, and Moon, in the second, fifth, and sixth houses, are not "visited" by John's planets in this House Comparison. However, an unoccupied house in an individual's birthchart which is "visited" by the partner's planets immediately becomes stimulated. In John and Jackie's House Comparison most of the "visiting" planets fall in already occupied houses, but John's Uranus does fall in Jackie's unoccupied fourth house of home, while Jackie's Uranus falls in John's empty house of work and health, thus activating these otherwise less important areas.

There are 20 listed house placements to record as you will note from the comparison

BELOW President Kennedy's absorption in his work was self-motivated.

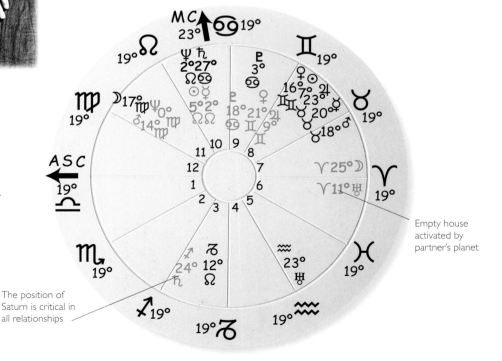

RIGHT Chart of President John F. Kennedy, born 3:00 p.m. EST, May 29, 1917, Brookline, Mass., USA. His partner's planetary placements are illustrated in red.

The position of Saturn is critical in all relationships

Empty house activated by partner's planet

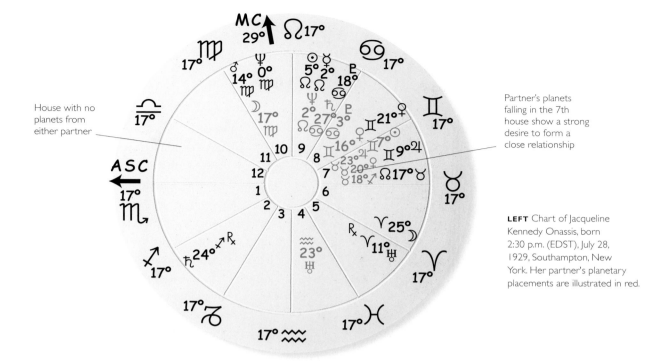

House with no planets from either partner

Partner's planets falling in the 7th house show a strong desire to form a close relationship

LEFT Chart of Jacqueline Kennedy Onassis, born 2:30 p.m. (EDST), July 28, 1929, Southampton, New York. Her partner's planetary placements are illustrated in red.

chart form on pages 148 and 149, ten planets in two charts, which are divided into Angular, Fixed, and Mutable house connections. Marital or sexual relationships should reveal an emphasis on Angular and Fixed connections whereas casual and working relationships fare best mainly with Mutable placements. A lack of connections between any houses should also be recorded. In John and Jackie's chart comparison the first, second, fifth and 12th houses are unoccupied by partner's planets. It is rare in a successful lasting relationship for more than four houses, as in their case, to lack connections as this indicates that the couple are operating individually and may have little in common.

The strongest are Angular house connections as these signify immediate impact and couples who claim to have fallen in love at first sight should exhibit a strong preponderance of them. Fixed house connections are vital, too, because they relate to monetary and sexual relationships. A comparison showing a high level of Fixed house associations is slow to ignite but usually stands the test of time. Ideally, a successful enduring relationship should consist of an equal proportion of Angular and Fixed connections with a smattering of Mutable links. A comparison with powerful Mutable connections rarely relates to romantic attachments unless the relationship is based on communication requirements. Strong Mutable contacts are vital, however, in casual relationships such as those between teacher and pupil.

LEFT Jackie, seen here with son John, left, and nephew Anthony, had strong family principles.

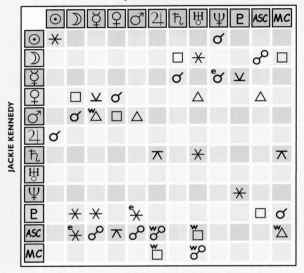

KENNEDY HOUSE COMPARISON

JOHN KENNEDY

ABOVE This chart shows the aspects between John and Jackie Kennedy's planets in their birthcharts.

HOUSE POSITIONS

His ☉ is placed in her 7th hse.
Her ☉ is placed in his 10th hse.
His ☽ is placed in her 11th hse.
Her ☽ is placed in his 7th hse.
His ☿ is placed in her 7th hse.
Her ☿ is placed in his 10th hse.
His ♀ is placed in her 8th hse.
Her ♀ is placed in his 9th hse.
His ♂ is placed in her 7th hse.
Her ♂ is placed in his 11th hse.
His ♃ is placed in her 7th hse.
Her ♃ is placed in his 8th hse.
His ♄ is placed in her 9th hse.
Her ♄ is placed in his 3rd hse.
His ♅ is placed in her 4th hse.
Her ♅ is placed in his 6th hse.
His ♆ is placed in her 9th hse.
Her ♆ is placed in his 11th hse.
His ♇ is placed in her 8th hse.
Her ♇ is placed in his 9th/10th hse.

TOTAL NUMBER OF ASPECTS: 37

Beneficial – 17
Detrimental – 20
Generational – 0

DOUBLE ASPECTS

☽ - ASC = ☍ ✳ = *variable*
♀ - ♇ = ⊼ ✳ = *good*
♀ - ASC = △ ⊼ = *variable*

NODAL CONTACTS

His NN 12 degrees – 18
Her NN 17 degrees – ☌
His ☽ 17 degrees ♍
△ her NN 17 degrees ☌

OTHER COMMENTS

No 1st, 2nd, 5th, or 12th house connections

HOUSE POSITIONS

Angular – 9
Fixed – 6
Mutable – 5

DEGREE OF ORB

☌ □ ☍ △ = 6 degrees
✳ = 3 degrees
⊼ ⊼ = 1 degree

HOUSE COMPARISON

ANGULAR HOUSE CONNECTIONS
1st, 4th, 7th, and 10th

Angular links are common in comparison charts but are particularly important in romantic and family associations. Planets falling in the other person's first house affect their personality – for better or for worse – while planets in their fourth house probe deep into the heart and emotions of the subject. Planets falling in their seventh house are very important as they indicate a powerful urge to form a close relationship with the subject. The tenth house (and MC) are also important in relationships and are often stronger in House Comparisons than the seventh house. More than 50 percent of people form permanent relationships with someone whose Sun or Ascendant is the sign on the cusp of their seventh or tenth house (or the MC).

The most important planets in House Comparison are the Sun, Moon, Venus, Mars, and Saturn. Sun falling in the possible partner's Angular house urges the subject to identify with the Sun individual on a deeply personal level. In the first house the ego of the Sun and the personality of the first house blend well and the couple project a united image. In the fourth house, the subject feels the heat of the Sun on an intense, emotional level and they enjoy setting up home together. Sun falling in another's seventh heralds a strong relationship as the couple enjoy being together. Sun occupying partner's tenth is excellent for the prestige of the tenth house person who is spurred on by the Sun to aim for better things in life.

Moon falling in an Angular house of the other person is also a potent influence. In the first house it may cause the subject to project a protective or tearful image toward the partner. In the fourth the couple are remarkably attuned to the domestic needs of each other. The seventh is generally beneficial, especially when the Moon of one falls in the seventh of the other, but both partners may be emotionally dependent on one another. Moon in the partner's tenth can bring success or recognition to the tenth house but the Moon person may be overprotective about their partner's ambitions.

Venus placed in the other person's Angular house nearly always forms loving, harmonious links. In the first house Venus projects a pacifying effect on the subject, and the couple resonate well together. In the fourth house the subject "loves" setting up home with Venus. The seventh produces powerful love feelings between the two individuals, while Venus in the partner's tenth appreciates and encourages the subject's aims and ambitions.

Mars falling in the other person's Angular house provides energy, excitement, and sexual attraction, or anger and resentment in the subject. In the first house, the subject's personality may become more assertive or aggressive with the need to show overt sexuality or dominance. Mars in the partner's fourth house can cause arguments or tension within the home, while Mars in the partner's seventh creates great sexual attraction but also antagonism as to who should be dominant. Mars in the tenth house pushes the subject in their aims – sometimes too far.

The position of Saturn is critical in all relationships. Its energy is slow and insidious and happy couples in the first throes of love may be unaware of its presence. Saturn takes its toll as relationships progress but because it also signifies stability and endurance, most lasting relationships feature Saturn strongly in their House Comparisons. Angular placements create most obstacles in relationships. Placed in the partner's first house, Saturn inhibits the subject's personality. Such repression is accepted for a while but eventually the strain tells and the couple become frustrated with one another. In the fourth house Saturn allows no leeway in domestic affairs, often causing the house subject to be unhappy within the home environment. Saturn falling in the partner's seventh is good for stable, enduring relationships but does not augur well for overall happiness. In the tenth Saturn can be both restrictive and encouraging. Saturn wants the tenth house person to succeed and will do anything to help without really comprehending the underlying issues.

Mercury, Jupiter, and the outer planets can all be important when placed in the partner's Angular houses. Mercury brings communication and freedom of speech within the respective area. Jupiter expands the partner's expectancies, often bringing good fortune, especially when falling in the seventh. Uranus heralds changes, excitement, and surprises – not all beneficial, while Neptune may encourage chaos, escapist tendencies, idealism, or spiritual awareness. Pluto's movement is too slow to be of great influence in House Comparison.

HOUSE COMPARISON

FIXED HOUSE CONNECTIONS:
2nd, 5th, 8th, and 11th

Fixed house connections relate to endurance, stability, money, and sexual proclivities, and are often more important for the continuing success of relationships than the Angular houses. They are also vital if partnerships are to become permanent. Although planets falling in Angular houses are responsible for the initial feeling of falling in love and its glorious sensations, planets falling in Fixed houses provide a powerful, consuming blend of material, emotional, creative, sexual, and friendship aspects as they deal realistically with the central core of a relationship. To begin with, a strong Fixed house comparison may seem dull and uninspiring but this situation is a metaphor for Aesop's fable of the hare and the tortoise – where the hare represents Angular house connections and the tortoise Fixed. And the tortoise always wins. A relationship which requires durability will fall by the wayside without the presence of Fixed house connections. Planets falling equally in Angular and Fixed houses generate the best opportunities for fulfillment within relationships.

Fixed houses are associated with the various degrees of sexuality. The second house relates to basic animal instincts, earthy sensuality, and lust. Fifth house sexuality is more refined – romance and affection combine with sexual desire to broaden the relationship potential. Eighth house sex is deep and meaningful within well-estab-

lished, loving relationships, but when strong eighth house connections occur without substantial Angular house links, relationships can become sexually obsessive or deviant. The 11th house progresses beyond physical sex into the spiritual realms of unconditional, platonic love. The fifth and eighth houses also relate to procreation – the eighth rules conception, pregnancy, and birth and the fifth governs offspring and aspirations within the family unit. The second and eighth also refer to the financial side of the relationship, the second dealing with money or possessions gained, while the eighth refers to the partner's financial status.

All the planets except Saturn heighten the sexual and materialistic inclinations of the relationship. Saturn may incite desire but

ABOVE Fixed house connections strengthen the core of a relationship and are vital if it is to stand the test of time.

RIGHT 5th house connections between two charts can result in sexually romantic liasions.

unless patience and understanding are observed, its energy will also encourage limitation and frustration. Sun, Moon, Venus, Mars, and Jupiter all work in a highly productive, or overproductive, manner when occupying the partner's Fixed houses. Though less powerful, Mercury's effect is useful as a communicative outlet on sexual, procreative, and financial matters. The outer planets can be highly influential especially when they form major aspects to the subject's personal planets.

Any planet falling in the partner's second house in the relationship creates desire for monetary gains, acquisition of possessions, release of basic sexual urges, and possible re-evaluation of outworn principles and attitudes. Saturn will inhibit responses but other planets will expand influences according to their own energy streams.

Planets falling in the partner's fifth house provoke romantic, pleasurable, or procreative feelings. Saturn's heavy, serious energy will tend to delay, frustrate, and irritate but the

underlying encouragement of fifth house matters will remain.

One of the main purposes of the eighth house is to perpetuate and magnify the attributes of the seventh. The seventh-house is "falling in love" and the eighth-house is "staying in love." Relationships which contain strong seventh- and eighth-house connections, such as John and Jackie Kennedy's, have a good chance of survival. Eighth-house connections provide the intense emotional and sexual feelings required to keep the relationship going. The eighth house is also very much concerned with receiving – sex, emotion, money. In House Comparison, both partners give and receive but the eighth house individual is the true "receiver." Planets falling here also encourage procreative and psychic matters.

When the other person's planets fall in the 11th house, the relationship is usually enduring but tends to be more spiritual in nature. The couple are well attuned without necessarily forming a sexual attachment. Much depends on where the rest of the planets fall as to whether or not a physical relationship occurs. Sun, Venus, Jupiter, Saturn, and Pluto will create a close, lasting bond whereas Moon, Mercury, Mars, Uranus, and Neptune indicate a more stimulating or unique connection. Sun, Venus, and Jupiter are good for both parties and the most likely to provide unconditional love.

LEFT The relationship of couples with strong 7th and 8th house connections such as can be seen in the Kennedys' charts have a good chance of lasting.

LEFT When there are 5th house connections, the couple will enjoy playing and romanticizing.

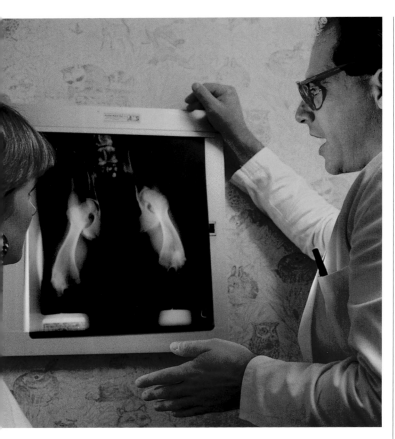

HOUSE COMPARISON

MUTABLE HOUSE CONNECTIONS
3rd, 6th, 9th, and 12th

Mutable houses govern communication of all kinds – in work and health, with animals, in travel, in religions, and within institutions. Mutable connections in House Comparisons are likely to feature mainly in casual, intermittent relationships such as those between doctor and patient, teacher and pupil, boss and employee, owner and pet, but they also play a lesser role in marital and other permanent partnerships. Many relationships survive best when adaptability, variety, imagination, and communication are injected regularly into them. If too many Mutable connections overshadow the Angular and Fixed within romantic attachments, the relationship will only be successful if communication and variety are more important than love, emotion, and sexuality. A relationship between two highly Mutable people (lots of planets in Gemini, Virgo, Sagittarius, and Pisces) will occasionally last purely because of the strongly restless and adaptable natures of both partners.

Mutable connections usually propel the house individual into movement or communication at some level. Third-house links stimulate short-distance travel, educational matters, communication, and interaction with relatives. Saturn may delay, limit, or frustrate third-house activity and is generally unhelpful when falling in another's third. Jackie Kennedy's Saturn falls in John's third suggesting that he might have felt restricted in his movement and ability to communicate when Jackie was around. Mercury falling in the third helps the house individual to communicate well, especially if there are no natal house placements. Sun, Venus, and Jupiter are also beneficial – Venus (and, to a degree, Neptune) may highlight communications related to love such as love-letters, while Moon, Mars, Uranus, Neptune, and Pluto tend to be exciting or different in their influence but may also cause restlessness or dangerous elements during daily movement.

Sixth-house connections are important in work and health relationships although Saturn's heavy energy may cause the house individual to succumb to depression, anxiety, or weakened health. Saturn's influence in the work environment may also be difficult to handle. Saturn is, however, a great teacher, and its position in a House Comparison is the main area of life where the recipient has much to learn from the Saturn person. Great progress can be made when Saturn's words are heard. Jupiter, here, is highly beneficial for the subject's health and work. This is an excellent connection for a doctor and patient or a boss and employee. Sun and Venus are also good for casual relationships but Neptune may bring confusion or deception. Mars is always energizing and can give vital assertive qualities or aggressive attitudes in work or health relationships.

Planets falling in the ninth will encourage the house individual toward higher learning, philosophical or theosophical activity, or long-distance travel. Sun, Mercury, Venus, Mars, and Jupiter make interesting traveling companions but the emotional sensitivity of the Moon, the restriction of Saturn, the excitability and self-ishness of Uranus, the chaotic nebulosity of Neptune, and the intensity of Pluto – may be less welcome when traveling overseas.

Twelfth-house connections relate mainly to powerful karmic lessons or necessary adjustments and are therefore difficult to comprehend and manifest on a positive level. When the personal planets of one person fall in the 12th house of another, there are almost certainly karmic debts to be paid off and sacrifices to be made, usually by the 12th-house individual. Strong 12th- house connections are not common but neither are they rare. Those who are well on their way to discovering their true spiritual identity and physical worth will tend to have more 12th-house connections than those who are not yet ready to face up to such difficult connections. Twelfth-house relationships are draining but surprisingly enduring for a Mutable connection. The house individual finds it difficult to dispense with the planet person even when the relationship is over. In reality, 12th-house connections are rarely finalized because the karma involved is too strong. Mars, Saturn, Uranus, Neptune, and Pluto induce difficult, violent or traumatic relationships, whereas Sun, Moon, Mercury, Venus, and Jupiter tend to be beneficial and, with the exception of Mercury, usually relate to previous, karmic, love relationships that have gone askew. Twelfth-house relationships are often carried out in secret.

BELOW The physician's Jupiter in the patient's 6th house can result in a beneficial rapport between them.

SYNASTRY IN ACTION: STAGE 3

★ ★ ★ ★ ★ ★ ★ ★ ★ ★ ★ ★ ★ ★ ★ ★

RIGHT The synastry between the Kennedys enabled them to present a united front to the world.

ASPECT COMPARISON

While House Comparison supplies the basic outer structure of a relationship, it is Aspect Comparison that reveals the quality of the foundations. Are they deep and strong or are they shallow and weak? A powerful House Comparison will support an inadequate Aspect Comparison for quite a long time but, eventually, the fabric will collapse and destroy the outer shell in the process.

Strong Aspect Comparisons contain many connections; the most successful are when the beneficial aspects outweigh the detrimental connections. The Ascendant, Midheaven, Moon's Nodes, and all the planets are taken into account and the aspects are written onto the Comparison Sheet in the central grid as in the chart for the Kennedys. The degrees of orb for the aspects are slightly less than those allowed for natal charts – six degrees for a conjunction, square, trine, and opposition; three degrees for a sextile; and one degree for a semi-sextile or quincunx. Some astrologers will allow more, others less, but the closer the aspect,

the more potent the effect. Using these orbs, comparisons containing between 40 and 50 aspects are strong and more than 50 aspects indicates powerful, solid foundations. The number of aspects is important, but quality is often better than quantity and a comparison with 25 beneficial aspects may be more helpful than one with 40, mainly detrimental, connections.

Generational aspects are formed between the outer planets when two people of a similar age form a relationship. These are of little consequence within synastry but they should always be included in the comparison and taken into account in the total number of aspects. Too many generational aspects will boost the total and make the comparison appear stronger than it really is. Generational aspects do not occur in relationships with a significant age gap (around eight years or more.) In the Kennedy example, John and

BELOW Aspect comparison is the key to discovering the true basis of a relationship.

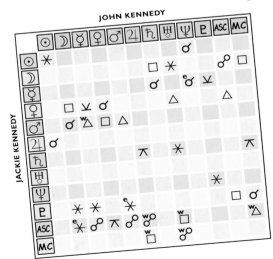

JACKIE KENNEDY

JOHN KENNEDY

Jackie do not possess any generational aspects because of their 12-year age difference. The House Comparison is much stronger in their overall synastry than the Aspect Comparison which is slightly below average in quantity and quality: 37 aspects with 20 detrimental. This type of combination is typical of many relationships which manage to endure because of the strength of the House Comparison. A strong Aspect Comparison with a weak House Comparison is a much rarer combination, because it is more difficult for a couple to get to know one another and reveal the aspect connections when the House Comparison bears little initial impact.

The most important aspects in synastry are those involving Sun, Moon, Venus, Mars, and Saturn, but aspects to the remaining planets can be relevant in certain relationships. As with natal charts, conjunctions are the most powerful aspects and may be variable in effect, depending on planets involved.

ASPECTS TO THE ASCENDANT AND MIDHEAVEN

These aspects should be reviewed in the same way as planetary connections. When the Ascendant is highly aspected, the personality and appearance are affected for better or for worse, and when the Midheaven is highly contacted, the aspirations and fulfillment area (denoted by the house position) are strengthened or weakened according to the planetary contacts.

THE MOST ASPECTED PLANET

Some planets receive more aspects than others and the most aspected planet is usually indicative of the central core of the relationship. Sometimes the Ascendant or Midheaven will be the most heavily contacted, as with the Kennedys, where Jackie's Ascendant receives seven aspects from John's planets, suggesting her personality and appearance were greatly affected by John's influence. Pluto and Venus were Jackie's most aspected planets – showing that the marriage on her side was based on deep love. John's most aspected planet was Uranus, an indication that Jackie helped him reveal his individuality and talents but also inadvertently encouraged his self-centeredness and detachment.

DOUBLE ASPECTS

Any connection which is repeated, regardless of the aspects involved, is called a double aspect. Many double aspects in a comparison add depth and strength to a relationship. In John and Jackie Kennedy's comparison there are only three double aspects, which is quite a low figure. Two of these involve the Ascendant – Moon–Ascendant and Venus–Ascendant in variable combinations. Good combinations are those in which both aspects are benign; variable connections refer to one benign and one challenging aspect, while difficult combinations are those formed by two detrimental aspects.

LEFT Jackie may have unintentionally encouraged John's emotional detachment as his most aspected planet from her chart was Uranus.

ASPECTS TO THE SUN

A very important chemical reaction takes place when a person's Sun makes contact (forms an aspect) with someone else's planets. Because the Sun is the central core of our ego, individuality, and self-awareness, any major aspects from another person's planets can change our perspective of ourselves – either heightening or deflating the ego according to the planet(s) and aspect(s) formed. If the Sun is barely touched (unaspected or almost unaspected) by the other person's planets, especially when an important relationship is involved, the individuality of the person concerned will remain unaffected by the partnership.

SUN–SUN contacts are best when trine or sextile to one another. Opposite Suns attract and repel at the same time but Suns in square aspect may clash badly.

SUN–MOON conjunctions are traditionally the best indication of happiness in a relationship, especially when they involve the man's Sun and the woman's Moon. Any major aspect between these two planets will incline toward attraction but squares and oppositions will invariably attract antipathy and create a love-hate situation.

SUN–MERCURY connections relate mainly to ease of communication when benign, and tense communication when difficult. Beneficial contacts are always useful.

SUN–VENUS connections denote love of a very high caliber – sometimes unconditional or platonic. When combined with physical contacts such as Mars-Venus, the effect can be wondrous. Difficult aspects still produce love but the energies create tension and obstacles which are difficult to overcome.

SUN–MARS contacts are vibrant, physical, and assertive. Despite the immense physical attraction that can occur, these forceful energies relate better in nonsexual relationships between the same sex. On an intimate level, Mars may try to dominate the Sun, physically or sexually. Anger, irritation, aggression, or violence can erupt with difficult (square, quincunx, or opposition) connections.

SUN-JUPITER aspects are excellent for all kinds of associations. The planetary energies complement one another and bring good fortune, harmony, and optimism to a relationship. The positive effects are somewhat mitigated when forming difficult aspects and may attract aggressive attitudes and power struggles between the two people.

SUN–SATURN connections are extremely common in

BELOW Stressful Sun–Mars connections such as quincunx between two charts can create irritation and anger in a relationship.

synastry and all bear a degree of difficulty, but the challenging aspects between the completely opposing energies of Sun–Saturn (conjunction, square, quincunx, and opposition) are especially demanding. The Sun views Saturn as inhibited, overserious, and humorless, while Saturn regards the Sun as irresponsible and thoughtless. When other planetary connections such as Sun-Venus, Sun–Moon, or Venus–Mars occur, a Sun–Saturn couple will struggle to overcome the adversities but may never feel totally at ease with one another.

SUN–URANUS combinations are dynamic and exciting when beneficial but disruptive, callous and demanding when difficult. Contacts from Uranus may lead an otherwise easy-going Sun person into all sorts of rebellious situations but the Sun is inspired by Uranian uniqueness and the glare is just what Uranus needs to draw attention to itself. Together they form a formidable but highly assertive duo.

SUN–NEPTUNE is an appealing, etheric combination, but in reality these two planets are poles apart and do not relate well. They may project love or empathy toward one another in the early stages but, in time, Neptune's innocuous influence erodes the individuality and pride of the Sun. Occasionally, the dissolving, softening effect of Neptune can work wonders when the Sun person's ego is overdeveloped but there need to be many compatible elements within the framework to draw two such individuals together in the first place. Trines and sextiles are the most advantageous as these allow them both to relate on a higher level.

SUN–PLUTO contacts are similar to those of Sun–Mars but more profound in effect. Pluto intensifies everything and everyone it touches, sending out currents of emotional and sexual vibrations in a sometimes obsessive or controlling manner. When Pluto falls exactly on another person's Sun, the effect can be hypnotic for both parties. The Sun individual falls easily under the spell of the Pluto person. Pluto, in return, admires the ego and fortitude of the Sun. Contact between these two planets can provide a lifetime of intense emotional-sexual compatibility (common with the conjunction, sextile, and trine) or a traumatic relationship that involves excessive feelings, heightened anger, and emotional or sexual obsessions.

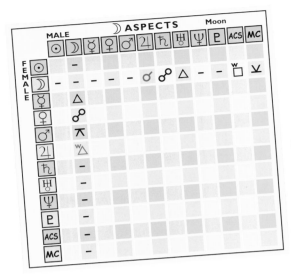

☽ ASPECTS Moon

FEMALE \ MALE	☉	☽	☿	♀	♂	♃	♄	♅	♆	♇	ACS	MC
☉		–				♂	♊	△	–	–	w □	⋎
☽	–	–	–	–	–	–						
☿	△											
♀	♊											
♂	⊼											
♃	w △											
♄	–											
♅	–											
♆												
♇	–											
ACS	–											
MC	–											

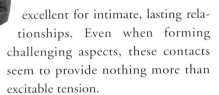

ABOVE Difficult Moon–Jupiter connections can create relationship problems, but benign aspects work well when the rest of the comparison is strong.

BELOW Moon–Jupiter contacts can lead to cloying behavior from the Moon subject which could crowd the Jupiter partner.

ASPECTS TO THE MOON

Aspects between the Moon and another person's planets affect the emotional reactions within a relationship and are vitally important, especially for a woman, when marital or long-term commitments are being considered. The Moon readily absorbs and takes on the qualities of the aspecting planets.

MOON-MOON contacts are excellent when benign (conjunction, sextile, and trine), but remarkably challenging when difficult (square, quincunx, and opposition). Moon square Moon is thought to be one of the most difficult synastric connections. The couple's emotional responses, habits, and attitudes are in total conflict but it is not until they set up home together that the potential trauma of this aspect is revealed.

MOON–MERCURY connections help the communication of emotional responses when beneficial, but hinder the same reactions when in difficult aspect.

MOON–VENUS contacts are extremely common in all kinds of relationships. The combination of emotional responses (Moon) and loving feelings (Venus) is excellent for intimate, lasting relationships. Even when forming challenging aspects, these contacts seem to provide nothing more than excitable tension.

MOON–MARS is a highly charged, sexually exciting combination which is common in intimate relationships but extremely difficult to handle successfully even when forming easy aspects (sextile and trine). The feminine, emotional sensitivity of the Moon does not blend well with the brash, physical energy of Mars. Attraction-repulsion can occur and unless there are other more compatible connections, the relationship will easily collapse.

MOON–JUPITER may seem benign but is not an easy combination. Jupiter's abundant energy is outgoing, optimistic, and loud whereas Moon's energy is soft, passive, and melancholy. Rather than combine to create balance, Jupiter tends to expand the emotions of Moon to produce overdependency, excessive sensitive reactions and cloying behavior. Benign aspects (conjunction, semi-sextile, sextile, and trine) can work well when the comparison is strong.

MOON–SATURN connections are always difficult but less so than Sun–Saturn. Both planets are feminine and passive by nature but the Moon is restless and emotional and Saturn is calm and unemotional. Beneficial aspects between the two can work well – each accepting the other and recognizing the good points – but difficult aspects are common in permanent relationships and unless understood and treated with care, they can create antagonism and resentment.

Moon regards Saturn as oppressive and unfeeling whereas Saturn sees Moon as fickle, gullible, and over-emotional.

MOON–URANUS is another combination which unites two planets that have nothing in common apart from the need for excitement which probably brought them together in the first place. The Moon will be forever trying to understand what makes Uranus tick, while Uranus is only interested in itself. The benign aspects can work well in a good comparison but the difficult connections tend to cause disruption and unhappiness.

MOON–NEPTUNE are very much in tune with each other and no aspect between them is truly difficult. The conjunction, trine, and sextile work beautifully to create the typical romantic, idyllic relationship which has inspired poets and artists. The couple may live in a dreamworld but they are happy. Stronger contacts are required in order for the relationship to gain solid foundations.

MOON–PLUTO are both feminine and passive and therefore compatible with each other but further similarities are few and far between. The powerful energy of Pluto will always surpass and control the weaker energy of the Moon – who is, however, a willing victim to the hypnotic charms of Pluto. Difficult aspects may prove to be traumatic with the Moon regarding Pluto as overbearing and Pluto labeling the Moon irresponsible and ineffectual.

ASPECTS TO MERCURY

Aspects to Mercury will often indicate the level of communication within a relationship. Beneficial Mercury aspects are helpful in any situation but only become important when communication is the main function of the relationship. Difficult connections between Mercury–Saturn, Mercury–Mars and Mercury–Pluto should be avoided.

MERCURY–MERCURY benign aspects are excellent for communication. Partners may out-talk each other when difficult aspects occur.

MERCURY–VENUS gives good verbal communication about love matters. Rarely difficult even when challenging aspects are formed.

MERCURY–MARS provides stimulating conversation when easily aspected but when difficult aspects occur, this can turn into argument and abuse.

MERCURY–JUPITER expands the communicational instincts of Mercury – either positively or detrimentally according to the aspect.

MERCURY–SATURN aspects are seldom desirable as Saturn limits or inhibits. Difficulties get worse as the relationship develops.

MERCURY–URANUS produces stimulating, unusual conversation even when difficult aspects are formed, though the latter might be more outspoken or rude.

MERCURY–NEPTUNE leads to confusion and disorientation of the communicative skills of Mercury, but also encourages romanticism.

MERCURY–PLUTO produces a volcanic, intense communication which can be hard for both parties to assimilate. Verbal abuse may occur with the difficult aspects.

ABOVE
Mercury–Venus aspects between two charts can enhance a relationship by encouraging discussion about love.

ASPECTS TO VENUS

Venus contacts in relationships often indicate powerful feelings of love and harmony even when forming difficult aspects.

VENUS–VENUS beneficial aspects are excellent and always add harmonious elements to a relationship, while difficult aspects often add dissension and incompatibility.

VENUS–MARS is a highly desirable connection between lovers. It relates to immediate physical attraction and though not always an indication of enduring love, its effect is very supportive when other aspects such as Sun–Moon or Sun–Venus are around. As with many contrasting energies, difficult aspects can simultaneously attract and repel but this usually ensures that the relationship does not get stuck in a downward spiral.

VENUS–JUPITER is a beautiful combination which expands feelings of love even when forming difficult connections.

VENUS–SATURN is restrictive and difficult though conducive to permanent attachments. It works better where there are large age differences and in relationships which have already passed the test of time.

VENUS–URANUS is common in intimate, sexual relationships due to the excitement and individuality that Uranus gives. Benign aspects survive the test of time remarkably well (both planets rule fixed signs: Taurus and Aquarius), but difficult aspects create upsets, anger, and incompatibility.

VENUS–NEPTUNE is similar to Moon–Neptune but slightly more active and positive in expression. Difficult aspects can cause disillusionment for the Venus partner.

VENUS–PLUTO creates powerful love feelings which can turn dangerously close to obsession or possession when difficult aspects occur. Seldom an easy contact, but a lasting fulfilling relationship is possible as long as both partners never glance elsewhere.

ASPECTS TO MARS

Mars contacts nearly always relate to sexual, sporting, or physical connections and are highly important in compatibility analysis.

MARS–MARS trines, sextiles, and conjunctions provide a supportive energy. Oppositions are sexually attracted but are on totally different wavelengths while squares and quincunxes are argumentative and mainly incompatible.

MARS–JUPITER is a very potent, assertive combination which expands the sexual and physical needs of both partners. These planets work well together but power struggles may ensue with the difficult aspects.

MARS–SATURN contacts rarely encourage a positive outlook, although benign aspects are easier to handle. Mars' energy is inhibited and nullified by Saturn who considers Mars to be rash, impulsive, and thoughtless.

MARS–URANUS is a powerful combination which excites in a physical and mental capacity. The difficult aspects can cause anger, violence, or disruptive attitudes.

MARS–NEPTUNE contacts weaken the vitality of Mars. These two are physically attracted and benign aspects can lead to successful attachments but difficult aspects can trigger resentment or anger from the Mars person.

MARS–PLUTO is a profoundly physical combination which can trigger obsessional sexual desires or power struggles. Anger, aggression, or violence can occur with difficult contacts. Not an association which bodes well for successful relationships, but certain forceful characters can handle and enjoy the contact.

ASPECTS TO JUPITER

Aspects between Jupiter and the outer planets are usually less significant than between Jupiter and the personal planets. Jupiter–Saturn gives and takes in equal proportions, Jupiter–Uranus is galvanizing and compatible, while Jupiter–Neptune and Jupiter–Pluto are only mildly conflicting. (See pages 115 to 120 for Jupiter with other planets.)

ASPECTS TO SATURN, URANUS, NEPTUNE, AND PLUTO

Aspects between these planets are usually generational and do not help the personal

interpretation of a Comparison Chart. (See pages 114 to 122 for analysis with personal planets.)

THE MOON'S NODES

Nodal contacts appear to be very common in compatibility analysis and highly indicative of karmic commitment. A very low orb of one degree for any aspect is allowed. The degree contact is more important than the actual aspect although exact conjunctions, squares, and oppositions often denote a more powerful and difficult karma than other aspects. In the Kennedys' comparison, John's Moon is exactly trine Jackie's North Node at 17 degrees of Taurus which suggests an easy or straightforward karma which is nearing its end. Double nodal contacts are uncommon but signify a relationship that is extremely binding and often difficult. About one-quarter of permanent relationships have no nodal contacts, suggesting that the association is in its infancy or karmically complete.

LEFT Difficult Mars–Pluto connections within a relationship can lead to an uprising of violent anger.

HIGHLY COMPATIBLE SYNASTRIC CONNECTIONS

* The personal planets (or Jupiter) of one person falling in the Angular houses of the other person
* Angular and Fixed house connections in fairly equal proportion
* A high proportion of aspects -- 45 or more -- which do not include many generational connections
* More beneficial than detrimental contacts
* More than five double aspects, preferably good or variable, with Sun, Moon, Venus, or Mars representing the most aspected planet
* Exact nodal degree contacts

SYNASTRY IN ACTION: STAGE 4

* * * * * * * * * * * * * * * * *

ABOVE The Kennedys' composite chart shows that the public displays of affection may not have been echoed in the home.

COMPOSITE CHARTS

Though seldom used before the 20th century, the popularization of Composite Charts in synastric interpretation was initiated by Robert Hand when his book *Planets in Composite* was published in the 1970s. The system is proving highly credible and more astrologers are now using it.

A Composite Chart combines the natal planetary positions of two charts to create a third, unique chart which represents the relationship as a complete entity. This new chart is the essential core of the relationship and reveals why apparently difficult House and Aspect comparisons appear to work while other, good comparisons fall apart.

The structure of a Composite Chart is made by taking the midpoints (see box, right) of the Ascendants and paired planets from two separate birthcharts to form a single new chart. As with natal charts, the Ascendant must be calculated first, then the midpoints between the two Suns, the two Moons, the two Mercuries, and so on until all the planets are placed in position on the single chart. The Composite Midheaven is also placed into position. When complete,

RIGHT Princess Diana had the same Pluto–Mars conjunction as the Kennedys' composite chart in her 9th house. This was being activated by a square from transiting Pluto in her 12th house at the beginning of September 1997 when she died in tragic and violent circumstances.

the chart is interpreted in a similar manner to a birthchart, bearing in mind always that it refers to a partnership-relationship rather than an individual.

As with House comparisons, Angular and Fixed house positions in the Composite Chart are the most important. At first glance John and Jackie Kennedy's Composite Chart (right) does not seem to possess very firm foundations – five planets in Mutable houses with only one weak Angular house placement – but the nine planets in the top half of the chart reveal that their relationship was essentially for the public. On closer inspection, the four planets in sensitive, homely Cancer are very important. Not only do the composite Sun and Moon form an exact conjunction at six degrees in this sign, but they are also joined by the ruler of the chart, Pluto, and the potentially violent Mars, all of which are forming very difficult squares to Saturn in the secretive, and sometimes destructive, 12th house. The shocking, violent ending to the relationship was very apparent in this chart – difficult Pluto–Mars aspects (especially conjunctions) are often present when violent deaths occur. John and Jackie's unusual and unfortunate Composite Chart speaks volumes, but happily, most Composite Charts have a more positive tale to tell.

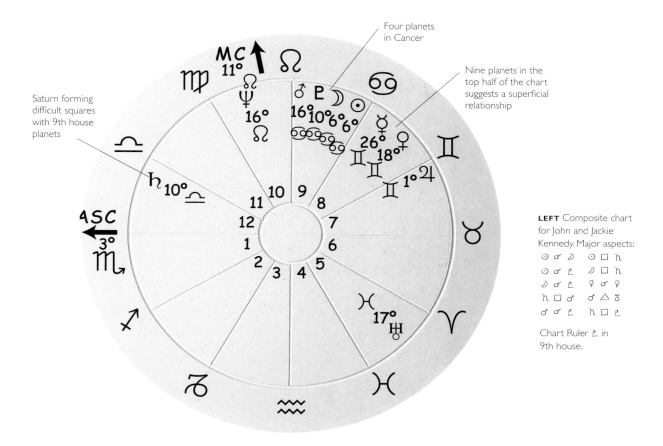

Four planets
in Cancer

Nine planets in the
top half of the chart
suggests a superficial
relationship

Saturn forming
difficult squares
with 9th house
planets

LEFT Composite chart
for John and Jackie
Kennedy. Major aspects:

☉ ♂ ☽   ☉ □ ♄
☉ ♂ ♇   ☽ □ ♄
☽ ♂ ♇   ♀ ♂ ♀
♄ □ ♂   ♂ △ ♅
♂ ♂ ♇   ♄ □ ♇

Chart Ruler ♇ in
9th house.

HOW TO WORK OUT MIDPOINTS

Midpoints are exactly what they seem – the halfway point between any two planets or astrological points. In Composite Charts it is only the midpoints between like planets – Sun–Sun, Moon–Moon, and so on, which are used, but in other branches of astrology, midpoints between any planets can be worked out and analyzed. One method of working out midpoints is as follows:

Take the shortest distance between the two planets or Ascendants. For example, if one Ascendant is at 14 degrees of Virgo and the other at two degrees of Aquarius, the shortest distance is 138 degrees from

Virgo to Aquarius (Aquarius to Virgo in the other direction would be 162 degrees). Divide this amount by two to find the midpoint degree: that is, 138 divided by 2 = 69. Then add these degrees onto the original Virgo Ascendant to arrive at a position of 23 degrees Scorpio. Check this by subtracting the 69 degrees from the other Ascendant of two degrees Aquarius which should work out to the same positional degree of 23 degrees Scorpio, which is the Composite Ascendant. Place in the chart in the usual left-hand position and continue to work out Sun–Sun, Moon–Moon, and so on in exactly the same way. Alternatively, the Zodiacal degree chart used to calculate the Part of Fortune illustrated on pages 132 and 133 could also be used with the following formula:

Ascendant 14 degrees Virgo = 164 degrees

plus Ascendant 2 degrees Aquarius = 302 degrees + 164 degrees = 466 degrees

Divide by 2 (to halve): 466 ÷ 2 = 233 degrees

233 degrees = 23 degrees of Scorpio = Composite Ascendant

PART NINE

CHART ANALYSIS

★ ★ ★ ★ ★

The birthchart has been erected, all the necessary data assembled, and you are now in a position to attempt a complete analysis of your subject. The mass of strange symbols and information may appear daunting, but keen interest and ability soon breed familiarity. The method of interpretation is less important than the ability to view the chart as a whole and create a reading that is both simple and systematic. Intuition is a bonus but not essential.

RIGHT Most novices can glean quite a lot of information from their first chart.

The first thing to do with your birthchart is to divide the reading into two stages. The first considers the broad outline of the chart and takes into account all the extraneous details such as the elements, quadruplicities, chart shaping, and so on. The second makes an in-depth analysis of the 12 signs and houses with their planetary placements, aspects, and major configurations. Some charts are easier to read than others and perseverance is often required to make sense of all the information placed before you, but the rewards are beyond compare. You now have before you the unique structure of someone who may be a total stranger to you — but not for long.

CHART ANALYSIS: ELVIS PRESLEY/1

★ ★ ★ ★ ★ ★ ★ ★ ★ ★ ★ ★ ★ ★ ★

THE BIRTH OF ELVIS

The birthchart of Elvis Presley is based on a birth time of 4:35 a.m. CST January 8, 1935 in Tupelo, Mississippi, USA. Although this birth time has been quoted in several biographies and is thought to have come from hospital records, a time of 12:20 p.m. has been quoted in other books. After studying both charts, however, I believe that 4:35 a.m. is correct.

ABOVE Elvis was born under the Sun sign of Capricorn with keywords such as dutiful, ambitious, reserved, wise, and sensual all ringing true.

ABOVE The position of the planets within Elvis' birthchart are in a Splash shaping.

BROAD OUTLINE

Chart Shaping: Despite the stellium (three planets) in Capricorn, Elvis' chart is basically a Splash shaping, indicating that he had a restless nature, was multitalented, and interested in a diverse range of activities. The lack of concentration and stamina often manifest within this shaping are verified by the Mutable Ascendant, Moon in Pisces, and a very powerfully placed Neptune, but other factors such as the strong, stable Capricorn and Saturnian influences and the ruler of the chart (Jupiter) appearing in a Fixed sign, more than compensate for any lack of consistency.

The Polarities: (Active-Passive Ratio) Elvis' polarity ratio was surprisingly biased toward passivity and introversion (three active, seven passive) and as a child he was excessively shy, often insecure, and generally regarded as a loner. His Ascendant, Sagittarius, a highly positive, outgoing sign, obviously helped him conceal this innate shyness and project a livelier, confident image as he grew older. The combination of passive

planetary positions and an active Ascendant is advantageous on the surface as it allows the subject to project an aura of confidence, but it is always difficult for them to handle and only those close to them are truly aware how insecure and helpless they really feel.

The Elements: The polarity imbalance also causes an inequality in the elements with a shortfall here of both Fire and Air. The Sagittarian Ascendant once again helps to alleviate the unevenness and create an illusion of fiery enthusiasm and warmth, but the overflow of Earth – three personal planets in Capricorn and Neptune–Midheaven in Virgo cannot help but allow the serious and shy, but logical and materialistic, qualities of this element to peep through and eventually take hold. Three planets in Water plus an angular Neptune show that Elvis was very sensitive, highly emotional, imaginative, caring, and protective of himself and other

LEFT Elvis' ascending sign of Sagittarius allowed him to hide his insecurities and project a confident, outgoing image to the world.

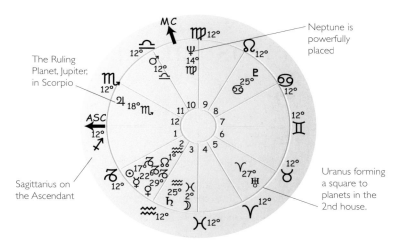

The Ruling Planet, Jupiter, in Scorpio

Sagittarius on the Ascendant

MC

Neptune is powerfully placed

ASC

Uranus forming a square to planets in the 2nd house.

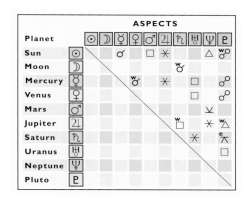

Planet	⊙	☽	☿	♀	♂	♃	♄	♅	♆	♇
ASPECTS										
Sun ⊙	⊙	☌		□	⚹				△	⚼
Moon ☽		☽					☌			
Mercury ☿			☿	☌		⚹		□		☍
Venus ♀				♀				□		☍
Mars ♂					♂				⚻	
Jupiter ♃						♃	□		⚹	△
Saturn ♄							♄		⚹	⚼
Uranus ♅								♅		□
Neptune ♆									♆	
Pluto ♇										♇

people. The low proportion of planets in Air is intensified by the position of constrictive Saturn in Air-sign Aquarius, which no doubt contributed greatly to his shyness and the difficulty he found with communication, especially during his childhood.

The Quadruplicities: It is always amazing how quiet, insecure signs like Cancer and Capricorn consistently manage to assert themselves and reach positions of prominence and authority. This is entirely due to their cardinal qualities – Elvis' chart is rich in cardinal placements which were, no doubt, the main driving force behind his ambition and yearning for recognition and his ability to stay at the top.

Aspect Patterns: Elvis' chart possesses a wide variety of aspects in a fairly high concentration, repeating his diversity of character and emphasizing an interesting, eventful life. He had several T-squares involving the Sun–Mercury–Venus grouping in Capricorn with Pluto and Uranus – all indicative of stress and tension on a personal, creative, and materialistic level. There is also a Yod involving Pluto and the Midheaven with Saturn as the focal point. This is an interesting configuration that shows much karmic talent with the serious and limiting, but enduring, qualities of Saturn highly supportive of success in the latter half of life

RULING PLANET — ♃
RULER'S HOUSE — 12th
RISING PLANETS(S) — —
POSITIVE — 3
NEGATIVE — 7
FIRE — 1 (+ASC)
EARTH — 4 (+MC)
AIR — 2
WATER — 3
CARDINAL — 6
FIXED — 2
MUTABLE — 2
ANGULAR PLANET(S) — ♆

LEFT Examining the planetary positions, aspect patterns, and the balance of the polarities and elements in Elvis' birthchart reveals a great deal about his character.

– suggesting that if Elvis had lived, his success would have continued and grown, perhaps allowing him to branch into other fields such as writing. Despite the abundance of aspects, the Moon forms only one connection – a weak conjunction with Saturn (seven-degree orb and planets placed in different signs) and almost stands alone in the chart, emphasizing his emotional, restless nature, his feelings of being "apart" from the crowd that plagued him when he was young, and his strong attachment to mother. Venus is at a critical, highly evolved degree (29) and five of the ten planets are placed in spiritual degrees that show him to have been an "old soul" who was facing forces of overwhelming karmic development during his lifetime.

CHART ANALYSIS: ELVIS PRESLEY/2

★ ★ ★ ★ ★ ★ ★ ★ ★ ★ ★ ★ ★ ★ ★ ★

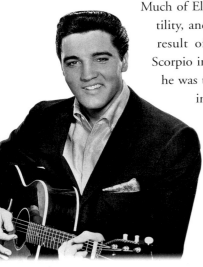

RIGHT The combination of Sagittarius and Scorpio projects a passionate and restless image.

ABOVE Elvis' appearance was typically Sagittarian in his youth. Sagittarius rising would also have contributed to his strong charisma.

RIGHT The second house governs financial matters, and this area is emphasized in Elvis' birthchart.

IN-DEPTH HOUSE ANALYSIS

FIRST HOUSE (ASCENDANT):
APPEARANCE AND OUTER PERSONALITY
Empty house, Ascendant Sagittarius with ruler, Jupiter, posited in Scorpio in the twelfth house

Much of Elvis' charisma, versatility, and endurance was a result of his Sagittarius–Scorpio image. In his youth he was typically Sagittarian in his appearance with a lean frame and long face but as he grew older, the intense, dark eyes and square-set features of Scorpio became more apparent. Because Jupiter is an expansive, larger-than-life planet, all those who come under its rulership tend to put on weight as they grow older and Elvis was no exception in the years before his death.

People with Sagittarius rising are fun-loving, adventurous, restless, candid, and often thoughtless. Elvis projected all of these qualities in his outer personality but because ruler, Jupiter, is placed in a very secretive, solitary area (the 12th house) in an equally covert, but passionate sign (Scorpio) he was also emotional, sensitive, shrewd and determined. The combination of the elements Fire (Sagittarius) and Water (Scorpio) produces steam, and no one could deny that Elvis' image was hot and steamy.

Jupiter forms five aspects, four of which are beneficial. The sextiles to Sun and Mercury are excellent for popularity and helped Elvis to be optimistic and expansive in his communication. The sextile from Jupiter to Neptune is perhaps the most important in his chart as Neptune is the main indicator of musical talent, spiritual awareness, and mass idolatry which, when combined with the majestic qualities of Jupiter, gave him intangible, mesmeric powers. The weak, difficult square from Jupiter to Saturn did in many ways limit his ability to communicate and feel at ease with certain people but it also contributed to the serious, reverential side of his nature and his responsible attitude toward elders.

SECOND HOUSE: MATERIAL AND
MONETARY CONCERNS, POSSESSIONS,
VALUES, APPETITE, BASIC SEXUAL INSTINCTS
Capricorn on the cusp, with ruler, Saturn in the third house

The second house of Elvis' chart contains three planets (a stellium) – Sun, Mercury, and Venus in the sign of Capricorn, as well as his North Node at one degree Aquarius. His potential for earning money and gaining material possessions was therefore extremely pronounced. The staunch principles, strong ambitions, and serious inclinations of this sign were all projected into Elvis' attitudes concerning material matters. Capricorn is, however, a very insecure sign,

especially during adolescence, and the security fear represented by attaining material wealth can be very inviting when placed on the cusp of the second. Many people with Capricorn or Saturn in the second become millionaires, although they are often miserly or retentive when it comes to sharing their hard-earned wealth. Elvis took his principles and responsibilities seriously in this respect – supporting his parents from an early age and not spending money on anything that he considered to be frivolous. He dressed in an unusual, glamorous manner in later years but this was due more to Neptune's influence than Capricorn's. Venus in the second certainly helped to mitigate the starkness and stringency of Capricorn, but there must have been many times when Elvis felt unsure about his financial success and worried whether he would have enough for the future.

Capricorn is an earthy, sensual sign with strong physical needs which are slow to develop and are only asserted when a favorable reception is assured. Capricorn people can be surprisingly naive and uncertain about their abilities. Elvis was overtly sexual but, according to some of the women with whom he had relationships (including his wife Priscilla), he was sexually immature and very unsure of himself. The second house often depicts the manner in which money is earned. Before becoming famous, Elvis had a wide variety of jobs, most of which related to the practical elements of Capricorn, such as trucking, construction, and factory work.

The second decanate of Capricorn (ten to 19 degrees) comes under the jurisdiction of the sign of Taurus and is greatly influenced by music and singing. The second house is also the natural house of Taurus and Elvis' Sun at 17 degrees of Capricorn in the second house is at a particularly potent musical degree. Elvis was able to earn money in many different ways but it seemed inevitable that he would eventually exploit his most precious talent – music!

LEFT At the age of 42, Elvis had piled on weight – a typical influence of the planet Jupiter when ruling the chart – but his success and sex appeal showed no signs of waning.

BELOW Even though Elvis was openly sexual in his performances (seen here in *Jailhouse Rock*), he was still unsure of himself in intimate relationships.

CHART ANALYSIS: ELVIS PRESLEY/3

★ ★ ★ ★ ★ ★ ★ ★ ★ ★ ★ ★ ★ ★ ★

IN-DEPTH HOUSE ANALYSIS

THIRD HOUSE: EDUCATION,
SHORT-DISTANCE TRAVEL, ALL
RELATIVES EXCEPT PARENTS, MUNDANE
DAILY MATTERS, AND COMMUNICATION
*Aquarius on the cusp, with ruler Uranus
in Aries in the fifth house*

The third house in Elvis' chart is almost as strong as the second but far more complex to analyze. The planets Saturn and Moon in weak conjunction there do not go well together but they are at least in different signs. Elvis must have been an enigma to many of his relatives, teachers, and casual acquaintances. Aquarius on the cusp of the third with Saturn at 25 degrees of this universally friendly but personally detached sign emphasizes the sense of solitariness and uniqueness he must have had during childhood and adolescence. He was quiet, dutiful, and polite in class according to his teachers who seem not to have noticed him very much. Although he obviously kept his feelings to himself (Saturn conjunct Moon inhibits emotional expression), Elvis must have been hurt at being constantly ignored. He was not a fast learner (Saturn acquires knowledge slowly) but he had the knack of absorbing information intuitively (Moon in Pisces).

ABOVE Elvis as a boy must have been both a loner and lonely but his Sagittarian Ascendant meant he was also playful and adventurous.

The Saturn–Moon conjunction can be held responsible for many of the difficulties Elvis experienced in communication during his younger years. He stuttered slightly (a Saturn affliction), found it difficult to form lasting childhood friendships, and was described as being "different" (typically Aquarian). It was not until he started to play guitar that his ability to communicate took an upturn. Saturn starts to develop and lose some of its insecurities at the time of the Saturn return, which occurs between the ages of 28 and 30, so it is unlikely that Elvis was able to gain complete self-confidence before then. The Saturn–Moon conjunction also infers that Elvis desperately needed the company of women to talk to and for casual relationships, even though he may have made life difficult for them at times.

The third house also represents brothers and sisters and it is on record that Elvis felt

BELOW Elvis' bond with his wife Priscilla grew even stronger after his mother died. The couple are seen here with singer, Tom Jones.

176

acutely the loss of his twin brother, who died at birth. Saturn in the third is often indicative of a single child, or a lonely childhood, but Elvis' Moon accompanies Saturn which indicates that he desperately needed the companionship of a brother or sister. The Moon (and the tenth house) usually represents the mother and Elvis was known to be very attached to Gladys Presley. Rather than form easy-going, loving relationships, Saturn tends to cling or hang onto people, especially when conjuncting the Moon, because of an inner fear of detachment. It seems that Gladys Presley perhaps became the twin brother and companion that he had lost. He apparently said that Priscilla, his wife, was "like a sister to him," implying she, too, was a substitute sibling who became even more important after his mother died.

FOURTH HOUSE: HOME ENVIRONMENT, FAMILY CONCERNS, FATHER, EMOTIONAL ROOTS
Empty house, Pisces on the cusp, ruler Neptune in Virgo on the angle of the tenth house

The areas of life relating to empty houses are rarely as "active" to the individual as those which are occupied. Pisces posited on the cusp of Elvis' fourth suggests that although he was sensitive to his surroundings, he was not unduly attached to his home and did not feel the need to form strong domestic roots. He thought people and possessions were more important. His dream home, Graceland, was a way of parading his wealth and stature, an attitude which is highly indicative of the ruler Neptune placed in the tenth house of career, aims, and ambitions. Neptune is a planet with many different guises, however, and as well as promoting glitz and glamour, it is also vague, confused, and escapist. Elvis liked the prestigious public image his home represented, and in later years he enjoyed its seclusion but it is doubtful whether he ever truly felt the need to stabilize his roots.

Neptune, ruler of the fourth house (father), placed in the tenth (mother), suggests that Elvis' parents shared parental roles and both acted in a maternal capacity, though Vernon Presley, his father, is less strongly depicted in the birthchart than Gladys. Pisces and Neptune dominate the parental axis of Elvis' chart suggesting that although he loved and revered his parents and they adored him, in many ways Elvis felt that he was not part of them and that they were somehow totally alien to him. The religious and spiritual inclinations that attracted him deeply throughout his life were inherited karmically from both parents but the link from his mother was particularly strong.

ABOVE Elvis' attachment to his dream home Graceland was probably more about presenting a prestigious public image than planting roots.

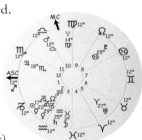

ABOVE Elvis' empty 4th house is suggestive of a lack of connection with home and family.

CHART ANALYSIS: ELVIS PRESLEY/4

* * * * * * * * * * * * * * * * *

IN-DEPTH HOUSE ANALYSIS

FIFTH HOUSE: LOVE
AFFAIRS, CREATIVE OUTLETS, GAMBLING,
SPORTS, HOBBIES, CHILDREN
*Aries on the cusp, with ruler Mars in
Libra, 11th house*

The fifth house, though not heavily occupied, is without doubt the most vital and self-assertive area of Elvis' chart. Aries is always a dynamic influence but the sparks really fly when the uniquely talented rebellious Uranus falls in this sign. Both Aries and Uranus are completely self-absorbed and thrive on excitement and danger. Elvis' well-known predilection for love-affairs is just one example of this powerful placement of Uranus. His film roles and musical talents were also enforced by this position – the quiet, shy loner suddenly transformed into a positive vibrating surge of electric current with no inhibitions whatsoever. What a contrast! When Elvis flicked the switch to his fifth house, he commanded attention, became popular, and gained the support of many loyal companions (ruler Mars in the 11th house of friends.)

Even as a child Elvis would emerge frequently from his shell to reveal a playful, adventurous streak very much aligned to his Sagittarius Ascendant and Uranus in Aries. Uranus has, however, several difficult squares to Mercury, Venus, and Pluto which in turn form some highly tense T-squares in his chart. Elvis loved to take risks and live

ABOVE
Uranus in Aries
makes for a
rebellious, risk-
taking lifestyle.

dangerously in a whirl of social pleasure (Uranus in Aries), but the strong disciplinary restraints of Capricorn were at odds with Uranus and often held him in check. The act of suppressing a powerful planet like Uranus can create a build-up of tension and anger. Although in control of himself for most of the time, Elvis must have let go and exploded angrily on many occasions to his friends and girlfriends, but not to his relatives or parents. Despite the fact that he was stimulated by love affairs and social activity, Uranus is a cold and detached planet and he must have blown hot (Aries) and cold (Uranus) within those relationships.

Apart from music, Elvis enjoyed horseriding and martial arts, both of which

RIGHT In his films,
Elvis had a strong
mesmerizing and
electrifying quality, due
to his powerfully
placed Uranus in the
5th house. He is seen
here in *GI Blues*.

are appropriate to Uranus in Aries. Any dangerous fast sport would have appealed to him, but the Saturn-Moon conjunction and the squares from Uranus to the planets in Capricorn probably prevented him from participating to any degree, which is just as well as there is also an element of danger and a risk of accidents where Uranus is concerned. His natural restraint must have spared him on many occasions.

Elvis' attitude toward his only child, Lisa, must have been complex – a mix of coldness, protectiveness, physical warmth, and detachment. He probably enjoyed showing her to his friends and surprising her with outings and treats but the tense T-squares which inhibited his ability to express feelings must have made it hard to give her the love she needed. Despite his inner detachment, however, Elvis was highly paternal and overprotective and would dearly have loved to father more children.

SIXTH HOUSE: WORK, SERVICE GIVEN AND RECEIVED, HEALTH, PETS, SMALL ANIMALS

Empty house, Taurus on the cusp, Venus ruler in Capricorn second house

As well as being practical and earthy, Taurus rules music. Taureans love to sing and their solid build and powerful lungs often give them powerful vocal strength – as was, of course, the case with Elvis. After his youthful attempts at conventional, blue-collar occupations, Elvis turned, of course, to music and singing. There is a lazy element to the influence of

LEFT Elvis' difficulty with expressing his true feelings must have affected his relationship with his only child, Lisa.

Taurus–ruler Venus in Capricorn which was probably apparent in his early working life, but when he was involved in something he enjoyed, such as music, he worked extremely hard at it. His birthchart indicates that he enjoyed singing less for financial gain than as a creative pursuit or status enhancer.

With no planets in the sixth house, Elvis had an indifferent attitude toward health. His was a robust constitution (Taurus) with just a few weak points – one of them, unfortunately, being the throat. The strong Capricorn–Saturn influences made him susceptible to bone and skin problems such as arthritis and eczema and his legs from the knees downward may have given him trouble as he grew older. Psychological factors were, however, the principal cause of his health breakdown and early death and these can be attributed to the repressive qualities of Saturn combined with the nebulous, addictive traits of Neptune.

ABOVE
The musical sign of Taurus in the house of work suggests Elvis' forte.

CHART ANALYSIS: ELVIS PRESLEY/5

* * * * * * * * * * * * * * * *

IN-DEPTH
HOUSE ANALYSIS

SEVENTH HOUSE: MARRIAGE
AND PARTNERSHIPS
*Empty house, Gemini on cusp, ruler
Mercury in Capricorn in the second house*

Although people who never marry rarely possess an occupied seventh, a lack of planets in this house does not necessarily indicate a lack of relationships. It suggests that the subject does not need to be married and will usually commit themselves to a permanent relationship for reasons other than lasting companionship. Those without planets in the seventh tend to hop in and out of marriages more easily than most people. The position of the ruler of the house is vitally important. Elvis was not keen to get married. He enjoyed the romantic, non-committal elements of relationships (Uranus in the fifth) and deferred marrying Priscilla for as long as possible. Gemini (the sign on the cusp) can be fickle wherever it falls and dual-natured. Placed on the seventh it suggests infidelity, an inclination for concurrent relationships, and divorce. Even though he loved Priscilla, Elvis is known to have been unfaithful to her. The clue to his true feelings about Priscilla and marriage lie in the position of the ruler of the seventh house, which is placed in the second – the house of possessions. Elvis viewed Priscilla as his property – someone to nurture and mold in his own style. Capricorn, (Mercury, ruler of Gemini in Capricorn), however, is noted more for its disciplinary judgment and

honorable principles than its compassion or warmth. Elvis did what he thought was right by Priscilla and cared deeply for her in his own way, but his conception of a happy marriage was obviously very different from Priscilla's. He needed lots of communication from a partner, especially about the material, practical matters of the relationship, but his inability to express his own inner feelings must have made it difficult to make this known to Priscilla.

Elvis was undoubtedly attracted to Mutable sign women (Gemini, Virgo, Sagittarius, and Pisces) as these are the signs on the important angles of his chart. Priscilla is a Sun Gemini with a Capricorn Ascendant – a highly compatible combination with his seventh house Gemini and Sun–Mercury conjunction in Capricorn. On the whole, however, Elvis' chart does not lend itself to successfully maintaining permanent relationships – a fact which eventually took its toll on his marriage.

ABOVE The empty 7th house of marriage suggests that Elvis did not need to be married.

LEFT In his music, Elvis found a way of expressing himself but his true feelings in relationships remained difficult to fathom.

EIGHTH HOUSE: SEXUAL AND MONETARY CONCERNS IN RELATIONSHIPS, BIRTH, INHERITANCE, SPIRITUAL MATTERS
Cancer on the cusp, ruler Moon in third house

The planet Pluto is placed in Elvis' eighth house which, taken on its own merit, looks good – it's posited in a harmonious Water sign and in its natural Water-ruled house (Scorpio). On closer inspection, however, the challenging aspects unfortunately outweigh the beneficial connections five to one and must have created difficulties in this highly secretive, intense house. Pluto here emphasizes the importance of sexual activity in Elvis' life. It could have been an area of deep release and spiritual fulfillment for him if Pluto had not been so badly aspected, but tension within his relationships, opposing forces relating to money and materialistic concerns, and perverse or immature sexual direction were all fairly evident.

Elvis must have experienced many deep, enlightening impressions about the process of life and probably found fascinating the complete cycle of birth, death, and reincarnation. But the practical side of his nature depicted by Capricorn in the second house was at odds with the intense emotional-spiritual attunement of Pluto in the eighth, and he no doubt repressed many urges to delve into the depths of the unknown.

People with planets in the eighth house usually receive or gain a great deal, both physically and materially, from other people. Elvis would have experienced great generosity and devotion from those close to him but, once again, the Capricorn contingency (stellium in the second) insisted on independence and self-support. Pluto in Cancer is highly protective and nurturing and Elvis obviously felt these qualities within his marriage and close relationships but was rarely allowed to project them openly.

The ruler of the eighth house, the Moon conjunct Saturn, points to Elvis' inner loneliness within his relationships. The immaturity of the Saturn–Moon conjunction combined with the difficult aspect to Pluto indicate a man unable to relate to the emotions and sexual content of a relationship in the normal way. Although Elvis learned in his later years how to nurture and care for others, in his earlier days he himself was the one who needed mothering and it is this desperate, apparently unfulfilled longing which holds the key to his complex character.

ABOVE The birth of his daughter must have been an important event in Elvis' life – usually it was he who needed nurturing; now he had a paternal duty.

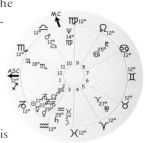

ABOVE Pluto in Cancer shows Elvis' protective and nurturing side.

CHART ANALYSIS: ELVIS PRESLEY/6

* * * * * * * * * * * * * * * *

IN-DEPTH
HOUSE ANALYSIS

NINTH HOUSE: LONG
DISTANCE TRAVEL,
HIGHER EDUCATION,
RELIGION, PHILOSOPHY
*Empty house, Leo on the cusp,
ruler Sun in second house*

ABOVE
An empty 9th
house shows a lack
of interest in
expanding horizons.

Ninth-house matters were not very pronounced in Elvis' life – his strong religious and spiritual inclinations came mainly from tenth house Neptune and 12th house Jupiter. He disliked long-distance traveling and journeyed overseas only when forced by circumstances to do so, the most famous of which was his posting to Germany during conscription into the US Army. Life in the armed forces suits the regimented ideals of Capricorn subjects so this period of his life was no great hardship for him.

Fixed signs such as Leo take a lot to get them moving and it is rare for a Fixed sign without planets, placed on the cusp of the ninth, to enjoy far-flung adventures. Elvis liked to pretend that he was always ready to go anywhere and do anything (Sagittarius on the Ascendant), but this was far from so. When Fixed sign, ninth-house subjects do make up their minds to travel or expand their mental horizons, they often follow conventional paths.

ABOVE Elvis was not born to travel but his posting to Germany was probably made easier by the fact that army life suited his nature.

In Elvis' chart, Sun, the ruler of the ninth, placed in Capricorn in the second house, emphasizes his reluctance to travel far and wide. The fears and insecurities surrounding the sign of Capricorn appear insurmountable, and with three planets in this sign Elvis obviously had many deep-rooted fears, some of which are known while others may have been too deep for him to acknowledge. Elvis made few attempts to expand and improve his mind with higher education and his religious–spiritual involvement came mainly from hereditary, inspirational, and intuitional influences.

TENTH HOUSE: AIMS, AMBITIONS, CAREER, MOTHER
*Virgo on the cusp,
ruler Mercury in the
second house*

The tenth house, with planet Neptune placed supremely on the angle, is another key area in the life of Elvis Presley. His musicianship and acting talents, the hypnotic charisma, and the adoring public were all due to the positive, divine influence of Neptune in his birthchart. Unfortunately, the downside of Neptune – drug addiction, loneliness, escapism, and the inability to cope with fame – became more apparent as he grew older. Many highly creative and charismatic individuals have Neptune powerfully placed in their charts – people like English poet

ABOVE Neptune powerfully placed is a characteristic chart feature of creative, talented personalities.

Robert Browning, singer and film star Cher, dancer Rudolf Nureyev, film star icon Marilyn Monroe, singer and poet Bob Dylan, and crime-fiction writer Agatha Christie, for instance – and some of them do manage to cope well with the nebulous fluctuations of this planet but just as many of them fall by the wayside. Elvis struggled hard throughout his life to transmute the negative influences of Neptune into the positive channels of his music, but the added challenge of the Capricorn planets, Saturn conjunct Moon, and a difficult aspect to Pluto, eventually wore him down. Neptunian people love the idea of glamour, fame, and adulation but they struggle to cope with the effects in reality and yearn to

escape back into their secluded inner worlds. Neptune is an enigma and those born under its shrouded influence are sensitive souls who need to have something or some place to hide to recharge their batteries. Elvis attempted to hide his problems from the public, and to a certain extent was successful, but after his death much came into the open.

One of the most important influences in Elvis' life was his mother, Gladys Presley. Any tenth-house planet can represent the mother or mother-figure, but Neptune here indicates all kinds of complex, contradictory feelings that Elvis must have experienced through his mother. Part of him idolized her but it is fairly certain that part of him also needed to escape her cloying influence – Gladys Presley adored Elvis and was highly dependent on him. Good or bad, the bond between them was ironclad and never broken. He was also profoundly influenced by her spiritual beliefs and was tempted several times during the height of his fame to forgo everything and retreat into religious or spiritual anonymity. Fortunately for the fans, but perhaps less so for his peace of mind, Elvis was easily persuaded (Neptune) that his future lay elsewhere.

ABOVE Elvis had a strong bond with his mother, Gladys. He is seen here bidding her, and his father, Vernon, farewell on the eve of his conscription into the army.

RIGHT In common with Elvis, Marilyn Monroe had a strong Neptune placement in her chart and, while she loved the glamour of fame, she was unable to cope with its effects.

CHART ANALYSIS: ELVIS PRESLEY/7

* * * * * * * * * * * * * * * *

IN-DEPTH
HOUSE ANALYSIS

ELEVENTH HOUSE: FRIENDS
AND GROUP ACTIVITIES
Libra on the cusp, ruler
Venus in the second house

ABOVE
Strong friendships
are indicated by the
position of Mars in
the 11th house.

Mars, the bringer of energy, enthusiasm, and assertiveness, is strategically placed exactly on the cusp of Elvis' 11th house. It forms no other aspects apart from a square to the Sun and a weak semi-sextile to Neptune. Although weakened by sign (Libra) and position (11th house), Mars here can be beneficial for group-cult leadership and vibrant friendships. Despite childhood problems, Elvis grew into a sociable adult who enjoyed the company of dynamic individuals, particularly male friends. He was a natural leader in his chosen circles and was usually charming and fair in his distribution of favors (Libra on the cusp), but the square from Mars to the Sun does reveal an angry or impatient side to his nature, especially when his principles were questioned by those close to him, and there are several indications in Elvis' chart that suggest he liked to have his own way. Mars in the 11th can be demanding and pushy in friendships and Elvis doubtless managed to alienate people from time to time. Generally, however, he was popular and well-respected and he would have enjoyed participating in martial arts and other sporting activities with his chosen group of friends.

TWELFTH HOUSE: HOSPITALS,
LARGE INSTITUTIONS, KARMA, SPIRITUAL
ACTIVITY, CHARITIES, SECRETS,
SACRIFICES, AND HIDDEN AGENDAS
Scorpio on the cusp,
ruler Pluto in the eighth house

The depth of feeling and imagination relating to Elvis' 12th house is quite phenomenal, not only through the intensity of Scorpio on the cusp (with ruler Pluto in the secretive, sensitive sign of Cancer in the eighth), but through the added influence of Jupiter, the ruler of the chart being posited here. Elvis obviously possessed a dark hidden side to his character and undoubtedly there is much about his inner thoughts and habits which was never revealed, even to close friends. At certain points in his life when he was left

ABOVE With the
chart ruler in the
12th house, a deep
spiritual awareness
is indicated.

BELOW Elvis loved
the company of
dynamic men and is
seen here with
Frank Sinatra.

alone, Elvis must have retreated into his own fathomless world, a place which was probably the source of his creative inspiration. He was a very spiritual person and, karmically speaking, an old soul. He possessed powerful psychic ability but it was usually the practical influences of Capricorn and Saturn–Moon which dominated his reactions and lifestyle. There was a deep charitable side to his nature and he probably made donations to the needy or religious funds without advertising the fact. Apart from a weak square to Saturn, Jupiter is nicely aspected and quite at home in this 12th-house position – being the old ruler of Pisces, natural sign of the 12th house – and it certainly provided Elvis with an expansive imagination, a deeply creative mind, and a wealth of spiritual knowledge.

THE DEATH OF ELVIS

Although we can learn much by studying the distribution of the planets at a time of major events, it is the positions at birth and death that provide the most interesting information. One or more of the three outer planets, Uranus, Neptune, and Pluto, nearly always feature strongly at the moment of death, usually forming conjunctions to personal planets, although squares and quincunxes are also quite common. Sudden deaths nearly always involve Uranus or Pluto in aspect to Sun or Mars. On August 16, 1977, the day of Elvis' death, Pluto had formed an exact conjunction to Mars, indicating a traumatic, untimely death – and Neptune, the most important outer planet in Elvis' natal chart, had just passed the degree of his Ascendant (12 degrees of Sagittarius). Although Elvis died of a heart attack (the Sun, ruling heart, was conjunct transiting Saturn, planet of restriction on this day), the real cause of death was his addiction to prescribed drugs – sedatives and tranquilizers. All drugs are poisons and are ruled by Neptune so it is therefore appropriate that Neptune was in such a prominent position on the day of his death. There were many close quincunxes around on that day and Venus was in the eighth house of death, opposing the Sun, and fast approaching Pluto, the ruler of birth and death. There is no doubt that death, when it came, was a welcome release for Elvis, a man who had such attunement with the spiritual world. If he has not returned already, it is certain that he will be back and someone, somewhere, will grace the world once more with his charismatic talent.

GLOSSARY

* * * * * * * * * * * * * * *

ANGULAR PLANETS
Any planet placed within an eight degree orb either side of the four angles of the birth chart (forming a cross) or conjuncting the Midheaven.

ARABIAN PARTS
An ancient system of calculating hypothetical points within a set formula using two planets and the Ascendant or Midheaven (Z + B = D) which relate to important themes in life such as marriage, divorce, finance, luck, health etc. The Part of Fortune (Ascendant + Moon - Sun) is the most commonly used.

ASCENDANT
Also known as Rising Sign. The sign of the zodiac rising over the eastern horizon at the time of birth.

ASPECTS
The measurement of various angles and degrees between planets in a birthchart which form easy or difficult relationships known as **major** or **minor** aspects. For example, two or more planets placed 120 degrees apart form a major aspect known as a trine which is regarded as beneficial. Other major aspects are the conjunction (0-8 degrees apart), semi-sextile (30 degrees), sextile (60 degrees), square (90 degrees), quincunx (150 degrees) and opposition (180 degrees). Minor aspects are not deemed to be so important in their influence and involve less obvious degree connections. The most commonly used of these are the semi-square (45 degrees), sesquiquadrate (135 degrees), quintile (72 degrees) and the bi-quintile (144 degrees).

CHART SHAPING
Refers to the outer appearance (shape formation) and related characteristics of the birthchart. There are seven known chart shapings (Bowl, Bucket, Bundle, Locomotive, See-Saw, Splash, Splay), plus several lesser known newer ones (Fan, Undefined).

CUSP
The cusp is the dividing line between two signs or houses in the birthchart. Planets or the Ascendant and Midheaven are said to be "on the cusp" or "cuspal" in a birthchart if they fall extremely close to the end of one sign or house and the beginning of the next sign or house. For instance a planet placed between 29 degrees of Gemini and 0 degrees of Cancer would be regarded as cuspal.

DECANATES
Each of the twelve signs consists of 30 degrees. Decanates (or decans) are the division of these 30 degrees into three groups of 10 degrees, amounting to 36 decanates in all. When using the Equal House system of division the houses of the birthchart can also be divided into 36 decanates. The first 10 degrees of any sign or house (0-9) are always called the first decanate, likewise the second ten degrees (10-19) the second decanate and the last ten degrees (20-219) the third decanate.

DIGNITIES
An ancient system of placing the planets into three sign groupings entitled **exalted**, **fall** and **detriment**, which is not used greatly in modern astrology. Planets placed in signs where they are "exalted" are said to work well whereas planets in signs of "fall" or "detriment" are deemed to be badly placed.

DIRECT
A planet is said to be in "direct" motion when it moves from a stationary or retrograde (backward) movement.

ELEMENTS
The signs of the zodiac are divided into four elements - Fire, Earth, Air, and Water, each forming characteristics specifically related to their element. The Fire signs are Aries, Leo, and Sagittarius, the Earth signs Taurus, Virgo, and Capricorn, the Air signs Gemini, Libra, and Aquarius and the Water signs Cancer, Scorpio, and Pisces.

EMPTY HOUSES (UNOCCUPIED)
These are houses on the birthchart which do not contain any **planet**. (They may, however, contain Arabian Part, Nodes or other mathematical points used in the birthchart.)

EPHEMERIDES (Singular Ephemeris)
Publications in book or booklet form which contain all the astronomical data required to set up a birthchart.

EVENT CHART
A chart set up for a particular event (e.g. a marriage or house move) using the date, time, and town in which the event takes place.

GRAND CROSS
A major aspect configuration, renowned for its difficulty, involving four squares and two oppositions (four or more planets) which make a "cross" formation when placed into the birthchart.

GRAND TRINE
A major aspect configuration which is considered to be highly beneficial, involving three trines (three or more planets) which make a "triangular" formation when placed into the birthchart.

HORARY ASTROLOGY
An ancient form of predictive astrology which answers questions. The date, place, and time the querent forms the question is noted and a chart erected for this data. Different planets and areas of the chart are studied according to the question asked, but the ascendant always rules the querent (questioner).

HOUSE DIVISION / HOUSES
The zodiac circle is usually divided into sectors which are called houses. The size and number of these sections varies according to the method of house division used. The three major systems used nowadays are **Equal**, **Koch** and **Placidus**. Both Equal and Koch always divide the circle into twelve segments, but in the Equal House system the divisions are equal – each containing 30 degrees – whereas in the Koch system the sectors vary slightly in the number of occupied degrees. House sizes in the Placidus system vary enormously depending upon the country of birth, with extreme northern latitudes producing a combination of very large and very small (or non-existent houses) – one reason why this system has waned in popularity during the twentieth century. Each of the twelve houses represents a different area of life and may or may not contain planets, depending upon the time of birth. The 1st, 4th, 7th, and 10th houses are known as **angular**, the 2nd, 5th, 8th, and 11th are known as **succedent**, and the 3rd, 6th, 9th, and 12th are called **cadent** houses.

GLOSSARY

* * * * * * * * * * * * * * * *

**IMMUM COELI
(IC or NADIR)**
The lowest point below the
horizon in the chart where the
ecliptic crosses the local
meridian which is always
exactly opposite the
Midheaven (MC).

LUNAR RETURN
A monthly method of predictive astrology using the return
of the Moon to the place it
occupies in the birthchart and
erecting a new chart for this
position.

MIDDLE PLANETS
Relates to planets Jupiter and
Saturn which are too far away
from the earth to be regarded
a personal, but too close to be
viewed as outer planets.

**MIDHEAVEN
(MEDIUM COELI,
MC or ZENITH)**
The highest point above the
horizon in the chart where the
ecliptic crosses the local
meridian which is always
exactly opposite the IC.

NODES
Theoretical points formed
when a moving body (usually
a planet) crosses the axis of
the ecliptic in the north and
south. The most commonly
used nodes are those of the
Moon, which are often
known as the **Dragon's Head**
(North Node) and the
Dragon's Tail (South Node).

OUTER PLANETS
Refers to Uranus, Neptune,
and Pluto which are the three
discovered outermost planets
in our solar system.

PERSONAL PLANETS
These are the Sun and Moon
(referred to as planets for astrological purposes) and Mercury,
Venus, and Mars – the three
closest planets to the earth.

POLARITIES
The division of the signs of the
zodiac into two distinct groups
entitled **active/passive**, or
masculine/feminine, or **posi-
tive/negative**. Active signs are
Aries, Gemini, Leo, Libra,
Sagittarius, and Aquarius and
Passive signs are Taurus,
Cancer, Virgo, Scorpio,
Capricorn, and Pisces.

PRE-NATAL EPOCH
A specialized form of
predicting the sex of a baby
when the time of conception
is known.

PROGRESSIONS
A form of predictive astrology
using the daily progressive
movements from the birth
date onward (using an
ephemeris) of the personal
planets and interpreting them
into yearly forecasts.

QUADRANTS
The four sections of the
birthchart divided by angles
of 90 degrees. Houses 1-3
represent the first quadrant,
houses 4-6 the second quadrant, houses 7-9 the third
quadrant, and houses 10-12
the fourth quadrant.

QUADRUPLICITIES
The division of the twelve
signs of the zodiac into three
groupings called **Cardinal**
(Aries, Cancer, Libra, and
Capricorn), **Fixed** (Taurus,
Leo, Scorpio, and Aquarius)
and **Mutable** (Gemini, Virgo,
Sagittarius, and Pisces). Each
group contains one sign from
each element, and have certain
characteristics in common.

QUERENT
Refers to the person asking
the question in **horary
astrology**.

RETROGRADE
The apparent backward
movement of a planet.

RULING PLANET
The planet which rules the
chart is always the ruler of the
Ascending sign. For example,
somebody with Gemini rising
would have Mercury, the ruler
of Gemini, as their ruling
planet. In general terms the
ruling planet can refer to any
planet ruling any sign. For
example, the ruling planet of
an empty house which has
Sagittarius on the cusp would
be Jupiter.

**SATELLITIUM/
STELLIUM**
Different terms used to
describe a group of three or
more planets in one sign or
house.

SIDEREAL TIME
Sidereal time is "true" time
measured from the movement
of the planets wherein a
normal day is slightly shorter
(approximately 4 minutes)
than a clock day. Sidereal
time is needed to find the sign
and degrees of the Ascendant
and Midheaven in order that
the rest of the chart can be
calculated.

SIGNIFICATOR
A term mainly used in **horary
astrology** referring to the
"person" or "subject" being
enquired about.

SINGLETON
Generally used when referring
to a planet sitting along in
one half of the chart.

SOLAR RETURN
A method of producing yearly
forecasts which uses the date
and time each year when the
Sun returns to the exact position it occupied at birth.

SUN SIGNS
The general term for the star
signs as used in magazine and
newspaper columns. Solar
charts based upon the sign
position of the Sun at birth
are used for such readings.

SYNASTRY
Used as a general term for the
various methods of compatibility analysis between two
charts within any kind of relationship.

TRANSIT
The daily movement of the
planets.

T-SQUARE
A major aspect of configuration involving two squares
and an opposition, which
indicates tension.

UNASPECTED PLANET
A planet which does not form
any of the seven major aspects
with another planet.

YOD
(Also known as the Finger of
God). A major aspect configuration involving two
quincunxes and a sextile, with
a variable influence.

ZODIAC
The part of the sky which the
planets orbit around the Sun
when viewed from the earth
(also known as the ecliptic).
In order to measure the
progress of the planets the
zodiac is divided into 360
degrees and twelve signs of 30
degrees which we refer to as
the Sun signs.

ZONE STANDARD
The standard "clock" time
used in different countries,
which may be behind or
ahead of GMT and therefore
requires to be converted to
GMT before a correct
birthchart can be calculated.

NAME:

EQUAL HOUSE SYSTEM

QUALITIES

RULING PLANET _ _ _ _ _ _ _ _
RULER'S HOUSE _ _ _ _ _ _ _ _
RISING PLANET _ _ _ _ _ _ _ _
MASCULINE _ _ _ _ _ _ _ _
FEMININE _ _ _ _ _ _ _ _

TRIPLICITIES

FIRE _ _ _ _ _ _   AIR _ _ _ _ _ _
EARTH _ _ _ _ _   WATER _ _ _ _ _

QUADRUPLICITIES

CARDINAL _ _ _ _ _ _ _ _ _
FIXED _ _ _ _ _ _ _ _ _
MUTABLE _ _ _ _ _ _ _ _ _
ANGULAR _ _ _ _ _ _ _ _ _

ASPECTS

NOTES:

BIRTH DATE	d	m	y
PLACE			
LATITUDE	°	′	
LONGITUDE	°	′	
BIRTH TIME as given am/pm	h	m	
ZONE STANDARD E−/W+			
RESULT am/pm			
SUMMER TIME			
G M T am/pm			
SID. TIME NOON/M.N. 0°			
INTERVAL am−/pm+			
RESULT			
ACC. ON INTERVAL am−/pm+			
RESULT			
LONG. EQUIVALENT E+/W−			
RESULT			
ADJUSTMENT ± 12/24h			
LOCAL SID. TIME			

FURTHER READING AND USEFUL ADDRESSES

* * * * * * * * * * * * * * * * *

REFERENCE BOOKS
(used for calculation and construction of birthcharts)

THE CONCISE PLANETARY EPHEMERIS FOR YEARS 1900–2000 (The Hieratic Publishing Co.)

THE AMERICAN EPHEMERIS FOR THE 20TH CENTURY (A.C.S. Publications)

THE AMERICAN EPHEMERIS FOR THE 21ST CENTURY (A.C.S. Publications)

RAPHAEL'S TABLES OF HOUSES FOR NORTHERN AND SOUTHERN LATITUDES (W. Foulsham & Co.)

RAPHAEL'S YEARLY EPHEMERIDES (W. Foulsham & Co.)

LONGITUDES AND LATITUDES U.S.A. (American Federation of Astrologers)

LONGITUDES AND LATITUDES THROUGHOUT THE WORLD (American Federation of Astrologers)

GENERAL READING

ARROYO, Stephen, RELATIONSHIPS AND LIFE CYCLES (C.R.C.S. Publications, 1993)

CUNNINGHAM, Donna, AN ASTROLOGICAL GUIDE TO SELF-AWARENESS (C.R.C.S. Publications, 1994)

HUNTLEY, Janis, THE ELEMENTS OF ASTROLOGY (Element Books, 1990)

HUNTLEY, Janis, ASTROLOGICAL VOIDS (Element Books, 1991)

MOORE, Marcia and Mark Douglas, ASTROLOGY. THE DIVINE SCIENCE (Arcane Publications, 1977)

SAKOIAN, Frances and Louis S. Acker, THE ASTROLOGER'S HANDBOOK (Penguin, 1989)

SAKOIAN, Frances and Louis S. Acker, THE ASTROLOGY OF HUMAN RELATIONSHIPS (Harper and Row, 1989)

SASPORTAS, Howard, THE TWELVE HOUSES (Thorsons, 1988)

TOMPKINS, Sue, ASPECTS IN ASTROLOGY (Element Books, 1990)

USEFUL ADDRESSES

Federation of Australian Astrologers Inc
www.faainc.org.au

Association Canadiennes des Astrologues Francophones
CP 1715
Succ "B"
Montreal H3B 3LB
Canada
Tel: +1-514-831-4153
Fax: +1-514-521-1502

Astrolinguistics Institute
2182 Cubbon Drive
Victoria
British Columbia V8R 1R5
Canada
Tel +1-604-370-1874
Fax: +1-604-370-1891
e-mail:
ablack@islandnet.com

Astrological Society of New Zealand
5266 Wellesley Street
Auckland 1003
New Zealand

Astrological Foundation Incorporated
41 New North Road
Eden Terrace
Auckland 1003
New Zealand
Tel/Fax: +64-9-373-5304

Astrological Society of South Africa
PO Box 2968
Rivonia 2128
South Africa
Tel: +27-11-864-1436

The Astrological Association of Great Britain
Unit 168
Lee Valley Technopark
Tottenham Hale
London
N17 9LN
Tel: + 44 (0) 208 880 4848
Fax: + 44 (0) 208 880 4849
http://www.astrologicalassociation.com

The American Federation of Astrologers
6535 S. Rural Road
Tempe
AZ 85283-3746
USA
http://www.astrologers.com
Email: AFA@msn.com

Association for Astrological Networking
8306 Wiltshire Blvd
PMB 537
Beverley Hills
CA 90211
USA
http://www.afan.org

INDEX

* * * * * * * * * * * * * * * * *